Experiencing
Spirituality

JEREMY P. TARCHER/PENGUIN
a member of Penguin Group (USA)
New York

Experiencing Spirituality

FINDING MEANING
THROUGH
STORYTELLING

Ernest Kurtz and
Katherine Ketcham

JEREMY P. TARCHER/PENGUIN
Published by the Penguin Group
Penguin Group (USA) LLC
375 Hudson Street
New York, New York 10014

USA · Canada · UK · Ireland · Australia
New Zealand · India · South Africa · China

penguin.com
A Penguin Random House Company

Stories of Reb Yerachmiel reprinted with permission from Rabbi Rami Shapiro, author of *Open Secrets: The Letters of Reb Yerachmiel ben Yisrael* (Monkfish Book Publishing).
Excerpts from William J. Bausch, *A World of Stories for Preachers and Teachers and Storytelling: Imagination and Faith* reprinted with permission from Twenty-Third Publications, Mystic, CT.
Excerpts from Anthony de Mello, *The Prayer of the Frog* (vols. 1 and 2), *One Minute Nonsense*, and *More One Minute Nonsense* reprinted with permission from Gujarat Sahitya Prakash (bookgsp@gmail.com).
Excerpts from Lao Tzo, *Tao Te Ching: A New English Version*, by Ursula K. Le Guin. Copyright © 1997 by Ursula K. Le Guin. Reprinted by arrangement with The Permissions Company, Inc., on behalf of Shambhala Publications Inc., Boston, MA, www.shambhala.com.
"How Wisdom Comes" by Leila Fisher from the book *Wisdomkeepers* by Steve Wall and Harvey Arden. Copyright © 1990, reprinted with permission from Beyond Words Publishing, Hillsboro, OR.

Most Tarcher/Penguin books are available at special quantity discounts for bulk purchase for sales promotions, premiums, fund-raising, and educational needs. Special books or book excerpts also can be created to fit specific needs. For details, write: Special.Markets@us.penguingroup.com.

Library of Congress Cataloging-in-Publication Data
Kurtz, Ernest.
Experiencing spirituality : finding meaning through storytelling / Ernest Kurtz and Katherine Ketcham.
p.   cm.
Includes bibliographical references and index.
ISBN 978-0-399-16417-0
1. Storytelling—Religious aspects.   2. Spirituality.   I. Title.
BL628.7.K87   2014   2013050986
204—dc23

Printed in the United States of America
1   3   5   7   9   10   8   6   4   2

Book design by Emily Herrick

DEDICATION

Gratefully, we dedicate this book to and acknowledge the contributions of all who have taught us over the years: formal teachers and professors, diverse writers, good friends, many "in the rooms"—all those whose quiet example of dedication to truth helped us to experience spirituality.

ACKNOWLEDGMENTS

A special acknowledgment to Linda Loewenthal, our literary agent; Sara Carder, our editor, and Joanna Ng, her assistant; and especially to our long-suffering but tolerant spouses, Linda Kurtz and Patrick Spencer.

We also wish to note here our debt to Anthony de Mello, Jesuit priest, gifted storyteller, and profound spiritual guide. A great collector as well as teller of stories, Father de Mello died suddenly on June 1, 1987, and we appreciate the help of his brother, Bill deMello, whose biography— *Anthony deMello: The Happy Wanderer*—is an enriching read. Bill also aided our project by connecting us with Father Jerry Sequeira, S.J., provincial of the Jesuit province of Gujarat and director of Gujarat Sahitya Prakash, the first publisher of Tony's books, who helped us put Tony's storytelling work in context.

Contents

Introduction

W hat are you doing for an encore?" So ran an occasional
conversation starter from friends after the 1992 publica-
tion of our book *The Spirituality of Imperfection*.

"Back to reading and thinking," came our usual answer.

But then something new arrived in our lives! Even as the
Internet was dawning, at the very beginning of e-mail, individuals began to contact us offering more or slightly different stories (some of which appear in this book). What a gift! Eventually, as
we read and listened to those gifts, this book began to take
shape. But only barely and very slowly, for our other reading,
thinking, and life adventures combined with the stories, old and
new, to lead us down diverse pathways pondering what we were
experiencing.

In our non-writing lives, meanwhile, Kathy was raising three
children into and through the adventurous teen years, and Ernie
confronted a cascade of body-part-replacement and other surgical
events that led to his retirement from mainline academia. In contact through those years, despite the some 2,200 miles that separate us, we continued to exchange discoveries and insights. Slowly

the themes that make up this book emerged, hammered out on the hard anvil of our life experience at least as much as in the soft tissue of our brains.

Once upon a time we had dared to write a book on "spirituality," but now, two decades later, had we learned any more from our own experience trying to *live* that spirituality?

We hope so. We think so.

The governor resigned his exalted office and came to the Master demanding to be taught.

"What is it you wish me to teach you?" asked the Master.

"Wisdom," was the reply.

"Ah, my friend! How gladly would I do that were it not for one major obstacle."

"What?"

"Wisdom cannot be taught."

"So there's nothing I can learn here."

"Wisdom can be learned. But it cannot be taught."

❧

AND SO THE FIRST TRUTH with which we had to become comfortable was that anything we wrote would do no good. At least not directly. Once again we turned to experience—both our own ongoing experiences over the intervening twenty years and the experiences captured and encapsulated in the traditions we had mined for the stories that conveyed the themes of a spirituality of imperfection. Because it is impossible directly to transmit or convey experience—for experience itself attests that it must be *experienced*—we again turn to stories: Experience is best awakened within story. Many of these stories and themes are light, even humorous, but some are dark, perhaps uncomfortable. Both experiences, after all, fall within the experience of most of us.

As we reviewed those themes and the comments we had received, one question repeatedly struck us: Why is it that the most profound truths seem to be simplistic, even clichés? Probably, the stories seemed to say, because through much experience those who came before us discovered many of the most important truths about *be*-ing humanly° . . . and having learned them, they did try to pass them on. As many wisdom thinkers had observed: The good seeks to diffuse itself. But as their own experience taught, all they had to offer was . . . their own experience.

When seekers searched out those whose lives revealed a certain *something*—a quality variously named spirituality, sanctity, bliss, serenity—and earnestly asked, *What must I do?* they consistently received the only possible answer: *Come, follow me; see how I live.*

There was once a Sufi who lived alone. He was sought out by a young man who wanted enlightenment, and he allowed him to come and live nearby, and said and did nothing to discourage him.

° A word about *be*-ing: "How irritating! Don't they know better than to put a stupid hyphen in the middle of an ordinary word?" Yes, we do. But how, then, are we to convey, in our language as it is ordinarily used, the phenomenon of *is*-ness, the practice of *is*-ing?

"How do you be?" is not an inquiry into one's health; it is an honest question into how we conduct our daily life. This question might also be expressed by the more purely philosophical query, "What is existence like for you?"

The problem, perhaps, is in the mundane routine of our daily existence, for we tend to overlook the fact that our most important task—no, better, our basic responsibility—is to *be*. Be-ing (*is*-ing) has many specifications: to *be* a good citizen, to *be* a good parent, to *be* a friendly neighbor, to *be* a responsible employer/employee, to *be* generous with our time and our goods, to *be* a loving spouse, to *be* helpful. . . .

So when you see the word *be*-ing within these pages, please, after a brief wince, try to think "all of the above."

At length, having no teaching and little to think about, the young man said, "I have never seen you eating, and I marvel at how you sustain life without food."

"Since you joined me," said the Sufi, "I have stopped eating in front of you. Now I eat in secret."

The young man, even more intrigued, said, "But why should you do that? And if you wanted to deceive me, why do you now confess?"

"I stopped eating," said the sage, "so that you might marvel at me, in the hope that you would one day stop marveling at irrelevancies and become a real student."

The young man asked, "But could you not have simply told me not to marvel at superficialities?"

"Everyone in the world," said the Sufi, "and that includes you, has already been told precisely that, at least a hundred times. Do you imagine that one more handful of words on this subject would have had any effect on you?"

⸺⳾⸺

FOR WHAT THE SPIRITUAL masters—and, we hope, this book—offer is a *retail* spirituality. In this area, as in just about every other, there is always the whispering voice of someone who knows "shortcuts" or "can get it for you wholesale." And as just about everyone who has ever fallen for such a scam knows, you get what you work for, what you pay for in whatever currency. There is no such reality as "discount spirituality": Stories invite thought and may indeed impose effort even as they convey experience.

Nothing trumps experience. It is not the aim of this book to teach, persuade, or convince; rather, we hope to present, to those who are ready, realities that their experience might approach. And so in *Experiencing Spirituality* we continue to follow what we began in *The Spirituality of Imperfection*: telling stories of the spiritually adept, the stories that they told those who sought to follow them, the stories that were their lives—the stories that may help us answer the most meaningful question of all: How do we *be?*

A NOTE TO THE READER

"It has been said that all wisdom is plagiarism;
only stupidity is original."
HUGH T. KERR

Even a passing glance within the pages of this book will lead to the discovery that many of the stories we tell are not "new." Very true, but stories are usually presented within a context. So, although the reader may have heard or read one or another of these stories before, this reading should be different. Stories do not just hang in space as discrete entities; they are rather embedded in a context. The context changes the meaning and the impact of the story.

Also, although we have tried to keep this to a minimum, we do bring in bits and pieces of quotes and stories from *The Spirituality of Imperfection*, for these two books are deeply connected. As earlier, then, we borrow from the past in order to enrich the present and future. We offer not so much new stories as new contexts in which to appreciate some stories that have withstood the test of time precisely because they have different meanings in different contexts.

Please understand that although some of our stories may provoke a smile, we are not trying to be funny. Similarly, though some tales may lift your spirits, we are not attempting to be inspiring. We rather try to present here an invitation to a new way of seeing, at times by placing together ideas and images not usually witnessed in embrace. In this, we endeavor to follow in the footsteps of one of the great storytellers, Martin Buber:

> *I stand in a chain of narrators, a link between links; I tell once again the old stories, and if they sound new, it is because the new already lay dormant in them when they were told for the first time.*

We also walk with Buber in that more than 15 percent of our stories have a Jewish—mainly Hasidic—context. This happens not by accident but because of the richness of this tradition and the many joys of both our exposures to it. Although neither of us is Jewish, we each have had Jewish mentors and guides who introduced us to the wealth of that story tradition. We are grateful to them, and to that tradition.

A further word about the stories: Neither the stories nor their placement is haphazard. On many occasions, both will be obvious. At other times, the reader may puzzle: "Why *this* story, *here*?" We respectfully suggest that the puzzled reader pause to ponder that question. For there will always be *an* answer, even if it is not *the* answer. Spirituality in none of its forms can be commanded. That is one core of its affinity with stories. We can grasp only if we reach; and while it is true that not every reach results in a sure grasp, it is even more true that we have been made to reach: Grasping is the gift of grace. What is that "grace"? Anne Lamott has come perhaps as close as anyone to describing it: "I do not at all understand the mystery of grace—only that it meets us where we are but does not leave us where it found us."

Finally, a word about the Notes: This is not an academic work, and so we offer only an occasional footnote. On the other hand, many who pick up this book will want to know more about the sources of some of what we offer. To meet this need, we offer Notes for each segment; these appear at the end of the book, beginning on page 301. Also in those Notes we occasionally offer additional thoughts or extensions that do not fit into the body of the text.

We use the word *segments* rather than *chapters* because "chapters" implies a greater degree of continuity and connection, with one chapter leading seamlessly to the next. This book is different—it is intended to be read in an "open wherever you want" kind of way. One day, a title, word, or phrase may catch your eye; at another time, a particular story, read at a certain moment in time, might draw your attention; on yet another occasion, some occurrence may move you to thumb through the index. Here, within these pages, asymmetry is preferred to symmetry, inconsistency to uniformity, the unpredictable to the foreseeable.

Each segment in *Experiencing Spirituality* is thus a discrete piece that can be read out of order and savored out of context. When taken together, however, the segments form a whole—the whole of the experience of spirituality.

Stories pose a special challenge. Most of the stories that we re-tell are, in one way or another, classic: They have been around for a long time—for so long a time, often in widely diverse places, that it is impossible accurately to "source" them with any confidence. In general, then, we offer attributions only for less familiar stories. The unattributed stories may readily be found in many places, in varying versions—in most cases in more than one source, both online and printed. Some books in which some of these stories appear are listed on page 329. Online sources for the classic or common "old chestnut" stories may generally be found by searching for the story's punch line.

In presenting these stories, we identify with storyteller Anthony de Mello, who more than once explained of his own use of them:

> *The stories in this book come from a variety of countries, cultures, and religions. They belong to the spiritual heritage—and popular humor—of the human race.*
>
> *All that the author has done is to string them together with a specific aim in mind. His task has been that of the weaver and the dyer. He takes no credit at all for the cotton and the thread.*

Thank you, and enjoy!

BEYOND
"SPIRITUALITY"

The problem with the term spirituality *is that its meaning has been distorted for us by hearing the word used mainly in the phrase "spiritual rather than religious." This connection has fogged up our idea/understanding of "spirituality," has led it to have an almost negative connotation, by in a very real way defining it by what it is not—"cus we all know what 'religion'" is.*

What has been lost is the reality that signifies some profound change in be-ing.
MARILYNNE ROBINSON

A Hasid burst into the study of Reb Yerachmiel ben Yisrael. "Rebbe," he said breathlessly, "what is the way to God?"

The rebbe looked up from his studies and answered: "There is no way to God, for God is not other than here and now."

"Then, Rebbe, tell me the essence of God."

"There is no essence of God, for God is all and nothing."

"Then, Rebbe, tell me the secret that I might know that God is all."

"My friend," Reb Yerachmiel sighed, "there is no way, there is no essence, there is no secret. The truth you seek is not hidden from you—you are hiding from it."

SPIRITUALITY IS STUCK: not the reality, but its name.

Or perhaps also, to some extent, the reality: Realities take on the qualities of the names in which we encase them. And so, as in the story, spirituality is not hidden; but its reality has become such that we too easily hide from it.

That hiding is facilitated by a phrase that has become more popular than either of its conjoined terms: "spiritual rather than religious." Most people do not seem to give much thought to what is "spirituality," but they are certain of this one thing about it: It is *not* religion.

One problem with *not*-ing°—knowing mainly what some reality is not—is that the more we talk about it, the less we seem to know. It often helps to have a clear idea about what something is not; but when that is *all* that we know about it, we really know nothing. It is difficult—perhaps impossible—to experience nothing. It is even more hopeless to attempt to communicate that experience. And so, how can we talk about some reality when the main thing we know about it is what it is not?

A couple of generations ago, Episcopal priest turned Zen teacher Alan Watts, frustrated by the apparent inability of the available theologies to grasp the nature of change, proclaimed that his (and

---

° The benefits of knowing what something is *not* after developing a clear idea of what that thing really is are explored in greater detail in the segments on Forgiveness and Memory.

our) task is to find a way of communicating that which cannot be spoken … or in his inimitable phrase, to "eff the ineffable"—to speak that which cannot be put into words … and more.

Stories, in a way, "eff" the ineffable: They convey experience not by "talking about" (which never works), but by opening hearts and minds in ways that make them capable of experiencing that which cannot be described. There are still limits. No words or story will ever convey the taste of chocolate ice cream or the scent of a rose. A story may, however, enable a trace of recognition of the meaningfulness of the welcoming smile of a lover.

> *He opened his eyes and looked at her. She greeted him with a mocking, enigmatic smile in which was a poignant gaiety. Over his face went the reflection of the smile, he smiled, too, purely unconsciously.*
>
> *That filled her with extraordinary delight, to see the smile cross his face, reflected from her face. She remembered that was how a baby smiled. It filled her with extraordinary radiant delight.*
>
> *"You've done it," she said.*
>
> *"What?" he asked, dazed.*
>
> *"Convinced me."*
>
> *And she bent down, kissing him passionately, passionately, so that he was bewildered. He did not ask her of what he had convinced her, though he meant to. He was glad she was kissing him. She seemed to be feeling for his very heart to touch the quick of him. And he wanted her to touch the quick of his being, he wanted that most of all.*

D. H. LAWRENCE, *Women in Love*

༺ↂༀ

IF, AS THE TRADITIONS of primitive peoples seem to bear out, religion *and* spirituality began not in fear but in awe and gratitude, an *openness* to such experience is the true beginning of any spirituality. But what does such "openness" mean? What does it involve?

Imagine—picture—a hand . . . your hand. You use it in several ways each day. Much of the time, it is grasping something—a pen, a knife or fork, a book, the steering wheel of a car, the hand of another person. At other times, the hand is resting. Most of the time, when my hands are at rest, the palms tend to be held down or inward, fingers slightly flexed, relaxed. But there are also times when I hold out my hand, palm up. On many such occasions, I am waiting or hoping to receive something, to have someone place something in my hand. Also, from habit or training—I am not sure which—my hands are held open, palms up, when I meditate—when I relax and let go and try to be open to reality-as-it-is.

Spirituality begins in such openness. OPENNESS: Most of the time, our human tendency is to want to grasp, to command, to bring about, to *do* . . . but when dealing with the spiritual, the attempt to control or manipulate makes that which we seek, that which we hope for, vanish. We might as well try to capture soap bubbles with a fork. Awe and control are impossible bedfellows.

And yet . . . we can hope to influence without claiming to control. How readily and naturally, for example, when faced with some tragedy or sorrow, do we desire—yearn—to "make it better." Surely there is nothing "wrong" with this longing that seems so deeply engraved in our very being: Spiritual traditions encourage not only the good work of helping others but also prayer, and specifically prayers of petition, especially prayers for the good of others. We are made to want to help because in many ways *we are made in order to help.* That, the first deep "lesson" of spirituality suggests, is why we are here. On some level so profound that we most often experience it without being aware of it, we are made for each other.

Time before time, when the world was young, two brothers shared a field and a mill. Each night they divided evenly the grain they had ground together during the day. Now as it happened, one of the brothers lived alone; the other had a wife and a large family. One day, the single brother thought to himself: "It isn't really fair that we divide the grain evenly. I have only myself to care for, but my brother has children to feed." So each night he secretly took some of his grain to his brother's granary to see that he was never without.

But the married brother said to himself one day, "It isn't really fair that we divide the grain evenly, because I have children to provide for me in my old age, but my brother has no one. What will he do when he is old?" So every night he secretly took some of his grain to his brother's granary. As a result, both of them always found their supply of grain mysteriously replenished each morning.

Then one night the brothers met each other halfway between their two houses, suddenly realized what had been happening, and embraced each other in love. The story is that God witnessed their meeting and proclaimed, "This is a holy place—a place of love—and here it is that my temple shall be built." And so it was. The holy place, where God is made known, is the place where human beings discover each other in love.

NON-SPIRITUALITY IS wrapped up in self-as-center-of-the-universe. We all begin life in this way; it is part of the necessary baggage of infancy. Slowly, however, maturity should dawn—the maturity of the realization that self is not the center of the universe, that others are at least as worthy as we, that we truly fulfill ourselves only with and through others, and that we serve those others in the same way.

An old creation-myth story sometimes told to children—or to adults on a religious "retreat"—describes the infinite God as from all eternity looking over the world and seeing the need for some particular, specific task to be done, some role to be filled. And so God forms the being who will do that task, who will fulfill that function, who will *be* that being: That is how and why each one of us is created. Each of us exists not only to do something that no other being can do, but even more to be that being that no other being can be. Each of us is unique, an individual like no other, and in this resides our dignity. In a very singular sense, in this story, the infinite God needs each one of us as we are. That is why we are here.

> The devotee knelt to be initiated into discipleship. The Master whispered the sacred mantra into his ear, warning him to reveal it to no one.
>
> "What will happen if I do?" asked the devotee.
>
> Said the Master, "Anyone to whom you reveal the mantra will be liberated from the bondage of ignorance and suffering, but you yourself will be excluded from discipleship and suffer damnation."

No sooner had he heard these words, than the devotee rushed to the marketplace, collected a large crowd, and repeated the sacred mantra for all to hear.

The disciples reported this to the Master and demanded that the man be expelled from the monastery for his disobedience.

The Master smiled and said, "He has no need of anything I can teach. His action has shown him to be a Master in his own right."

∞

WHAT COMPLICATES our stories is that one part of our dignity as human beings, our ability to *do*, tends to outrun our *be*-ing. We love to manipulate, to bring about, to control—and we should do so for, again, that is one reason we are here. But our *be*-ing is more important, and there are some realities, *realities* essential to our very *be*-ing, that—as the forked soap-bubble image reminds—we cannot control. Indeed, the effort—the demand—to control them destroys not only them but ourselves. Spirituality is one of those realities.

Yet as is the case with love, another of those realities, its attractiveness and desirability are so great that some claim not only to grasp them but to make them available to others . . . for a price. But there are some realities—spiritual realities—that price destroys: As economist Joan Robinson observed a half-century ago, bought sex is just not the same. The world of material things requires the kind of control that is commerce; one genius of civilization is to be found in the diverse ways in which commerce, the exchange of material things, has been developed and facilitated. But such commerce can be a treacherous form of control, and genuine spirituality eludes all attempts at control. Spirituality is not a possession. In fact, most often, those who have it don't seem to realize that they have it.

A cobbler approached Rabbi Isaac of Ger, seeking advice. "Tell me," the cobbler asked with a heavy heart, "what shall I do about my morning prayers?" He went on to explain that his clients were poor men who had only one pair of shoes. He picked up the shoes late at night, when the men returned from work, and then he worked all night to repair the shoes. But when dawn came around, there were still shoes left to be repaired and so he often missed his morning prayers.

"I don't know what to do," the cobbler said, his head bowed down in shame.

"What have you been doing so far?" the rabbi asked.

"Well, sometimes I rush through the prayers, which makes me feel bad," the cobbler admitted. "Other times I am so busy that I will let the hour of prayer go by, and at those times I feel even worse. Lifting my hammer, I can almost hear my heart sigh, realizing what an unfortunate man I am that I cannot find the time to say my morning prayers."

"If I were God," the rabbi said, "I would value that sigh more than the prayer."

❦

"SPIRITUAL RATHER than religious." Theologians, social scientists, spiritual directors, poets, and novelists have commented richly on the problematic nature of that distinction. All who seriously examine the matter agree that spirituality is surely more than "*not*-religion." Spirituality, they all seem to say in one way or another, in some way involves an experience of *beyond*—it "be-yonds" us. All observers agree that genuine spirituality begins by looking outside the self, beyond the subjective. If religion is founded, as Robert Bellah suggests in his monumental study *Religion in Human Evolution*, in "awareness of an alternative reality," then spirituality involves a *consciousness of contact with* that alternative reality. In this sense, spirituality is beyond religion.

Master Shaku Soen liked to take an evening stroll through a nearby village. One day he heard loud lamentations from a house and, on entering quietly, realized that the householder had died and the family and neighbors were crying. He sat down and cried with them.

An old man noticed him and remarked, rather shaken on seeing the famous master crying with them: "I would have thought that you at least were beyond such things."

"But it is this which puts me beyond it," replied the master with a sob.

∞

GENUINE SPIRITUALITY is beyond the "spirituality" of those who see it as only or mainly "not-religion." Stephen Bamber, a British student of the role of spirituality in the healing of alcoholics and addicts, notes that too much of what passes as "the new spirituality is celebrated by those who, disillusioned by traditional religions, view it as a 'force for wholeness, healing, and inner transformation [that] provides a liberation and solace in an otherwise meaningless world.'" While that may be a laudable goal, he remarks, too often something is also missing, lost; for this "spirituality's" focus is on self, and that too easily leads to forgetting or ignoring the reality of "a higher, transcendent authority," a genuinely alternative reality.

Noting that the practices of traditional religion and classic spirituality aimed toward some transcendent reality and the softening of the boundaries of the self, Bamber goes on to point out that the goal of some contemporary so-called spiritualities appears to be the development of a more effectively defined self. Sadly, this does not work, for in reality, as several commentators have cautioned, "[genuine] spirituality is not knowing what you want but understanding what you do not need." The real tension, as psychotherapist and pastoral counselor Jeff Georgi points out in a similar context:

> ... *is not between religion and spirituality but between spirituality and materialism.... Spirituality is the sensitivity to, the celebration of and the participation in that which makes humans as a species special.*

Humans are not "special" because of *things*. We are literally "made for more"—but "more" not of material things or honors or degrees or workshops but "more" in the sense of *beyond*: We are "special" because in our very ordinariness we in some way *transcend* merely material reality. Things, most of us eventually learn, do not and cannot satisfy for long.... Soon we become sated, bored, and begin to look for some other "more." The same is true of a denatured "spirituality" that prioritizes self over transcendent reality. Like seed cast on rocky ground, such spring up rapidly only to as quickly die for lack of moisture and roots. Or perhaps a story from Southeast Asia captures more vibrantly and from a helpfully different angle what is actually going on here.

During the early days of the kingdom of Ava a caravan of hill men arrived with their merchandise at the market place. After selling their wares, they went from stall to stall with gold coins jingling in their pockets, looking for rare articles to be bought and taken home.

They paused before a stall selling fruit and looked in wonder at a bunch of coconuts on display.

"What are those?" asked the leader of the caravan.

"Coconuts, my friend," replied the woman stall-keeper. "They are very expensive and only kings and great lords can afford to buy them."

"Of course, I can afford to buy them," the caravan leader replied somewhat testily. "Name your price." Learning that the price was one silver coin for one coconut he bought the whole bunch with a lordly air.

The hill men then started on their journey homeward, and, after one or two days' travel, the caravan leader said, "My friends, let us now taste the wondrous coconut, which only kings and lords can eat." So saying, he cut the coconut, ate the outer fiber, and then threw away the nut, thinking it was a mere seed and not dreaming at all that there was sweet milk and a rich kernel inside. His friends followed suit with the other coconuts from the bunch.

The caravan leader then said, "Friends, kings and lords are foolish indeed to value this tasteless fruit."

❧

LIFE, REALITY, wisdom—call it what you will, even "spirituality"—throws curveballs: It is never exactly, or at times even nearly, what we expect. The deepest truths, the most profound realities—the sweet milk and rich kernel of a timeless spirituality—have a way of sneaking up on us, of being not quite what we anticipated, and so too casually we may throw them away. This may be the most profound wisdom that needs to be learned by those overly enamored of being "in control."

A rabbi once came to Reb Yerachmiel after a meditation workshop. "A member of my congregation, a philosopher at the state college, asked me to teach him how to meditate. How should I instruct him?"

Reb Yerachmiel replied: "Teach him the prayer for moving his bowels, and teach him to recite it every time he does so. Don't let him read on the toilet. He must just sit and pray."

 ⸎

ON ANOTHER occasion,

During a presentation on spirituality a woman rose and said: "I have no need of these practices. I feel spiritual all the time without doing anything."

Reb Yerachmiel looked at her for a moment and said: "The next time you have an urge to be spiritual, take a cold shower. Then dry off and do something kind for someone else."

As Reb Yerachmiel reminded in that same context, "Spirituality is no different than everyday life. It is doing everyday things with an attentive mind, which awakens us to the fact that we are both apart from and a part of everything else." Thus awakened, we discover simultaneously the reality of our emptiness and the reality of our connectedness. Reb Yerachmiel continues:

. . . spirituality is not a thing or a feeling. Spirituality is paying attention. Spirituality is being present to what is happening around and within you. Spirituality is living in the world with compassion and justice. Spirituality is making the world a little better for your having been born into it. Spirituality is meeting God in the ordinariness of our everyday lives.

Spirituality, then, implies a profound awareness, but within this, *spirituality is ordinary*. The "ordinary" is never spectacular, in large part because it concerns not our *doing* but our very *be-ing*. Genuine spirituality looks not at its nose nor in a mirror but *outside* the self, *beyond* the immediate and the subjective, and that very looking *be-yonds* us, conveys us away from the self-centeredness that is the human trap. Such spirituality asks: "Whom can I help today?" and "How can I be of service?"

When a learned but miserly man asked Rabbi Abraham of Stretyn for a drug to attain the fear of God, the rabbi offered him instead one for the love of God.

"That's even better," cried the man. "Just give it to me."

"It is the love of one's fellow men," replied Rabbi Abraham.

❧

AS STRANGE as the claim may sound, there is a God beyond "spirituality." And the God beyond spirituality is a quirky God:

One day, Mohammed was offering morning prayer and, among the crowd of people praying with the Prophet was an Arab aspirant.

Mohammed began to read the Koran and recited the verse in which Pharaoh claims, "I am your true God." Hearing this, the aspirant was filled with spontaneous anger and shouted, "The boastful son of a bitch!"

The Prophet said nothing, but after prayer was over, others began to scold the Arab. "Aren't you ashamed of yourself? Your prayer displeases God because not only did you interrupt the holy silence of prayer but you used filthy language in the presence of God's Prophet."

The poor Arab trembled with fear, until the angel Gabriel appeared to the Prophet and said, "God sends greetings to you and wishes you to get these people to stop scolding that simple Arab; indeed, his spontaneous profanity moved my heart more than the holy prayers of the others."

⊲⊳

WHAT, THEN, is spirituality? Twenty years ago we wrote:

The disciples were absorbed in a discussion of Lao Tzu's dictum:

"Those who know do not say;

those who say do not know."

When the Master entered, they asked him what the words meant.

Said the Master, "Which of you knows the fragrance of a rose?"

All of them knew.

Then he said, "Put it into words."

All of them were silent.

⊲⊳

WHAT IS SPIRITUALITY? To have the answer is to have misunderstood the question. Truth, wisdom, goodness, beauty, the fragrance of a rose: All resemble spirituality in that they are intangible, ineffable realities. We may know them, but we can never grasp them with our hands or with our words. These entities have neither color nor texture; they cannot be gauged in inches or ounces or degrees; they do not make a noise to be measured in decibels; they have no distinct feel as do silk, wood, or cement; they give no odor; they have no taste; they occupy no space.

And yet they exist; they are. Love exists, evil exists, beauty exists, and spirituality exists. These are the realities that have always been recognized as defining human existence. We do not define them; they define us. When we attempt to "define" spirituality, we discover not its limits, but our own. Similarly, we cannot prove such realities—it is truer to say that they "prove" us, in the sense that it is against them that we measure our human *be*-ing: the act and the process by which we exist.

Life is not what we "have," or even what we do, connected as these may be: We are what and how and who we are, and *be*-ing is a real activity. Like "love," spirituality is a way that we "be." This way of *be*-ing defies definition and delineation; we cannot tie it up, in any way package it or enclose it. Elusive in the sense that it cannot be "pinned down," spirituality slips under and soars over efforts to capture it, to fence it in with words. Centuries of thought confirm that mere words can never induce the experience of spirituality.

Thus began *The Spirituality of Imperfection*.

∞

MUCH HAS changed, yet little is different from the context into which we launched *The Spirituality of Imperfection* more than two decades ago. Spirituality remains impossible to define, but some brief, more recent descriptions may help frame understanding as we set out to explore it from the active perspective of *experience*:

Jesuit Retreat Master Edward Kinerk suggests that "the closest description [of spirituality] is life-style," continuing that any definition of spirituality "should contain the idea of personal growth.... What distinguishes the human condition is *growth beyond self*, self-transcendence."

Edward Sellner, scholar of Celtic spirituality, proposes that "Spirituality in its broadest sense is, quite simply, a way of life that reveals an awareness of the sacred and a relationship with the Holy One in the midst of our human fragility, brokenness and limitations."

According to Benedictine monk Jerome Dollard, "Spirituality is a lot like health—it is not something we can go out and buy, although a lot of people have tried that. We all have health; we may have good health or poor health, but it's something we can't avoid having. The same is true of spirituality: Every human being is a spiritual being. The question is whether the spirituality we have is the negative one that leads to isolation and self-destruction or the one that is more positive and life-giving."

And although not using the term *spirituality*, D. H. Lawrence observed that:

> *However smart we may be, however rich and clever or loving or charitable or spiritual or impeccable, it doesn't help us at all. The real power comes in to us from the beyond. Life enters us from behind, where we are sightless, and from below, where we do not understand. And unless we yield to the beyond, and take our power and might and honor and glory from the unseen, from the unknown, we shall continue empty.*

Finally, Sandra Marie Schneiders, perhaps our most profound contemporary student of the relationships between spirituality and religion, suggests that:

> *...spirituality, like personality, is a characteristic of the human being*
> *as such. It is the capacity of persons to transcend themselves through*
> *knowledge and love, that is, to reach beyond themselves in relationship*
> *to others and thus become more than self-enclosed material monads.*

In how many ways is it possible to say, "Spirituality is simple, ordi-nary"? Perhaps we need to return to an adventure of childhood when we may have asked about "spirituality" or "grace" or some other term we heard in a place of worship. If we were fortunate, our parents or other teachers told us to watch the wind. It is obvi-ously real, but you cannot see it, only its effects. Later we learned that air is a kind of fluid and the wind is like waves we could make in the water. But let's get de-sophisticated for a moment and think again of the wind as wind. We do not see wind as it is, but we see and feel what it does. And that's the way it is with spirituality. As Albert Einstein is said to have observed, "Not everything that counts can be counted."

∞

AND SO "what is spirituality?" Spirituality is to be found in the ordinary and everyday phenomena and activities of *be*-ing de-scribed in the following segments. Spirituality is *experienced* in our Listening, in our Forgiveness, in our Dark places, in our Confu-sions, in our stories—not so much in what we "do," but in what and how we *be* . . . by *how* we *experience* the realities that we meet.

Spirituality is, in briefest description, a *way of life*—a way of *being*.

For like "life" and "love," spirituality is a way that we "be." This way of *be*-ing defies definition and delineation; we cannot tie it up, in any way package it or enclose it. Elusive in the sense that it cannot be "pinned down," spirituality slips under and soars over all efforts to capture it, to fence it in with words. But because it is experienced, spirituality can be described.

What is spirituality?

I recently heard a story of someone asking a monk, "What is your life like as a monk?"

The monk replied, "We walk, we fall down, someone helps us up. We walk some more, someone else falls down. We help them up. That's pretty much what we do."

EXPERIENCE

There is no desire more natural than that of knowledge.
We try all ways that can lead us to it; where reason is wanting,
we therein employ experience.

MICHEL DE MONTAIGNE

Spirituality . . . denotes experience, a term that is itself very
difficult to define. . . . It implies that spirituality is not
an abstract idea, a theory, an ideology, or a movement
of some kind. It is personal lived reality. . . .

SANDRA MARIE SCHNEIDERS

Once some of the elders were in Scete and Abbot John the Dwarf was with them.

While they were dining, a priest, a very old man, attempted to serve them. But no one would take so much as a cup of water from him except John the Dwarf.

The others were shocked by this and later said to him, "How is it that you consider yourself worthy to accept service from that holy man?"

He replied, "When I offer people a drink of water, I am happy if they take it. Did you expect me to sadden the good man by depriving him of the joy of giving me something?"

⮎⮌

EXPERIENCE IS both noun—something that *is*—and verb, something one *does*. "What an experience!" "Well, you will just have to experience that for yourself." "Now *that* was an experience!" In how many ways do we experience *experience*?

"To experience" is to go through or endure something. An experience is not encountered: It is lived through. *Duration* is essential. That is why we need *story* to convey experience. *Experiencing* something means that some reality is seen, heard, and more—one's whole *be*-ing is involved, somehow touched, and insofar as possible brought into the experience.

A cowboy was riding across the desert when he came upon an Indian lying on the road with his head and ear to the ground.

"How ya doin', Chief?" said the cowboy.

"Big paleface with red hair driving dark green Mercedes with German shepherd dog inside and license plate number SDT965 going west."

"Gee, Chief, ya mean ya hear all that just by listening to the ground?"

"I'm not listening to the ground. The S.O.B. ran over me!"

⮎⮌

ONE OF the oft-quoted sayings of John Kolobos, the "John the Dwarf" whose story opens this segment, ran: "Unawareness is the root of all evil." But how does one achieve awareness? In conversation? By watching for it? By thinking about it?

"... Where reason is wanting, we therein employ experience." But is experience created or undergone? Is it possible to have *enough* experience? And what is the relationship between thought and experience? We will address these questions throughout this segment, throughout this book. Here, it is helpful to note that students of religious experience emphasize how many groups involve newcomers in *experience*, in "participation prior to a detailed exposure to the tradition's belief system"—a practice that takes advantage of the modern adage "Act yourself into a new way of thinking," as well as recapturing a too-often neglected classic insight.

As stories convey, both acting and thinking are experiences, and both experiences are involved in storytelling. There is a kind of circularity between experience and storytelling: According to Carol Christ in her rich study *Diving Deep & Surfacing: Women Writers on Spiritual Quest*: "Stories give shape to experience, experience gives rise to stories." And as William James observed and lived out in his own life, "My experience is what I agree to attend to."

A famous Viennese surgeon told his students that a surgeon needed two gifts: freedom from nausea and the power of observation.

He then dipped a finger into some disgusting fluid and licked it, asking each student to do the same. They steeled themselves and succeeded without flinching. Smiling, the surgeon announced, "I congratulate all of you on passing the first test. But not, I'm afraid, the second: not one of you noticed that the finger I licked was not the one I dipped in the fluid."

❧

THERE ARE two terms that, while their processes surely are included in *experience*, are anything but substitutes for it: "feel" and "think." The main problem with these terms is that each seems to exclude the other, or at least to downplay it. The special benefit of the word *experience* is that it includes all the senses and faculties mentioned above and more. In fact, a significant facet of many experiences is precisely their aroma and taste. Some experiences also engage the actual sense of touch—*feel*-ing in the precise first meaning of that term.

The scholar approached the Master, seeking enlightenment. "Can you offer me a revelation of greater weight than anything I can find in the writings?" he eagerly asked.

"Go out into the rain," the Master replied. "Lift your head and your hands to the heavens, and you will discover the first great revelation."

The scholar did so. Returning, he told the Master: "I went out into the pouring rain, lifted my head and my hands to heaven, and all I got for my efforts was water flowing down my neck. I felt like a complete fool."

"Well," said the Master, "that's quite a revelation for the first day, isn't it?"

❧

THE PROCESS of storytelling conveys certain experiences, even if these experiences are not talked about directly. These experiences, in fact, *cannot* be transmitted directly, by talking *about* them, but rather are conveyed *only* by means of "story," which invites identification. Identification begins when the similarities between two stories are realized. Identification is fulfilled in the sense of shared experience that springs from that realization.

Bare words fail because the primary responsibility of words is to convey ideas. Words tell. Conveying experience requires more. That "more" may be—usually is—dressed in words, as in the stories in this book. But what happens in such instances is that not only is an idea communicated, but an experience is genuinely shared in the classic true sense of that far too overused word. Such genuine sharing involves not merely communication but a kind of communion.

Tradition has it that the two sons of Rabbi Shmuel of Lubavitch were once playing the game of rebbe and Hasid. Rabbi Zalman Aaron, then seven years old, was playing rebbe while his younger brother, Rabbi Shalom Dov Baer, then five years old, played Hasid. The younger one girded his loins with a prayer sash and knocked softly at the door. When asked to enter, he timidly approached his brother and said, "Master, please give me a *tiqun* ('rectification') for my soul."

"What have you done?" the older one demanded.

"I did not say the blessing after eating an apple."

Zalman Aaron replied, "For the next forty days you are to recite a blessing out of the prayer manual after eating any food."

"You did not do it right!" Shalom Dov Baer reproached him.

"How can you say this?" Zalman Aaron argued. "I myself watched Daddy through the keyhole when a Hasid asked him the same question. I gave you his reply."

"I, too, watched Daddy," said the younger brother. "But you didn't do it right. Daddy always *sighs* before he answers."

∞

EXPERIENCE CARRIES numerous connotations. Many users have recognized both its strength and its slipperiness. Oscar Wilde is credited with "Experience is simply the name we give our mistakes." And although it did not originate with him, Randy Pausch's *The Last Lecture* (2007) is the most frequently cited source for "Experience is what you get when you don't get what you want." Because of the word's power, *experience* has at times been twisted and used in attempts to justify all kinds of aberrations, especially claims to certainty. Far more promising and attentive to reality is the description offered by philosopher Hans-Georg Gadamer:

> *. . . being experienced does not mean that one now knows something once and for all and becomes rigid in this knowledge; rather, one becomes more open to new experiences. A person who is experienced is undogmatic. Experience has the effect of freeing one to be open to new experience. . . . In our experience we bring nothing to a close; we are constantly learning new things from our experience. . . .*

The great rabbi was dying and, as we all know, deathbed wisdom is the best. So his students lined up, single file, to receive his last words. The most brilliant student was at the bedside, the second most brilliant behind him, and so on, till the line ended at a student who was a room and a half away. The most brilliant student leaned over to the slowly slipping rabbi and asked, "Rabbi, what is the meaning of life?"

The rabbi groaned, "Life is like a cup of tea." The most brilliant student turned to the second most brilliant student.

"The rabbi said, 'Life is like a cup of tea.'" And word was whispered from student to student till it arrived at the fellow who was waiting a room and a half away.

"What does the rabbi mean, 'Life is like a cup of tea'?" he asked. And his question was passed back up the line until the most brilliant student once again leaned over the dying rabbi. "Rabbi, what do you mean, 'Life is like a cup of tea'?"

The rabbi shrugged. "All right, so maybe life is *not* like a cup of tea!"

∽

IN THE twelfth century, Saint Bernard of Clairvaux urged his followers to practice a discourse—to use a language—oriented not toward learning but toward spirituality. Referring to a liturgical hymn, he said, "A canticle of this kind, fervor alone can teach; it can be learned only through experience. Those who have experienced it will recognize this. Those who have not experienced it, may they burn with desire not so much to know as to experience."

Experience, then—or at least openness to experience—is first an attitude: a *posture* of *be*-ing, the stance one takes in and before reality. Essential to this stance is an openness, even an eagerness, to learn. We all wish not so much to know more as to experience more. Looking at, thinking on, *experiencing* our marvelous sensory apparatus . . . it is meant to be *used*. *How* we use our senses to further our own experience—and the experience of others—is central to the experience itself. For problems can arise. As Wendy Doniger O'Flaherty observed, it can happen that "we arrange our talents and weaknesses like the foolish blind man and lame man in the old story: they agreed to team up, but the lame man carried the blind man on his shoulders."

A similar problem arises when someone for whatever reason lacks the courage to be open to experience.

Naaman, the army commander of the king of Aram, was highly esteemed and respected by his master, for through him, the Lord had brought victory to Aram. But valiant as he was, the man was a leper.

Now the Arameans had captured from the land of Israel in a raid a little girl, who became the servant of Naaman's wife. "If only my master would present himself to the prophet in Samaria," she said to her mistress, "he would cure him of his leprosy."

Naaman went and told his lord just what the slave girl from the land of Israel had said. "Go," said the king of Aram, "I will send along a letter to the king of Israel."

So Naaman set out, taking along ten silver talents, six thousand gold pieces, and ten festal garments. To the king of Israel he brought the letter, which read: "With this letter I am sending my servant Naaman to you, that you may cure him of his leprosy."

When he read the letter, the king of Israel tore his garments and exclaimed: "Am I a god with power over life and death that this man should send someone to me to be cured of leprosy? Take note! You can see he is only looking for a quarrel with me!"

When Elisha, the man of God, heard that the king of Israel had torn his garments, he sent word to the king: "Why have you torn your garments? Let him come to me and find out that there is a prophet in Israel."

Naaman came with his horses and chariots and stopped at the door of Elisha's house. The prophet sent him the message:

"Go and wash seven times in the Jordan, and your flesh will heal, and you will be clean."

But Naaman went away angry, saying, "I thought that he would surely come out and stand there to invoke the Lord his God, and would move his hand over the spot, and thus cure the leprosy. Are not the rivers of Damascus, the Abana, and the Pharpar better than all the waters of Israel? Could I not wash in them and be cleansed?" With this, he turned about in anger and left.

But his servants came up and reasoned with him. "My father," they said, "if the prophet had told you to do something extraordinary, would you not have done it? All the more now, since he said to you, 'Wash and be clean,' should you do as he said."

So Naaman went down and plunged into the Jordan seven times at the word of the man of God. His flesh became again like the flesh of a little child, and he was clean.

⸺⸺

THERE ARE ways other than story of conveying experience. Most of us would probably not choose them.

A big, tough samurai once went to see a little monk. "Monk," he said, in a voice accustomed to instant obedience, "teach me about heaven and hell!"

The monk looked up at this mighty warrior and replied with utter disdain, "Teach you about heaven and hell! I couldn't teach you about anything. You're dirty. You smell. Your blade is rusty. You're a disgrace, an embarrassment to the samurai class. Get out of my sight. I can't stand you."

The samurai was furious. He shook, got all red in the face, was speechless with rage. He pulled out his sword and raised it above him, preparing to slay the monk.

"That's hell," said the monk softly.

The samurai was overwhelmed. The compassion and surrender of this little man who had offered his life to give this teaching to show him hell! He slowly put down his sword, filled with gratitude, and suddenly peaceful.

"And that's heaven," said the monk softly.

※

ALL EXPERIENCE is limited. One difference between Europeans and Americans is that the former think one hundred miles is a long distance, while the latter think that one hundred years is a long time. We never transcend all our limitations, but as someone in early recovery from a serious illness once remarked: "Things are not good, but they sure are better." Few readers of this book are likely to meet samurai or Buddhist monks, but the image of that story clings. The images in the following two stories may offer sufficient contrast to make memorable the experiential stories in this segment.

A kind-hearted fellow was walking through Central Park in New York and was astonished to see an old man, fishing rod in hand, fishing over a beautiful bed of red roses.

"Tsk, tsk!" said the passerby to himself. "What a sad sight. That poor old man is fishing over a bed of flowers. I'll see if I can help." So the kind fellow walked up to the old man and asked, "What are you doing, my friend?"

"Fishin', sir."

"Fishin', eh? Well, how would you like to come have a drink with me?"

The old man stood, put his rod away, and followed the kind stranger to the corner bar. He ordered a large glass of vodka and a fine cigar.

His host, the kind fellow, felt good about helping the old man, and he asked, "Tell me, old friend, how many did you catch today?"

The old fellow took a long drag on the cigar, blew a careful smoke ring, and replied, "You are the sixth today, sir!"

❧

"EXPERIENCE IS not what happens to a man," said Aldous Huxley. "It is what a man does with what happens to him." There is one type of experience that generally defies complete or even adequate description: what goes on inside us, in the deepest core of our thinking, imagining, desiring. Even when we avidly *want* to be known, to make available to someone else our deepest experience of ourselves, our words never seem able to capture that reality, to make it comprehensible—graspable—by some other. Sometimes, of course, *we* are that "other," the one who cannot wrap our mind around what is being communicated. This problem may be larger than ourselves.

A man was riding his motorcycle along a California beach when suddenly the sky clouded above his head and, in a booming voice, the Lord said, "Because you have TRIED to be faithful to me in all ways, I will grant you one wish." The biker pulled over and said, "Build a bridge to Hawaii so I can ride over anytime I want."

The Lord said, "Your request is materialistic: think of the enormous challenges for that kind of undertaking: the supports required to reach the bottom of the Pacific and the concrete and steel it would take! It will nearly exhaust several natural resources. I can do it, but it is hard for me to justify your desire for worldly things. Take a little more time and think of something that could possibly help mankind."

The biker thought about it for a long time. Finally, he said, "Lord, I wish that I and all men could understand our wives; I want to know how she feels inside, what she's thinking when she gives me the silent treatment, why she cries, what she means when she says nothing's wrong, and how I can make a woman truly happy."

The Lord replied, "You want two lanes or four on that bridge?"

❦

SOME EXPERIENCES, both our own and the experience of others, will always mystify. Here, as in so many areas, our reach exceeds our grasp. William James, the great philosopher of experience, in an era when the most common mode of illuminating rooms was the use of gaslights, opined that turning introspection into a science is as impractical as "trying to turn up the gas quickly enough to see how the darkness looks."

There is another problem. Because particular circumstances differ, it may not be appropriate to transfer one person's experience to another, as a well-known Nasrudin story reminds:

Hussein told the Mullah, "I have terrible pain in my eye. What do you advise?"

Nasrudin thought for a moment, then said, "Pull it out."

Hussein said, "Nasrudin, you can't be serious."

The Mullah replied, "Well, last month my tooth hurt horribly for weeks, until I couldn't bear the pain anymore. So I had the tooth pulled out—and then I felt much better. If it worked for my tooth, it should work for your eye, too, shouldn't it?"

MORE MUNDANELY:

On the first day of school, about mid-morning, the kindergarten teacher said, "If anyone has to go to the bathroom, hold up two fingers."

A little voice from the back of the room asked, "How will that help?"

ARTISTS, ESPECIALLY poets, devised an underappreciated strategy to circumvent some of these difficulties, conveying *experience* by appealing to the *language of the heart*. Avoiding the trap of prioritizing either thinking or feeling, in their hands the *heart* becomes "mind as felt experience," experience insisting "the heart has its reasons." The "language of the heart" is necessary because of what the philosopher Mary Midgley has pointed out about "the Problem of Consciousness, the desperate ongoing attempt by many scientists to find ways of talking about human experience in 'scientific' language—language that has been carefully designed to make all such talk impossible."

A contributor to the Jewish newsletter *Aish* tells how he discovered this truth.

When I started to learn Torah 26 years ago, my insistence on my ability to know was perhaps my greatest obstacle to actually knowing God. My questions—about the Holocaust, the suffering of the innocent—were arrogant demands that the Infinite God fit into the confines of my three-pound brain. My turning point came when Rebbetzin Heller said to me, "This word, *olam* in Hebrew, comes from the root word meaning 'hidden.' God is essentially hidden in this world. No matter how smart you are, no matter how much you know, you will never fully know God." Then she added, "And would you really believe in a God that was no bigger than your finite mind's ability to grasp?"

When I gave up the presumption of knowing, on that day I started to learn.

❧

THE WIDE yet precise understanding of *heart* alluded to above has an ancient pedigree, running from the Egyptian Middle Kingdom and earliest biblical usage into the shtetls of Eastern Europe, through the early years of North American settlement to its continuing appearance in recent literature. As Michael Downey records:

In earliest Biblical and Christian usage, "heart" meant the whole, total person; the individual at this time was not understood as a being with the separate faculties of intellect and will, but as a unity. The heart, from this perspective, was not associated with the will, affections, or emotions as opposed to reason or the intellect. It was looked to as the single root of all thought and wishes and of the moral and religious life.

Later,

Rabbi Baer of Radoshitz once said to his teacher, the rabbi of Lublin: "Show me one general way to the service of God."

The zaddik replied: "It is impossible to tell men what way they should take. For one way to serve God is through the teaching, another through prayer, another through fasting, and still another through eating. Everyone should carefully observe the way his heart draws him to, and then choose this way with all his strength."

❦

AND NOT only heart:

A Chabad Hasid once came to visit Rabbi Mendel of Kotzk. In the course of their discussion, the rebbe asked the man what the prayers really meant to him. The Hasid launched into an elaborate discourse derived from intense study. Impatiently, Rabbi Mendel interrupted, "That's all very well. That is what it means to your head. But what does it mean to your *puppik* [bellybutton]?"

❦

IN WHAT became America, meanwhile, this continent's first great theologian, Jonathan Edwards, proposed in his *Treatise on Religious*

Affections (1746) that "true religion" resides in the heart, naming it the seat of affections, emotions, and inclinations.

> *[Edwards] opposed the effort to divide human nature into separate compartments of mind, will, and emotion, and insisted that all of these faculties are rooted in the heart, the center of human personality. Thus he believed that what we think is inevitably the product of the set of our wills, and that this in turn results from the basic direction of our hearts' desires.*

It is, then, this "heart" that *experiences*, "the heart" that, in Page Smith's words, "is a more reliable organ than the brain."

⚮

THE WISDOM of the heart's experience is not simply vision. It is *lived* vision—"personal lived reality," a source within self that synthesizes feeling and vision. A wise person does not simply garner and dispense insights, but rather has the heart to *live* those insights. As the heart muscle gives life to the whole body, so the experiencing heart centers life: It is the place where the currents of being and becoming, of what-we-are and what-we-are-not-yet, cross.

The heart thus understood is the frontier of our identity. Because we do not want to limit the self with the name of intellect alone, or will alone, or feeling alone, nor to see these as separate, we have invented the sensibly opaque name of *heart* for the identifying core of our own doing and *be*-ing.

Encompassing feeling, knowledge, desire, and decision, the human heart stands for the authentic self, the axis of our interiority, the core of our experience. Our experiential philosopher William James shared this insistence on the unity of the human, affirming, for example, that the modern case against religious faith was not proven. As James put it in his 1895 lecture at the Cambridge YMCA: "It was still intellectually permissible 'to believe in the existence of an unseen order of some kind in which the riddle of the natural order may be found explained.' What was no longer possible was the earlier dogmatic certitude—but that was less a loss than a gain, an opening to the enchanting world of 'maybe.'"

Which recalls the story of a Taoist farmer, recounted in the writings of Lao Tzu, illustrating well the dance of life's events and how difficult it can be to distinguish losses from gains.

When the farmer's horse ran away, his neighbors gathered to commiserate with him since this was such bad luck. He said, "Maybe."

The next day the horse returned, bringing with it six wild horses, and the neighbors came exclaiming at his good fortune. He said, "Maybe."

And then, the following day, his son tried to saddle and ride one of the wild horses, was thrown, and broke his leg. Again the neighbors came to offer their sympathy. He said, "Maybe."

The day after that, conscription officers came to the village to seize young men for the army. But because of his broken leg, the farmer's son was left behind.

When the neighbors came to say how fortunately everything had turned out, the farmer said, "Maybe."

❦

"UNCERTAINTY [IS] the key to *the ethic of maybe*. 'Not a victory is gained, not a deed of faithfulness or courage is done, except upon a maybe,' James insisted. Risk is the essence of life." It is also the essence of experience.

Opening one's eyes may take a lifetime. Seeing is done in a flash.

WONDER

In the name of God, stop a moment,
cease your work, look around you.
LEO TOLSTOY

"Concepts create idols; only wonder comprehends
anything." People kill one another over idols.
Wonder makes us fall to our knees.
JÜRGEN MOLTMANN

We lay and looked up at the sky and the millions of stars that
blazed in darkness. The night was so still that we could hear the
buoy on the ledges out beyond the mouth of the bay. Once or twice
a word spoken by someone on the far shore was carried across
the clear air. A few lights burned in the cottages. Otherwise,
there was no reminder of other human life. . . .

It occurred to me that if this were a sight that could be seen
only once in a century or even once in a human generation, this
little headland would be thronged with spectators. But it can be

seen many scores of nights in any year, and so the lights burned in
the cottages and the inhabitants probably gave not a thought
to the beauty overhead; and because they could see it almost
any night perhaps they will never see it.

RACHEL CARSON

A we. Wonder. Mystery. Reverence. How can we choose among these words a title for this segment? There is a two-sidedness to wonder: On the one hand, standing in awe of a reality that is incomprehensibly greater than "self," we experience our smallness, our relative insignificance in the presence of immensity; yet also, our very human capacity for that awe, that wonder, calls into experience what the author of the psalms [8:5] describes and the apostle Paul quoted with approval in his letter to the Hebrews [2:7]: "... you have made him a little lower than the angels, and have crowned him with glory and honor!" This exclamation expresses a double wonder: at the generosity of God or the magnificence of the universe, and at the majesty, the very wonder, of human *be*-ing.

Awe is a reflex of spirit.

ELPENOR

... our capacity for awe is the lens through which creation
passes.... So reverence should be thought of as prior to belief.
It is the human predisposition, perhaps as universal among us as
any other, to sense the grandeur of the event we call being, to
consider the heavens, to ponder the cunning of a hand.

> *. . . reverence is the great corrective to the tendency of*
> *belief to warp, contract, harden. This is true, I think, because*
> *reverence is a kind of awe, and awe is a kind of humility.*
>
> MARILYNNE ROBINSON

❧

AWE IS THE ORIGINAL spiritual act. Some have thought that religion—even spirituality—began in dread and fear. Their vision is of a cowering primitive humanity, terrified by the forces of nature, desperately hoping to control or at least to placate those forces.

But familiarity with primitive traditions such as those of Native Americans suggests otherwise. "Primitive" means *earlier*, not "stupid." In many things ecological, in fact, primitive means *purer* in the sense of "closer to the source." Yes, contact with powers and forces and realities greater than ourselves can evoke fear and the desire to control; but the more natural first response is the kind of awe that is wonder, a marveling that can become worship, a worship occasioned less by fear than by gratitude. The first prayer is not "Gimme" but "Wow!"

> *. . . when you come right down to it, there are only four basic*
> *prayers. Gimme! Thanks! Oops! and Wow! . . . Wow! are prayers of*
> *praise and wonder at the creation. Oops! is asking for forgiveness.*
> *Gimme! is a request or a petition. Thanks! is expressing gratitude.*
>
> MARC GELLMAN

Spirituality begins not in fear ("help/save me") nor in greed ("give or get for me") but in the sense of awe, wonder, and gratitude ("Wow!" "Thanks!") evoked at a realization of, in the aware presence of, beauty—whether perceived in the grandeur and magnificence of the universe or in the hint of infinity in a newborn infant.

"What is man, that you are mindful of him?" asked the psalmist in the verse preceding the one quoted previously. We do not ask questions like that anymore. Which may be why it is so difficult to believe the next verse's response: "...a little lower than the angels ... crowned with glory and honor."

∞

AWE IS not fashionable these days. The calculating mind—and those who live by it—refuses the limitation that wonder and mystery imply.

> *Awe and wonder are concepts that have fallen into extreme*
> *disfavor, if not actual contempt, in our culture. Rather than*
> *admiring what is greater and better than ourselves, we try to*
> *destroy it. We disfigure what is more beautiful than we are and*
> *ridicule what is more profound than we are and drag what is*
> *higher than we are down to our own level. We feel diminished by*
> *the existence of these things, whereas we should feel exalted. We*
> *shut ourselves off from everything that would lift us up.*
>
> WILLIAM H. HERR

"Today's mystery," runs the usual assumption, "is tomorrow's truism." And for the calculating mind, this is true: The only purpose of any limit, the only reason for its being, is to be overcome. But not all reality accepts calculation. Not all limits are contingent. The hammer, so useful in pounding in any kind of nail—indeed so effective for any kind of pounding—eventually meets the screw.

Screwdrivers exist, of course. But to believe that nothing can be beyond manipulative control is to believe that the universe is composed solely of nails.

A man traveled across land and sea to investigate the Master's extraordinary fame.

"What miracles has your Master worked?" he asked a disciple.

"Well, there are miracles and then there are miracles," the disciple replied. "In your land it is regarded as a miracle if God does someone's will. In our country, it is regarded as a miracle if someone does the will of God."

∞

SOCIAL THEORIES derived from the Enlightenment, which assume that scientific mastery over nature ought to "exorcise" fear and awe and thus make people feel more secure, cannot explain why so many feel more insecure than ever, why so many find it tempting, therefore, to think of ourselves as helpless victims of circumstances.

After several thousand years, we have advanced to the point where
we bolt our doors and windows and turn on our burglar alarms—
while the jungle natives sleep in open-door huts.

MORRIS MANDEL

From ancient times, civilizations have distinguished two ways of knowing. We are perhaps most familiar with naming them art and science. The Greeks called them *muthos* and *logos*. Both, then and after, were regarded as essential, and neither was viewed as privileged over the other. They were not in conflict but complementary, each enjoying its own sphere of competence. *Logos* ("reason") was the pragmatic mode of thought that enabled people to function effectively in the world. It had, therefore, to correspond accurately to that external reality. Science answers "How?"

But *logos* could not assuage human grief nor find any kind of ultimate meaning in life's struggle. For those needs, people turned to *muthos*, to forms of art such as stories. Art suggests "Why?" It makes no pretensions to historical exactness but rather offers ways of healing—making whole—the brokenness that is untouchable.

Through many long nights and years, the rabbis discussed and debated over that passage in Torah (Genesis 6:6), when just before the story of Noah and the Flood it says that G-d° "regretted that he had made man."

"How could Ha'Shem, perfect and unchangeable, 'regret'?" they asked. And the answer most commonly given was that this was a figure of speech, used to convey to mankind the depth of human departure from the divine.

But one rabbi, who remains nameless, argued otherwise. "No," he insisted, "if Torah says G-d regretted, then G-d regretted. For indeed, He had to: humans can regret, and their regret can be a good act. And whatever humans can virtuously do, that act must first be in G-d."

And so we know that, at least once, G-d said that word you never want to hear from your surgeon: "Oops!"

° Out of respect for Orthodox Jewish practice, when drawing on stories from that tradition, the name of the divinity will not be spelled out.

❦

MYTHIC STORIES, it has been suggested, never happened because they are always happening.

The experiencing mind—the mind open because it contemplates rather than calculates—recognizes the intractable reality of limitation. Boundaries hallmark the real. For beings destined to die, and knowing that, the recognition of finite should pose neither threat nor challenge. For even if a boundary or limit cannot be transgressed, crossed over, passed through, perhaps it can be looked across . . . seen beyond. And the only fit first response, the only possible initial reaction, to such glimpses of "beyond" is the wonder that is awe.

What is *beyond*? The literal meaning of the word's original form—*begeondan*—is "on the farther side." *Beyond* implies a sort of peekaboo with reality . . . or, better, reality playing peekaboo with us. An implication, then, of reality glimpsed rather than seen clearly and directly. And so one wishes to see more.

"Beyond" is the reason that reach exceeds grasp. Recognition of a beyond has sparked all human exploration, from mountain peaks to ocean depths, from the Silk Road to the space program. But there is another two-sidedness in our apprehension of "beyond." On the one hand, it is a goal, and as such perhaps can be reached, eventually. But that attainment, that reaching that finally does grasp, always discovers another goal, a further *beyond*.

Human beings seem made to reach—to *beyond*, in the verb form proposed by Kenneth Burke. Why? Could it be that we experience awe, we require awe, because there is engraved and ingrained in our very human *be*-ing the need to go beyond, a need for transcendence? We are "made for more." The question is: What kind of "more"? A related question may be, "What kind of faith might that 'more' require?"

Every day a farmer's daughter carried fresh milk to customers in nearby villages. One of her customers was a Brahman, and to reach his hut, the milkmaid had to use a ferry raft to cross a river.

The Brahman worshiped daily, offering the fresh milk to God. But one day the milkmaid was very late, and the Brahman grew angry.

"What can I do now with this milk?" he scolded her. "You are so late—it is of no use to me now."

"I started out early," replied the milkmaid, "but I had to wait a long time for the ferryman to bring me across the water."

The Brahman chided her: "What?" he said. "People have walked across oceans by repeating the name of God—and you can't cross this little river to get my milk to me on time?"

The milkmaid was ashamed, taking his words to heart. And from that day on, she brought the milk to him each day on time. One day he asked her why she was now able to bring the milk to him on time, never even a moment late.

"Just as you said," she replied, "I cross the river by repeating the name of God without waiting for the ferry. With God's name in my heart and on my lips, I walk across the water and my foot does not sink."

The Brahman shook his head in disbelief. "Can you show me how you crossed the river on foot?" he asked. Surely, he thought, if a simple milkmaid could walk on water, he could, too!

Walking with the Brahman to the water's edge, the milkmaid

stepped into the river, and began to walk across the surface of the water. Looking back, she saw the Brahman lift the hem of his garment as he began to mutter the name of God and enter the water. With just one step, he began to sink.

She called back to him as she continued her walk across the water. "Sir, it is no wonder that you are sinking! How is God to carry you over the water when in the very act of speaking his name, you lift up your garment for fear of getting it wet?"

⚬⚬

THE *WONDERFUL* hints an answer to the question "What kind of more?" What makes some thing, some phenomenon, some experience "wonder full"—full of wonder and, so, inspiring awe? The glib and at times sarcastic use of such words as *wonderful* and *awesome* more than suggest that the meaning of those terms has been lost. Too easily, the precious-treasured morphs into the precious-cute. But we can do better than that:

> *Wonder is the experience of mystery. It is a fascinated recognition*
> *of great beauty where a moment before we noticed only routine;*
> *it is an attitude of amazement and perplexity, and sometimes a*
> *stunned curiosity in the face of the astonishing and inexplicable.*
> *In some way, however strange, it is often a form of homage elicited*
> *by the presence of something larger than ourselves.*
>
> PAUL BROCKELMAN

If we have lost the meanings of awe and wonder, we have probably also lost the ability to sense them. Or, if we experience them, we do not know how to talk about them, which means that we are incapable of thinking about them. And unable to grasp them even tenuously in thought, their experience evanesces, fades into a kind of nothingness. And yet—

> *Reality is that which refuses to go away*
> *when I stop believing in it.*
> PHILIP K. DICK

A mother was watching her four-year-old child playing outside in a small plastic pool half filled with water. He was happily walking back and forth across the pool, making big splashes. Suddenly, he stopped, stepped out of the pool, and began to scoop water out of the pool with a pail.

"Why are you pouring the water out, Johnny?" the mother asked. "'Cause my teacher said Jesus walked on water, and this water won't work," the boy replied.

❧

PERHAPS WE have lost the sense of awe and wonder because we first lost the sense of mystery: "Wonder is the experience of mystery," Paul Brockelman observed. But from childhood, for most of us, a mystery is something to be solved. We have been taught that all mysteries, like all puzzles, have solutions. But there is a difference between a mystery and a puzzle, and that is precisely the point: Puzzles have solutions, but mysteries . . . well, genuine mysteries remain shrouded in mystery.

> *I'm for mystery, not interpretive answers. . . . The answer is*
> *never the answer. What's really interesting is the mystery.*
> *If you seek the mystery instead of the answer, you'll always be*

seeking. I've never seen anybody really find the answer,
but they think they have. So they stop thinking. But the job is
to seek mystery, evoke mystery, plant a garden in which
strange plants grow and mysteries bloom. The need for
mystery is greater than the need for an answer.

KEN KESEY

In an ironic and even cynical age, perhaps too much of our mis-education has been devoted to disenchanting us, to teaching us to "see through" not only appearances but things themselves. But as C. S. Lewis noted during the dark days of World War II:

You can't go on "seeing through" things forever. The whole point
of seeing through something is to see something through it.
To "see through" all things is the same as not to see.

⁂

WHAT IS *wonder*? "Something that causes amazement or awe, a marvel," suggests one dictionary. "Awe," the same dictionary suggests, has to do with "fear or reverence," an interesting combination.

The mysterious is the most beautiful thing we can experience. It is
the source of all true art and science. He to whom the emotion is a
stranger, who can no longer pause to wonder and stand wrapped
in awe, is as good as dead—his eyes are closed. The insight into
the mystery of life, coupled though it be with fear, has also given
rise to religion. To know what is impenetrable to us really exists,
manifesting itself as the highest wisdom and the most radiant
beauty, which our dull faculties can comprehend only in their

most primitive forms—this knowledge, this feeling is at
the center of true religiousness.

ALBERT EINSTEIN

One large problem flows from the mistrust of mystery, the willed blindness that denies awe and wonder: These refusals entail the forfeiture of miracle. The person unable to experience awe becomes incapable of encountering miracle. For "miracle," as Maurice Friedman reminds in his delightful *Dialogue with Hasidic Tales*, "is simply the wonder of the unique that points us back to the wonder of the everyday."

No, it's not fools who turn mystics. It takes a certain amount of
intelligence and imagination to realize the extraordinary queerness
and mysteriousness of the world in which we live. The fools, the
innumerable fools, take it all for granted, skate about cheerfully on
the surface and never think of inquiring what's underneath.

ALDOUS HUXLEY

∞

YET THERE is a problem with where we have been. We have treated "awe" and "wonder" as having to do with the *tremendum*— with the large, the gigantic. But the sublime may reside just as well at the other end of the size spectrum. A very real kind of awe and wonder can also be elicited by simplicity and innocence.

For thirty-five years, Paul Cézanne lived in obscurity, producing masterpieces that he gave away to unsuspecting neighbors. So great was his love for his work that he never gave a thought to achieving recognition.

He owes his fame to a Paris dealer who chanced upon his paintings, gathered some of them, and presented the world of art with the first Cézanne exhibition. The world was astonished to discover the presence of a master.

The master was just as astonished. He arrived at the gallery leaning on the arm of his son and could not contain his amazement when he saw his paintings on display. Turning to his son he said, "Look, they have framed them!"

༄

AWE AND wonder are a gift of innocence. Faced with the sublimity of the *tremendum*, we experience awe in the awareness of our own minusculeness in its presence. "What is man, that you are mindful of him?" A necessary aspect of healthily self-aware human *be*-ing is the recognition of a real simplicity, a necessary innocence in the face of the unimaginable immensity of greatness.

A little boy opened the big old family Bible with fascination, looking at the pages as he turned them. Suddenly, something fell out of the Bible, and he picked it up and looked at it closely. It was an old tree leaf that had been pressed in between the pages.

"Momma, look what I found," the boy called out.

"What have you got there, dear?" his mother asked.

With astonishment in the young boy's voice, he answered: "I think it's Adam's suit!"

༄

IS IT POSSIBLE not to "recapture innocence" but in some way to become again innocent? We have wondered about that recently, watching some very old (i.e., older than us) people, the parents of friends, slip into what is medically termed dementia. Yes, we have some idea about what is happening physiologically to their brain tissue. And so do some of them. But that does not seem to stop them from somewhat enjoying their visits to bad-memory lane. And at times they even seem puzzled that others do not. Observation suggests that it is more often the children rather than the parent who become upset over the parent's poor memory.

It may be a stretch to call this "innocence," but we are becoming more and more convinced that this is what innocence looks like: the simplicity of living thoroughly in the present when the present is all that one has. It has been suggested that *complex* means just that—necessarily not simple—while *complicated*, with its hint of an actual folding, denotes the unnecessarily un-simple, that which need not be folded. Liquid reality, and most people, are necessarily complex. Spiritual reality is uncomplicated.

A little boy wanted to meet God. He knew it was a long trip to where God lived, so he packed his suitcase with Twinkies and a six-pack of root beer and started off.

When he had gone about three blocks, he saw an old woman sitting in the park staring at some pigeons. The boy sat down next to her and opened his suitcase. He began to take a drink of root beer when he noticed that the old woman looked hungry, so he offered her a Twinkie. She accepted it and smiled at him. Her smile was so pretty that the boy wanted to see it again, so he offered her a root beer. Again, she smiled at him. The boy was delighted!

They sat there all afternoon eating and smiling, never saying a word. As it grew dark, the boy realized he was tired and started to leave, but before he had gone a few steps, he turned around, ran back to the old woman, and gave her a hug. She gave him her biggest smile ever. When the boy got home a short time later, his mother was surprised by the joy on his face.

She asked, "What did you do that made you so happy?" He replied, "I had lunch with God." Before his mother could respond, he added, "She's got the most beautiful smile I've ever seen!"

Meanwhile the old woman, radiant with joy, returned to her home. Stunned by the look of peace on her face, her son asked, "Mother, what did you do that made you so happy?" She replied, "I ate Twinkies in the park with God," adding, "You know, he's much younger than I expected."

❧

THERE IS a humility in simplicity, in innocence—a humility the more attractive because we realize it is so unaware. If one can abstain from self-conscious awareness of it, there is a similar humility in awe, whether that awe be awakened by the *tremendum* or the tiny.

❧

YOU WANT both *tremendum* and tiny?

A young man, when he was counseled to become a shohet [ritual slaughterer], replied, "Rebbe, I am afraid of such great responsibility."

The rebbe retorted: "So, what would you have me do—appoint one who is not afraid?"

∽

. . . the unwanting soul
sees what's hidden,
and the ever-wanting soul
sees only what it wants.

Two things, one origin,
but different in name,
whose identity is mystery.
Mystery of all mysteries!
The door to the hidden.

LAO TZU, Tao-Te-Ching,
as translated by Ursula K. Le Guin

COMMUNITY

All things are connected.
The art of community is discovering how.

MARK NEPO

A team of evangelical Christians invaded Shipshewana, Indiana, to bring the lost of Shipshewana to Christ. In front of Yoder's dry goods one of these earnest souls confronted a Mennonite farmer with the question "Brother, are you saved?"

The farmer was stunned by the question. All his years of attending the Peach Bloom Mennonite congregation had not prepared him for such a question—particularly in front of Yoder's.

Wanting not to offend, as well as believing that the person posing the question was of good will, he seriously considered how he might answer. After a long pause, the farmer asked his questioner for a pencil and paper and proceeded to list the names of ten people he believed knew him well.

Most, he explained, were his friends but some were less

than that and might even be enemies. He suggested that the evangelist ask these people whether they thought him saved since he certainly would not presume to answer such a question on his own behalf.

∽∾

WHOSE NAMES would you put on such a list? Most probably you would list people with whom you have experienced some sense of community. But what does that mean? "Community" implies a relationship based in some similarity, not of blood or family but of something else participated in. Communities can be based on place, but the term is also used to designate individuals who share some affinity, who have something in common.

Community, then, means "others," and others are, of course, in some way or ways *different*. Difference can be either enriching or threatening. For most people, history suggests, the perception of "different" more often implies potential threat than possible enrichment. We tend to "like" those who are like us, but our ability to perceive and recognize *likeness* varies. Too often, it seems, the very concept of *other* suggests competition rather than cooperation. Many reasons, personal and social, can be adduced why this is so, but let's look at one that may help change our experience by helping us to experience it differently.

Through some weird misconstrual of the phrase *survival of the fittest*, an individualistic culture has distorted that phrase beyond the intentions of Charles Darwin. The clearest exposition of the real meaning of those words appears in a turn-of-the-twentieth-century book by evolutionary theorist Peter Kropotkin, *Mutual Aid: A Factor of Evolution*. Arguing against the emphasis on interper-

sonal competition put forth by "social Darwinists," Kropotkin detailed his actual field observations "that it was an evolutionary
emphasis on co-operation instead of competition . . . that made for
the success of species." Those who survived, and especially those
who flourished, did so as participating members of families, clans,
tribes.

Within these communities, each participant accepted and lived
the axiom "You alone can do it, but you cannot do it alone." *Community* is not some large, theoretical concept but a place where our relationships with others are based on personal rather than market
considerations. *Community* is a setting where *helping* and *service* are
not by-products of calculation but flow from a way of seeing, a
way of *be*-ing that recognizes the deep connectedness that binds us
together in *need*, if not in love.

> *If I am not for myself, then who will be for me? And if I am*
> *only for myself, then what am I? And if not now, when?*
> RABBI HILLEL

With the advance of civilization—and even earlier, if E. O. Wilson
is correct—such groups need not require blood or kinship relationship. But it is such groups, and only such groups, that merit the
name *community*.

The Yid was asked: "In the Talmud it says that the stork is called
hasida in Hebrew, that is, the devout or the loving one, because
he gives so much love to his mate and his young. Then why is he
classed in the Scriptures with the unclean birds?"

He answered: "Because he gives love only to his own."

❧

"PAY ATTENTION to yourself," spiritual guides suggest, and the experience of truly attending to oneself requires developing an awareness of self as related to others, as a member of a community. *"I don't want to 'fit in': I want to belong,"* said a newcomer at an AA meeting. The sense of belonging is related to telling/listening to stories. Participation in community opens doors to a way of life that can be preserved and handed on only within a community, within a setting in which stories are explicitly or implicitly told and heard. In such a community we learn that the experience of spirituality is more than seeing, more than feeling, more than willing, more than doing—it is the interplay and interconnection of all four.

Classic spiritual traditions suggest as the criterion of spirituality that one seek out "the company of the saints." And so who are my "friends"? What kind of people do I like to be with? What kind of people seek me out? What do we do together? Am I, and are they, "better" for our time together? On whom do I rely? Who can rely on me? The first meanings of *rely* are to band together, to be devoted to, to adhere or to belong to.

> *He who travels alone travels fastest,*
> *but in the company of friends you go farther.*
> BREYTEN BREYTENBACH

There is an old rabbinic tale: The Lord said to the rabbi, "Come, I will show you hell."

They entered a room where a group of people sat around a huge pot of stew. Everyone was famished and desperate. Each held a spoon that reached the pot but had a handle so long it could not be used to reach their mouths. The suffering was terrible.

"Come, now I will show you heaven," the Lord said after a while.

They entered another room, identical to the first—the pot of stew, the group of people, the same long spoons. But there everyone was happy and nourished.

"I don't understand," said the rabbi. "Why are they happy here when they were miserable in the other room, and everything was the same?"

The Lord smiled. "Ah, but don't you see?" he said. "Here they have learned to feed each other."

※

COMMUNITY AND identity interweave. To be a member of a community requires a sense of personal identity, an awareness of who we are and who we are not, which suggests both what we can give to and what we need from the community. This in turn requires some degree of constancy, and one source of that constancy is some bond, some link, some firm connection to something larger than ourselves. Indeed, that deep and enduring connection is one function of "community." If we did not remain the same in some way from one day to the next, our relationships could not survive—relationships would become impossible. "Each day a new beginning" is at best a very partial truth. But perhaps not for everyone:

Don Parker was interviewing a ninety-four-year-old man in Port Washington, New York, as part of an American Civil Liberties

Union oral history project. At one point Parker asked him, "At this time in your life, what gives you the most satisfaction?"

The ninety-four-year-old man thought a moment then responded, "No peer pressure."

⚭

COMMUNITY REQUIRES a shared story—a story that is shared. Individuals "sharing" their separate stories—no matter how similar those stories may be—is not the same as "shared story." Community is not created: It is discovered.

"*Shared* story": Words sometimes fail because the primary responsibility of words is to convey ideas. Conveying *experience* requires more. That "more" may be—usually is—dressed in words. But what happens too often is that while some idea may be communicated, no experience is genuinely shared in the true sense of that far too overused word. Genuine *sharing* involves not merely communication but a kind of communion.

A little boy sits on the front steps of his home on a very hot day. He is tired and perspiring, but his home is not air-conditioned, so he stays out, hoping for a wisp of breeze. Suddenly his apron-clad mother comes out the screen door and hands him one of those old-fashioned two-stick Popsicles—the whole thing! Smiling, she pats him on the head and returns indoors to continue her chores.

The little boy cannot believe how cool that Popsicle feels as he gently removes the paper from it. The better to catch a possible breeze and so make his life perfect, he moves out to the curb. As he is seating himself, his best friend appears and sits down beside him. No word passes between the two, but our little boy carefully splits his Popsicle in half and offers his friend his choice of the halves.

And so they sit there, in silence, each communing with his Popsicle, but each even more enjoying the friendship of the other.

∽

THIS IS sharing in the deepest meaning of that overused word— giving someone part of what we have and enjoying (or at times suffering) it together, usually without words. For in the presence of such an experience, words are superfluous.

At such moments, indeed, words can be worse than superfluous—they can injure and destroy meaning, making not only communion but communication itself impossible. What are these words that have lost meaning as well as power, that have become meaningless and, worse, useless because they lie in wait to entrap careless speakers? They are words that pretend to convey experience. "Sharing" itself is a good example of what happens to a word forced to do more than a word can do. In one popular usage, this term—once so richly generous—has come to connote unwelcome intrusive behavior, as in "thank you for sharing"— a meaningless phrase, a cliché, words offered with little thought or insight, another way of saying, "Okay, let's move on."

∽

TRUE COMMUNITY begins in *attending*: Spirituality, wisdom, "that-which-all-seek" is transmitted from one person to another by *being present* in an open way, by listening in such a way that we are willing to surrender our previous worldview. What happens first, in any "community," is that those who would participate in it listen. But if we would listen, we must also tell—and community is the place where we can tell and listen. Those wrestling with spiritual dilemmas do not need answers but presence—permission to confront the dilemma and struggle with it aloud. This need not—indeed, *cannot*—be done perfectly. But as G. K. Chesterton pointed out, "Anything worth doing is worth doing badly."

Such community rests also on an openness to service.

The rabbi of Kotzk once said of a famous rabbi: "That's a zaddik in a fur coat." His disciples asked him what he meant by this.

"Well," he explained, "one man buys himself a fur coat in winter, another buys kindling. What is the difference between them? The first wants to keep only himself warm, the second wants to give warmth to others, too."

⚬⚬

SOME COMPLAIN about the lack of a sense of community. It is not always clear what they miss. But perhaps a rethinking of our attitudes toward others will help. If today our common life in society seems to lack shared purpose and commitment, if it has become a life with little in common, perhaps at least a part of the problem is that we have understood our common life mainly in terms of rights and entitlements, in terms of the language of obligation, and not in terms of a virtue like gratitude, of a practice such as generosity.

The difference between a "winner" and a
"whiner" is the sound of the "I."

ANONYMOUS

Depression seems an epidemic complaint in the postmodern world. As Thomas J. Scheff has incisively investigated, one possible source of depression, and a potent root of shame, is having no experience, as an adult, of being an accepted member of a real community.

Theologian Gilbert Meilaender poses a choice: "Either we should stop bemoaning the loss of community and common purpose in our society, or we should learn to talk not just the language of rights and duties but also the language of virtue." What does this mean? Well, for one thing, the "language of virtue" recognizes gratitude as an obligation that shatters the boundaries of our usual talk about duties; for gratitude is finally not a duty to be discharged but an attitude that pervades and shapes the whole of life.

It intrigued the congregation to see their rabbi disappear each week on the eve of the Sabbath. They suspected he was secretly meeting with the Almighty, so they sent one member to follow him.

This is what the man saw: the rabbi disguised himself in peasant clothes and served a paralyzed Gentile woman in her cottage, cleaning out the room and preparing a Sabbath meal for her.

When the spy got back, the congregation asked, "Where did the rabbi go? Did he ascend to heaven?"

"No," the man replied, "he went even higher."

◌◠◌

TO OBTAIN perspective, to come to see one's life from another point of view, requires others, or at the very least *an*-other.

However this takes place, it involves the kind of breaking through routine that is *greatness*—which Rabbi Hillel Goldberg described as "sensitivity to the needs of those around you . . . the capacity to see suffering and the courage to act."

A story about such greatness:

A Hasidic rebbe was in Siberia for seven years. One day, out of the blue, a hardened guard approached him and said: "Today, you are free. Just sign here." One problem. It was Shabbes, the Jewish Sabbath (when writing is forbidden). The rebbe said, "I won't sign." The guard said, "Then you stay here another year!"

Meanwhile, an old Jew, next to the rebbe, was also told, "Today, you are free. Just sign here." The old Jew was in a quandary. The rebbe didn't sign. How could he? So he refused.

The rebbe turned to the old man and said: "Sign." The old Jew wouldn't. So the rebbe said, "Give me the pen. I'll sign for him!" And the rebbe did.

The guard was baffled by the turn of events. No one had refused to leave Siberia ever before. And here, the one man who did would not violate the Shabbes by writing. But to help someone else leave, the same rebbe violated the Sabbath and signed.

"What's going on?" the guard demanded.

"Me? I made a calculation," said the rebbe. "I've been here seven years. I think I could survive another year. I feel up to it. So I have no right to violate the Shabbes. My life is not at stake. But this old Jew is weak. He wouldn't survive another year. So he has to sign, and if he won't, I must sign for him to save his life."

Amazed, the guard said: "For that, I am letting you both go."

⸎

COMING TO see our lives from "another point of view"—this is where community comes in. Community is the place where we "feel good" because we *fit*. "Fitting" is the meaning of *good*, a word that shares origin with *gather* and *together*: We "feel good" when we *are* "good," when we *fit*, like a hand in a glove or, better, like tired, cold feet slipped into a warm pair of perfectly fitting furry slippers after a trudge through winter's snow. In this comfortable setting we become able to see alternatives. Surrounded by others whom we see and accept as like ourselves, we become able to see and *to experience* a reality that is larger than our usual relatively narrow world.

Lawrence Kushner, in his *Book of Words*, calls up a special kind of community, an echo of *home*, by conjoining "family" and "Israel":

> *"Family—Israel": Home is where they have to let you in simply be-cause you're you. And family are the people who live there. They are the ones you get whether you like them or not. In the last tally, they may be all any of us have. As Adin Steinsaltz is once alleged to have quipped, "The worst thing about being a Jew is that you have to associ-ate with them."*
>
> *The power of congregational life comes from precisely this involun-tariness of association. We look about the room and realize these people are not friends or even acquaintances; we do not agree with them about much; these are simply people we are stuck with. The*

often cited teaching of the sages that "All Israel are intermingled with one another," probably means something more like "We are all stuck with one another." This generates a kind of love, both more intense and more complicated than the voluntary variety. These members of our community, just like the people in our family, literally make us who we are.

Page 17 of the AA "Big Book," *Alcoholics Anonymous*, offers a quietly profound observation: "We are people who normally would not mix."

❧

OVER THE AGES, many wise and even saintly people have presented spirituality as essentially a solitary experience. The American philosopher and psychologist William James, in his study *The Varieties of Religious Experience*, defined "religion" as "*the feelings, acts, and experiences of individual men in their solitude, so far as they apprehend themselves to stand in relation to whatever they may consider the divine*" [italics James's]. James cited not only David Brainerd and George Fox as exemplars of finding God "while walking in a solitary place," but also the late medieval saint John of the Cross and Persian mystic Al-Ghazali, who used "solitary" or "solitude" four times in one brief page.

Finding spirituality in solitude and solitariness expresses one point of view. The seeds of many practices in both Eastern and Western Christian spiritualities were first sown by the "Desert Fathers," who are often portrayed as solitaries. But a focus on this aspect of their lives overlooks the experience and teaching of the great Saint Basil, who, after touring Egypt and Palestine and trying his own vocation as a solitary recluse, came to see a community based upon the social nature of man as alone providing the opportunity of fulfilling the Christian commandment to love one's neighbor. For Basil, the defect of the solitary life was that it provided no opportunity to practice the virtues of humility and patience or to perform the practical works of mercy. "If you live alone," he asked, "whose feet will you wash?"

> *What makes loneliness an anguish*
> *Is not that I have no one to share my burden,*
> *But this:*
> *I have only my own burden to bear.*
> DAG HAMMARSKJÖLD

Martin Buber's life as well as his teaching drives this point home. In Buber's view, the dangerous consequence of presenting God as part of the psyche and doing away with God's transcendence, God's radical "otherness," is the concomitant loss of respect for the otherness of persons and hence the loss of real relationship.

Buber's writings suggest this practice as the key to the religious life: Seek God in and through meetings with others and the world. Seek the other as unique and different, as "other," for behind the other as human partner stands the eternal and transcendent other, the eternal Thou, God. The sense of the "other" in Judaism derives from the importance of developing a relation to the utterly other, the unseen and transcendent God. This respect for otherness also means that the other-than-me, the world and others, is of ultimate value.

Such respect involves *caring*, a word at times too cheaply used. A story about why Moses was chosen to lead the Chosen People conveys its real meaning . . . and importance.

Why Moses? Our rabbis have taught us that when our teacher Moses (peace be upon him!) was tending the flock of Jethro, his father-in-law, in the desert, a young kid escaped from him. He followed it until it reached a place where leek-plants were growing, and when the kid reached the plants it saw a pool of water and stopped to drink.

When Moses came up to it, he said: "I did not know that you ran away because you were thirsty: now you must be tired." So he picked up the kid, put it on his shoulder, and walked back to his flock.

The Holy One, blessed be He, said: "Because you have shown mercy in leading the flock of a mortal man, you shall surely lead my flock, Israel."

❧

BUBER UNDERSTOOD and embraced such respectful caring to the point that his core message became that the self can be known only as it relates to that which is other than it. To find its depth and destiny, the self must be embedded in ever-widening circles of responsible relationship to other persons, to family, community, and the world. Appreciation for ever-widening circles of relationship pushes one's temporal frame of reference out from the present, back to the past, and toward the future. Buber writes: "I begin to realize that in inquiring about my own origin and goal I am inquiring about something other than myself."

Two friends were walking through the desert. At one point they had an argument, and one friend slapped the other one in the face.

The one who got slapped, without saying anything, wrote in the sand: "TODAY MY BEST FRIEND SLAPPED ME IN THE FACE."

They kept walking until they found an oasis, where they decided to bathe. The one who had been slapped started drowning and his friend saved him. When he recovered from his fright, he wrote on a stone: "TODAY MY BEST FRIEND SAVED MY LIFE."

The friend who saved and slapped his friend, asked him, "Why, after I hurt you, you wrote in the sand, and now you write on a stone?"

The other friend replied: "When a friend hurts us, we should write it down in the sand, where the winds of forgiveness can erase it away. When something great happens, we should engrave it in the stone of the memory of the heart, where no wind can erase it."

⸺⧖⸺

MEMORIES OF suffering and shame and their impact on community infuse the work of Holocaust survivor Elie Wiesel, who offers a trenchant perspective on friendship.

What is a friend? Someone who for the first time makes you aware of your loneliness and his, and helps you to escape so you in turn can help him. Thanks to him you may remain silent without shame and speak freely without risk.

And another (nameless) Holocaust survivor told:

> *I learned about friendship in Auschwitz. When I was cold, strangers shielded me with their bodies from the blowing winds, for they had nothing else to offer but themselves.*

And so we circle back to the story of community, a story that does not preclude argument or dissension but instead celebrates a diversity of opinion and a broadening of perspective. Indeed, the nature of community can be surprising, at times even scandalous, to the uninitiated.

During a service at an old synagogue in Eastern Europe, when the Shema prayer was said, half the congregants stood and half remained sitting. The half that was seated started yelling at those standing to sit down, and the ones standing shouted at the ones sitting to stand up.

The rabbi, learned as he was, didn't know what to do. His congregation suggested that he consult a house-bound ninety-eight-year-old man who was one of the original founders of their temple. The rabbi hoped the elderly man would be able to tell him what was the actual temple tradition, so he went to the nursing home with a representative of each faction of the congregation.

The one whose followers stood during Shema asked the old man, "Is the tradition to stand during this prayer?"

The old man answered, "No, that is not the tradition."

The one whose followers sat said, "Then the tradition is to sit during Shema!"

The old man answered, "No, that is not the tradition."

Then the rabbi said to the old man, "But the congregants fight all the time, yelling at each other about whether they should sit or stand."

The old man interrupted, exclaiming, "THAT is the tradition!"

DARK

We are as forlorn as children lost in the woods. When you stand in front of me and look at me, what do you know of the griefs that are in me and what do I know of yours? And if I were to cast myself down before you and weep and tell you, what more would you know about me than you know about Hell when someone tells you it is hot and dreadful? For that reason alone we human beings ought to stand before one another as reverently, as reflectively, as lovingly, as we would before the entrance to Hell.

FRANZ KAFKA

. . . spiritual love is born of sorrow. . . . For men love one another with a spiritual love only when they have suffered the same sorrow together, when through long days they have ploughed the stony ground buried beneath the common yoke of a common grief. It is then that they know one another and feel one another, and feel with one another in their common anguish, and thus they pity one another and love one another. For to love is to pity; and if bodies are united by pleasure, souls are united by pain.

MIGUEL DE UNAMUNO

L ife is not always smooth. It is often not pretty. But beauty is a diverse reality.

Though they are more closely packed together, the stories in this segment less invite than compel pause for thought. "Meditation" can mean many different things. In the classic thought of the West, its practice involves story: visualizing, thinking on, or chewing over some narrative. "Lessons" rarely appear; there is rather the image, or the idea, that will not go away.

That is what these stories did for us . . . to us.

Early in World War II in Moscow there lived a woman named Lida. Her husband was a pilot, and she didn't love him very much, but they got along well enough. When the husband's plane is shot down, the widow attends his funeral. But two months later, a strange young man, very malnourished and pale, begins following her. "Don't you recognize me?" he asks. "I'm your husband."

Accepting his return without emotion, Lida accompanies him to the forest in which his plane crashed, where he wants her to bury the flight suit he'd left behind in a pit. After hours of shoveling, she realizes her husband has vanished. Back home, exhausted, she falls asleep. In her dream her husband comes to her and says, "Thank you, Lida, for burying me."

This visitation conjures a stark and unbreakable bond, all the more powerful in its lack of false tenderness. A husband returns from the grave not to rekindle love or remembrance but to get his ungrieving widow to grant him a decent burial. Duty, not love, is the marriage vow she must keep.

❧

FOR WHATEVER reasons, it is the Russian literary tradition that enriches us with the most memorable stories of sorrow and loss and grief. What can you remember from *The Brothers Karamazov*? Perhaps you recall the rampages of the drunken father, or the speech of the Grand Inquisitor. Our recollection of plotlines, even from standbys of the literary canon, is often hazy and uncertain.

But here's a different question: What can't you forget? One story, told in almost by-the-way fashion, has haunted many English-language readers since the novel's first translation in 1912.

Grushenka, a passionate "fallen woman," tells the tale of a wicked peasant who dies and is dragged by devils into a lake of fire. The peasant's guardian angel tries to save her by telling God of the single good deed the woman performed in her lifetime: she once pulled an onion from her garden and gave it to a beggar.

"Take that onion, then," God replies, "hold it out to her in the lake, and let her take hold." If the onion doesn't break, God continues, "let her come to Paradise." But as the angel draws the peasant out, other sinners cling to her, seeking their own rescue, and she selfishly kicks them away. The onion breaks, and down she sinks. So the angel wept and went away.

❧

AS THE intertwined masks over performance stages remind, tragedy and comedy are related: Each is dependent on the other. In their reception, however, there can be at least one large difference. The depth of tragedy touches most, if not all. Comedy, especially in the form of humor, bites in a different way.

Yaakov, a farmer living in Israel's lush Galilee region, was giving a tour of his farm to his new mother-in-law. The newlywed farmer genuinely tried to be friendly to his new mother-in-law, hoping that it could be a friendly, non-antagonistic relationship. All to no avail, though, as she kept nagging him at every opportunity, demanding changes, offering unwanted advice, and generally making life unbearable for Yaakov and his new bride.

While they were walking through the barn, Yaakov's mule suddenly reared up and kicked the mother-in-law, killing her instantly. It was a shock to all no matter their feelings toward her.

At the funeral service, Yaakov and his wife sat as well-wishers paid their respects. The rabbi, however, noticed that whenever a woman would whisper something to Yaakov, he would nod his head yes and say something. Whenever a man walked by and whispered to Yaakov, however, he would shake his head no, and mumble a reply.

Very curious as to this bizarre behavior, the rabbi later asked Yaakov what that was all about.

Yaakov replied, "The women would say, 'What a terrible tragedy,' and I would nod my head and say, 'Yes, it was.' The men would then ask, 'Can I borrow that mule?' and I would shake my head and say, 'Can't. It's all booked up for a year.'"

❧

WE WILL several times remind of those intertwined masks of comedy and tragedy. Always in the background, however, loom some words of Eugene O'Neill:

Laughter
means turning your back on suffering.
And on the hard truth that tragedy
writes the last act—always.

A story is told about a soldier who was finally coming home after having fought in Vietnam. He called his parents from San Francisco. "Mom and Dad, I'm coming home, but I've got a favor to ask. I have a friend I'd like to bring with me."

"Sure," they replied, "we'd love to meet him."

"There's something you should know," the son continued. "He was hurt pretty badly in the fighting. He stepped on a land mine and lost an arm and a leg. He has nowhere else to go, and I want him to come live with us."

"I'm sorry to hear that, son. Maybe we can help him find somewhere to live."

"No, Mom and Dad, I want him to live with us."

"Son," said the father, "you don't know what you're asking. Someone with such a handicap would be a terrible burden on us. We have our own lives to live, and we can't let something like this interfere with our lives. I think you should just come home and forget about this guy. He'll find a way to live on his own."

At that point, the son hung up the phone. The parents heard nothing more from him. A few days later, however, they received a call from the San Francisco police. Their son had died after falling from a building, they were told. The police believed it was a suicide. The grief-stricken parents flew to San Francisco and were taken to the city morgue to identify the body of their son. They recognized him, but to their horror they also discovered something they didn't know: Their son had only one arm and one leg.

❦

GRIEF, SORROW: Always, it seems, they come tinged with regret. "If only I had . . ." Sometimes we experience regret for our actions; more often, for our omissions. But all evidence suggests that regret is an essential, inseparable part of the human condition.

Despite that, regret is rarely anticipated.

Once upon a time there was a blind girl who hated herself just because she was blind. She hated everyone, except her loving boyfriend. He was always there for her. She said that if she could only see the world, she would marry him.

One day, someone donated a pair of eyes to her and then she could see everything, including her boyfriend.

Her boyfriend asked her, "Now that you can see the world, will you marry me?"

The girl was shocked when she saw that her boyfriend was blind, too. Hating her former blindness, she refused to marry him.

Her boyfriend walked away in tears.

Months later she received a letter. "Just take care of my eyes, dear," he wrote.

❦

FOR THE seasoning of grief and sorrow is love—the experience that gives these universal emotions their sweet/bitter aftertaste. Yet with how many foreign substances can love be mixed yet remain genuinely love? Who among us might ever claim "pure love"? The problem is not always "selfishness—self-centeredness." Sometimes it can be the relative ranking of our loves—not necessarily "Who/What comes first?" but "Who/What do we really *choose*?"

Once upon a time in the forests of Russia there lived a peasant named Ivan and his wife, Maria. They had many friends and they loved each other very much. But they were unhappy because they had no children.

One cold winter day they watched the village children playing in the snow.

"Let's build a child out of snow!" Ivan said, and they lovingly created a snow maiden with little arms and little legs, a nose, a chin, and a rosebud mouth. She was so beautiful that they regarded her with awe.

"If only she could speak!" Ivan cried.

"If only she could come to life and share our old age with us!" said Maria.

And the miracle happened. The lovely little snow girl began to run and dance and sing.

"I will stay with you forever," the snow girl told the old man and his wife, "unless you love me too little. And then I shall melt away and return to the land of ice and snow."

The old man and his wife were overjoyed, and during the long, cold winter days the snow girl brought much happiness into their lives.

One day the village children went into the forest to play and invited the little snow girl to go with them. But she wandered off and was lost. As darkness fell, she called out to the forest animals to help her return to the village. The little red fox agreed to help her.

Back in the village, the old couple watched the children return from the forest but their snow girl was not with them. They cried bitterly, believing that they had lost her forever.

In the dark of the night, the fox returned with the snow girl and with great tears of happiness they thanked the red fox and offered him a loaf of bread for his troubles. But the fox knew that he had returned a great treasure, and he was hungry and tired.

"Surely your beautiful snow girl is worth one of your chickens," said the fox.

Now, a chicken is a large gift and not to be taken lightly. "Surely a loaf of bread is a sufficient reward for his troubles," they grumbled.

Overhearing them, the little snow girl began to cry. "Because you love me less than you love your chickens," she said, "I must leave you and return to the land of ice and snow."

Then she was gone.

❧

SUCH A tale strikes deep: Who among us has not put a price on the very things that make our lives meaningful, realities that cannot in truth be possessed, bartered, or sold?

Perhaps it is time for a break, ever mindful of those twin masks of comedy and tragedy that guide our way.

A man was being tailgated by a stressed-out woman on a busy boulevard. Suddenly, the light turned yellow, just in front of him. He did the right thing, stopping at the crosswalk, even though he could have beaten the red light by accelerating through the intersection.

The tailgating woman was furious and honked her horn, screaming in frustration as she missed her chance to get through the intersection, dropping her cell phone and makeup.

As she was still in mid-rant, she heard a tap on her window and looked up into the face of a very serious police officer. The officer ordered her to exit her car with her hands up. He took her to the police station, where she was searched, fingerprinted, photographed, and placed in a holding cell. After a couple of hours, a policeman approached the cell and opened the door. She was escorted back to the booking desk, where the arresting officer was waiting with her personal effects.

He said, "I'm very sorry for this mistake. You see, I pulled up behind your car while you were blowing your horn, flipping off the guy in front of you, and cussing a blue streak at him. I noticed the 'What Would Jesus Do?' bumper sticker, the 'Choose Life' license plate holder, the 'Follow Me to Sunday School' bumper sticker, and the chrome-plated Christian fish emblem on the trunk.

"Naturally, I assumed you had stolen the car."

❦

AND THEN, neither comic nor tragic, there is the . . . plaintive?

Two men, both seriously ill, occupied the same hospital room. One man was allowed to sit up in his bed for an hour each afternoon to help drain the fluid from his lungs. His bed was next to the room's only window. The other man had to spend all his time flat on his back.

The men talked for hours on end. They spoke of their wives and families, their homes, their jobs, their involvement in the military service, where they had been on vacation.

Every afternoon when the man in the bed by the window could sit up, he would pass the time by describing to his roommate all the things he could see outside the window.

The man in the other bed began to live for those one-hour periods when his world would be broadened and enlivened by all the activity and color of the world outside.

The window overlooked a park with a lovely lake. Ducks and swans played on the water while children sailed their model boats. Young lovers walked arm in arm amid flowers of every color and a fine view of the city skyline could be seen in the distance.

As the man by the window described all this in exquisite detail, the man on the other side of the room would close his eyes and imagine the picturesque scene.

One warm afternoon the man by the window described a parade passing by.

Although the other man couldn't hear the band, he could see it in his mind's eye as the gentleman by the window portrayed it with descriptive words. Days and weeks passed.

One morning, the day nurse arrived to bring water for their baths only to find the lifeless body of the man by the window, who had died peacefully in his sleep. She was saddened and called the hospital attendants to take the body away.

As soon as it seemed appropriate, the other man asked if he could be moved to the bed formerly occupied by his friend. The nurse was happy to make the switch, and after making sure he was comfortable, she left him alone.

Slowly, painfully, he propped himself up on one elbow to take his first look at the real world outside.

He strained to slowly turn to look out the window beside the bed.

It faced a blank wall.

❧

A STORY about reading this segment?

A certain man planted a rose and watered it faithfully and before it blossomed, he examined it.

He saw the bud that would soon blossom, but noticed thorns upon the stem and he thought, "How can any beautiful flower come from a plant burdened with so many sharp thorns?"

Saddened by this thought, he neglected to water the rose, and just before it was ready to bloom . . . it died.

❧

CAN A dark story carry a bit of humor? Or vice versa?

The little boy ran into the house all upset, announcing that his pet turtle had rolled over and died. He was inconsolable. His mother called her husband, and when Daddy came home, he gathered up the boy in his arms as he sat crying in front of the dead turtle, telling him that maybe they could have a funeral for the turtle. Yes, and not only that, but Daddy would bury him in the little tin box in which they kept the candy. The boy stopped crying and listened intently. "Then," chimed in the mother, "we can have a party afterward." By this time the boy was smiling. Encouraged, his father went on, "Yes, and we'll have balloons and some of your friends over and everything." The boy began grinning from ear to ear. Then, suddenly, to the surprise of them all, the turtle rolled back on his legs and began walking slowly away.

The boy looked startled and exclaimed, "Oh, Daddy—let's kill it!"

∽

TOO MANY STORIES? Too much comic relief? Let's move to two tales of a very different kind.

Under the heading "Good Grief," the prominent sociologist Amitai Etzioni reflected on his own experience of grief in an op-ed piece in the *New York Times*:

> *Soon after my wife died—her car slid off an icy road in 1985—a school psychologist warned me that my children and I were not mourning in the right way. We felt angry; the proper first stage, he said, is denial.*
>
> *In late August this year, my 38-year-old son, Michael, died suddenly in his sleep, leaving behind a 2-year-old son and a wife expecting their next child. When, at Michael's funeral in Los Angeles, I was about to say a few words to the people assembled, the rabbi whispered that I need not fear speaking publicly—"Just go with the flow," she urged.*
>
> *On both occasions, I had a hard time not telling the free advice givers to get lost, or something less printable along the same lines. There is no set form for grief, and no "right" way to express it.*

. . . A relative from Jerusalem who is a psychiatrist brought some solace by citing the maxim: "We are not to ask why, but what." The "what" is that which survivors in grief are bound to do for one another. Following that advice, my family, close friends and I keep busy, calling each other and giving long answers to simple questions like, "How did your day go today?" We try to avoid thinking about either the immediate past or the bereft future. We take turns playing with Max, Michael's 2-year-old son. Friends spend nights with the young widow, and will be among those holding her hand when the baby is born.

I presume that many a psychiatrist and New Age minister would point out that by keeping busy we avoid "healthy" grieving. To hell with that; the void left by our loss is just too deep. For now, focusing on what we do for one another is the only consolation we can find.

A similar message is reported by Alida Gersie in her study of *Storymaking in Bereavement*:

This is what a woman whose daughter died of a brain tumor at the age of eight and whose twenty-year-old son became severely handicapped following a motorbike accident said:

Do not show us the road to recovery. Whatever recovery might mean. Allow us to find our own way through. To find comfort in your compassion, not in your consolation. To find strength in your helplessness, now that we feel so utterly helpless. Let us know that you too are speechless, wounded and outraged because the universe has done this to us and therefore to the human community. Listen to our guilt, when we think in spite of ourselves, that our child's death was some kind of divine punishment for our shortcomings. Hear the reality of these shortcomings. Do not diminish them in our own eyes, but help us also to see the strength of our love, and the solidity of our care. We have discovered that life can no longer be relied upon to safeguard us. Understand that therefore we feel in so many respects lost and lonesome. Try to comprehend our fear, and hear it. Do not try to remedy it, or to protect us against it. We need the full measure of our fear, so that we may discover the full strength of our courage. We also need the full measure of our self-accusation, so that we may experience the depth of our forgiveness.

People who talk at grief, instead of holding hands with grief,
are a menace. Words come later, but only after tears.

JOHN BOWKER

Miguel de Unamuno, whose words opened this segment, also wrote:

The chiefest sanctity of a temple is that it is a place
to which men go to weep in common.
. . . Yes, we must learn to weep! Perhaps that is the supreme wisdom.

"At the gates of paradise" stories usually have happy endings, albeit sometimes with a little twist. Here is one that may be more twisted than most.

A man arrives at the pearly gates, waiting to be admitted. God is reading through the Big Book to see if the man's name is written in it. After several minutes, God closes the book, furrows his brow, and says, "I'm sorry, I don't see your name written in the Book."

"How current is your copy?" he asks.

"I get a download every ten minutes," God replies. "Why do you ask?"

"I'm embarrassed to admit it, but I was always the stubborn type. It was not until my death was imminent that I cried out to you, God, so my name probably hasn't arrived to your copy yet."

"I'm glad to hear that," God says, "but while we're waiting for the update to come through, can you tell me about a really good deed that you did in your life?"

The guy thinks for a moment and says, "Hmm, well, there was this one time when I was driving down a road and I saw a giant group of biker gang members harassing this poor girl. I slowed down, and sure enough, there they were, about twenty of 'em torturing this poor woman. Infuriated, I got out of my car, grabbed a tire iron out of my trunk, and walked up to the leader of the gang. He was a huge guy, six-foot-four, two hundred and sixty pounds or more, with a studded leather jacket and a chain running from his nose to his ears. As I walked up to the leader, the bikers formed a circle around me and told me to get lost or I'd be next.

"So I ripped the leader's chain out of his face and yelled to the rest of them saying, 'Leave this poor innocent girl alone! You're all a bunch of sickos! Go home before I really teach you a lesson!'"

God, duly impressed, says, "Wow! When did this happen?"

"About three minutes ago."

⚬⚬⚬

SOME STORIES, though containing a touch of dark, also bring a kind of experience of light—albeit mainly to those who do not suffer a similar disability.

A farmer had some puppies he needed to sell. He painted a sign advertising the four pups and set about nailing it to a post on the edge of his yard. As he was driving the last nail into the post, he felt a tug on his overalls. He looked down into the eyes of a little boy.

"Mister," he said, "I want to buy one of your puppies."

"Well," said the farmer, as he rubbed the sweat off the back of his neck, "these puppies come from fine parents and cost a good deal of money."

The boy dropped his head for a moment. Then reaching deep into his pocket, he pulled out a handful of change and held it up to the farmer.

"I've got thirty-nine cents. Is that enough to take a look?"

"Sure," said the farmer. And with that he let out a whistle. "Here, Dolly!" he called.

Out from the doghouse and down the ramp ran Dolly followed by four little balls of fur.

The little boy pressed his face against the chain-link fence. His eyes danced with delight. As the dogs made their way to the fence, the little boy noticed something else stirring inside the doghouse.

Slowly another little ball appeared, this one noticeably smaller. Down the ramp it slid. Then in a somewhat awkward manner, the little pup began hobbling toward the others, doing its best to catch up.

"I want that one," the little boy said, pointing to the runt.

The farmer knelt down at the boy's side and said, "Son, you don't want that puppy. He will never be able to run and play with you like these other dogs would."

With that the little boy stepped back from the fence, reached down, and began rolling up one leg of his trousers.

In doing so he revealed a steel brace running down both sides of his leg attaching itself to a specially made shoe.

Looking back up at the farmer, he said, "You see, sir, I don't run too well myself, and he will need someone who understands."

With tears in his eyes, the farmer reached down and picked up the little pup.

Holding it carefully, he handed it to the little boy.

"How much?" asked the little boy.

"No charge," answered the farmer, "there's no charge for love."

⤜⤛

AND SO we depart this "dark" segment, the gentle—we hope— exploration of the grief and sorrow and pain that are part of the human condition of each one of us. Without such advertence, we think, no book that hopes to open to the experience of spirituality can approach completeness. For as perhaps our favorite story reminds:

A person died and stood before God.

God asked, "Where are your wounds?"

The person answered, "What wounds? I have none."

God said, "Was there nothing worth fighting for?"

LISTENING

We need a "way of thinking" that is a way of listening.
We can begin to think only after we hear the cry, but we
can also hear the cry only after we have begun to think.

DAVID MICHAEL LEVIN

The ear is the most spiritually determined of the senses.

SØREN KIERKEGAARD

Ever since what is called the "Enlightenment" took place in eighteenth-century Europe, cultures affected by it have emphasized *seeing* at the expense of *hearing.* Most metaphors for *knowing* are visual: "I see that" runs a common expression of mental grasp.

This approach shaped American psychological thinking, especially our understanding of how we ourselves function. The "Looking-Glass self" became the image of the interaction between how we see ourselves and how others see us. In this understanding, it is the detached act of looking, observing the way others respond to us, that moves us to shape our actions—and ourselves—as we strive to make the best impression on the social milieu in order to gain the most advantage from it.

But there was—and is—also another tradition:

Many years ago a great lord, nearing the end of his days, counseled his daughter:

"The green of the plum tree is gone and now is the time of blossoming. And yet, my child, you have not chosen a husband. Suitors come and go but you find none to your liking. Am I to die, then, and leave you alone?"

"No, my father," said the Lady Yumiyo. "I will create a drum of silk stretched upon a bamboo frame. He who hears the notes when my fingers strike is the man I will marry."

"Ah! Foolishness!" her father despaired. "A silken drum will make no sound. I fear that I shall never see a grandchild."

Lady Yumiyo made the drum nevertheless. Many would-be suitors came to listen, stretching forth their heads, listening closely, anxious to hear the sound of the silk drum. Some came because of Lady Yumiyo's radiant beauty. Some came for her wit and charm. Some came because they knew she would inherit great wealth. And some came for all three reasons.

But not one heard a sound when she struck the drum with her fingers.

"I told you so," said her father.

But Lady Yumiyo was silent and went on striking the drum as suitors came and went.

Then, one fine spring day, a young man appeared in the doorway. He was richly dressed, with a perceptive glance and the appearance of having traveled a long distance.

Bowing deeply to the old lord, he gave a slightly lesser bow to Lady Yumiyo.

"Tell us," the father asked, "from where have you come?"

"From beyond the mountains, seas, and valleys."

"And what have you come for, from such a faraway land?"

"I have come for your daughter, the Lady Yumiyo."

The old lord sighed. "She is for him who can hear the silk drum. No one has heard it. Do you mean to say that the sound has reached you beyond the mountains, seas, and valleys?

"No, my Lord," the young man responded with humility. "The sound of the drum has not reached me."

"Then why linger here?"

"I have heard its silence," said the young man.

With a smile, the Lady Yumiyo gently set the silken drum aside. She no longer had any need of it.

∞

LISTENING: HEARING may be the most difficult gift we ever give to anyone. We are so inclined to action, to attempt to "fix" situations, or at the very least—and too tragically often at the very most—we are driven to advise. And yet listening—hearing and truly *attending* to—requires a very explicit context of silence. Genuine, active, attentive *silence* is not only the setting but the most difficult *form* of this difficult gift.

Related to the posture of listening and the openness of silence is another practice, one whose name remains surprisingly uncorrupted in an era of individualistic competition: *compassion*. Some may scorn compassion, viewing it as a sign of weakness; most at least try to revere it. Compassion, its most profound students say,

... is experienced not when someone teaches us how to think or act, ... when we receive advice about where to go or what to do [or] when we hear words of reassurance and hope: ... What really counts is that in moments of pain and suffering someone stays with us. More important than any particular action or word of advice is the simple presence of someone who cares.

As McNeill, Morrison, and Nouwen in *Compassion* go on to point out:

Simply being with someone is difficult because it asks of us that we share in the other's vulnerability, enter with him or her into the experience of weakness and powerlessness, become a part of uncertainty, and give up control and self-determination.

In a time so filled with methods and techniques designed to change people, to influence their behavior, and to make them do new things and think new thoughts, we have lost the simple but difficult gift of being present to each other. We have lost this gift because we have been led to believe that presence must be useful.

⤳⤳

A RECOVERED alcoholic physician well describes what is at stake here—not only as the essential first step to sobriety, but for anyone's spiritual life:

Over the ensuing years I've learned more about surrender. I played with the idea that listening to and learning from everybody and everything might not only constitute surrender, but could define humility.... I began to equate listening with surrender.

I believe that if I try to listen without condoning and condemning, simply in order to understand what is being said, I am in a state of surrender. For example: if I take my troubles to a friend, and he or she listens to me with only one idea in mind—to understand what I am trying to say—then he or she will neither agree nor disagree with my words.

All my life I yearned to meet someone who would simply hear me—not advise me, nor criticize me, not even agree with me—just hear me. And my listening, nonjudgmental friend does just that. Being heard in this way makes me eager to tell more. And my friend knows that through really listening, he or she will connect with me. So he or she listens to me with even more intensity.

And the two of us connect through the art of listening.

&

DESPITE ALL the use of visual—SEEING—imagery in our understanding of knowledge, there is a kind of priority in hearing. Unlike seeing, where one can look away, one cannot "hear away" but must listen.... Hearing implies already belonging together in such a manner that one is claimed by what is being said. We don't have "earlids"!

Many have distinguished *listening* from *hearing*, but not always consistently. Most agree that to listen is to *attend* to, to *pay attention* to. There is less consensus about hearing. To some, it implies the simple act of distinguishing some sound, for example, hearing a noisy car radio while trying to carry on a conversation. Others locate a deeper meaning in hearing, taking it to signify absorption of the real meaning of what is heard, be it music or words: "I hear you." For the purposes of this segment, we substantially equate the meaning of *listening*, to attend to, with the second sense of *hearing*, to absorb the real meaning of what is being listened to. Truly listening to—hearing in the second sense—as opposed to merely "hearing" stories requires not the distancing of "objectivity" but the kind of "letting go" to, immersion in, asked by all works of art.

The valuing of *hearing* has a long tradition. For despite all the emphasis on the visual—seeing—and especially the use of its imagery when we think and talk about *knowing*, hearing historically enjoys a sort of priority. Judaism's *sh'ma*—"Hear, O Israel"—posits a logic based on hearing rather than seeing. Herbert Weiner, in his study of the Kabbala, points out the difference of this Jewish approach from the Greek emphasis on *theoria* (seen, beheld): "To the Jew, identification of truth with that which can be seen is the beginning of idolatry."

And not only "to the Jew." Attending—listening—is an essential component also of Christian spirituality. *Obsculta*—"Listen thoroughly"—insists the first word of the sixth-century Rule of Saint Benedict, the longest-flourishing monastic canon. Six centuries later, Saint Bernard of Clairvaux urged: "You wish to see; Listen. Hearing is a step toward Vision."

When a man whose marriage was in trouble sought his advice, the Master said, "You must learn to listen to your wife."

The man took this advice to heart and returned after a month to say that he had learned to listen to every word his wife was saying.

Said the Master with a smile, "Now go home and listen to every word she isn't saying."

Some might reasonably object that good listening is aided by clear communication. True, but all cases need not end as drastically as this one:

Down in rural central Georgia, a Catholic priest and a Baptist pastor who were friends were out fishing one day by the side of the road. They thoughtfully made a sign reading, "The End Is Near! Turn yourself around now before it's too late!" and showed it to each passing car.

One person driving by didn't appreciate the sign and shouted at them: "Leave us alone, you religious nuts!"

All of a sudden they heard a big splash. Looking at each other, the priest said to the pastor, "You think we should just put up a sign that reads 'Bridge out'?"

∞

OF COURSE, good listening may at times require a bit of imagination:

A little boy was doing his math homework. He said to himself, "Two plus five, that son of a bitch is seven. Three plus six, that son of a bitch is nine...."

His mother heard what he was saying and gasped, "What are you doing?" The little boy answered, "I'm doing my math homework, Mom."

"And this is how your teacher taught you to do it?" the mother asked.

"Yes," he answered.

Infuriated, the mother asked the teacher the next day, "What are you teaching my son in math?"

The teacher replied, "Right now, we are learning addition."

The mother asked, "And are you teaching them to say 'Two plus two, that son of a bitch is four'?"

After the teacher stopped laughing, she answered, "What

I taught them was, two plus two, THE SUM OF WHICH is four."

∽

THE WORLD has always needed good listeners, for only good listeners are truthful tellers. "Good listening" involves the surrender of a self-centered view of the world; it entails the equation of trust and love that flows from that surrender. To listen, to surrender, to trust, to love: these are to be open to the experience of *discovery*.

Spirituality flourishes in discovery, and especially in the discovery of shared story—the discovery that creates community. For community is where we can learn and practice storytelling and its virtues, "humility" and "obedience"—two painfully misunderstood qualities that are really the arts of listening. Humility involves the refusal to coerce, the rejection of all attempts to control others; real listening may be the most humanizing act of humility. Obedience—to obey—meant originally "to listen thoroughly."

One morning a group of teenagers asked Reb Yerachmiel: "What is the point of human life? Why are we here?"

The rebbe replied: "If a tree falls in a forest, does it make a sound?"

The children debated this for a while and then the rebbe replied: "Here is my understanding. Without an ear to register the vibrations of the falling tree, no sound is produced. Sound is not a thing but a transaction between things. For there to be sound there must be a falling tree and an ear to hear. Why are we here? We are the other half of the transaction. We are here to hear."

"But other beings hear!" a student said. "And dogs can hear sounds humans can't hear. Are dogs more important than us?"

"True," Reb Yerachmiel said, "dogs can hear what we cannot. But we can hear what even dogs cannot. We can hear the cry of a broken heart. We can hear the outrage of injustice. We can hear the whisper of empathy. We can hear the silence of death. You are here to listen not only to what everyone else can hear, but also to that which only you can hear."

⬡

WRITERS' FAVORITE metaphors convey their understanding of human development. A significant contribution of author Carol Gilligan is her resort, continually, to the metaphor of voice. For Gilligan, it is not by looking that the self develops but by talking and listening. It is through communication with others, through sharing their concerns and desires, that we come to understand ourselves and our responsibilities in the world. The self gains strength not in accumulating power but in becoming part of a web of relationships.

As Mihaly Csikszentmihalyi has pointed out, Gilligan's insight breaks from the understandings of selfhood implicit—and at times explicit—in the mainline tradition of American social science. According to this school of economics, the autonomous self is like a weasel hiding in its burrow, waiting to pounce on any unwary victim. Motivated by a fierce individualistic need to survive and prevail, it neither asks for nor gives quarter. By contrast, Gilligan suggests that care and responsibility for the well-being of others represent qualities at least as desirable as those associated with the more self-centered image of the self. Her more human self, responsive and dependent on others, is a definite improvement.

"Responsive and dependent on others": not only alert to the messages of others but replying in one's own way; not jealous over prerogative but open and willing to learn—sometimes by truly hearing only one small voice:

There was once a very ascetic man who consumed no food or drink while the sun was in the heavens. In what seemed a sign of heavenly approval for his fasting, a bright star shone above a nearby mountain, visible to everyone in broad daylight.

One day the man decided to climb the mountain. A little village girl insisted on going with him. The day was warm and soon the two became thirsty. The man urged the child to drink, but she said she would not unless he drank too. The poor man was in a quandary. He hated to break his fast; but he hated more to see the child suffer from thirst. Finally he drank. And the child drank with him.

For a long time he dared not look up to the sky, for he feared the star had gone. So imagine his surprise when, on finally looking up, he saw two stars shining brightly above the mountain.

֍

HEARING IS the key to the union of vision and feeling. Listening is the key to community, for hearing implies already *belonging* together in such a manner that one is being claimed by what is being said. As we listen, truly *hearing*, our understanding of the world changes from a self-centered focus to an other-oriented openness—we come to understand how we are connected with other realities, with other people.

A man tells the story of the day he was driving quietly along a country road and suddenly realized that he was lost:

> I stopped at a small farmhouse to ask for directions, and I saw an elderly woman sitting on the porch. An elderly man was working around the front yard, whistling nonstop. The whistling was loud and clear, but it seemed aimless and purposeless. There was no recognizable tune, just whistling.
>
> When I walked up to the man, I couldn't resist saying, "I see you're fond of whistling."
>
> "Oh," he said, "it's second nature to me now."
>
> Then, pointing to the woman on the porch, he explained that she was his wife, and that they had been happily married for thirty-eight years when she became blind. Coming as it did so late in life, the blindness had been a very frightening experience for her, and she was still feeling a deep-seated insecurity.
>
> The husband said, "I figured if I just keep whistling while I'm outside the house, she'll have the security of knowing that I'm still with her."

❦

A CLASSIC American axiom warns: "Don't try to think yourself into a new way of acting: Act yourself into a new way of thinking." We are used to learning by doing, by experience. A more ancient philosophy, but one that fits well with this pragmatic approach, suggests: "Listen yourself into a new way of seeing." For this is what is at stake: an ability to apprehend and comprehend what has been hidden from us or what previous generations have been seduced into ignoring.

A man came home from work late again, tired and irritated, to find his five-year-old son waiting for him at the door. "Daddy, may I ask you a question?"

"Yeah, sure, what is it?" replied the man.

"Daddy, how much money do you make an hour?"

"That's none of your business. What makes you ask such a thing?" the man said angrily.

"I just want to know. Please tell me, how much do you make an hour?" pleaded the little boy.

"If you must know, I make twenty dollars an hour."

"Oh," the little boy replied, head bowed. Looking up, he said, "Daddy, may I borrow ten dollars, please?"

The father was furious. "If the only reason you wanted to know how much money I make is just so you can borrow some to buy a silly toy or some other nonsense, then you march yourself straight to your room and go to bed. Think about why you're being so selfish. I work long, hard hours every day and don't have time for such childish games."

The little boy quietly went to his room and shut the door. The man sat down and started to get even madder about the little boy's questioning. How dare he ask such questions only to get some money?

After an hour or so, the man had calmed down, and started to think he may have been a little hard on his son. Maybe there was something he really needed to buy with that ten dollars, and he really didn't ask for money very often. The man went to the door of the little boy's room and opened it. "Are you asleep, son?" he asked.

"No, Daddy, I'm awake," replied the boy.

"I've been thinking, maybe I was too hard on you earlier," said the man. "It's been a long day and I took my aggravation out on you. Here's that ten dollars you asked for."

The little boy sat straight up, beaming. "Oh, thank you, Daddy!" he said. Then, reaching under his pillow, he pulled out some more crumpled-up bills.

The man, seeing that the boy already had money, started to get angry again. The little boy slowly counted out his money, then looked up at the man.

"Why did you want more money if you already had some?" the father grumbled.

"Because I didn't have enough, but now I do," the little boy replied. "Daddy, I have twenty dollars now. Can I buy an hour of your time?"

❦

A DIFFERENT kind of "at home" story about listening: A minister tells—

One Sunday I was entertained in a farm home of a member of a rural church. The intelligence and unusually good behavior of the only child in the home, a little four-year-old boy, impressed me.

Then I discovered one reason for the child's charm. The mother was at the kitchen sink, washing the intricate parts of the cream separator, when the little boy came to her with a magazine.

"Mother," he asked, "what is this man in the picture doing?"

To my surprise she dried her hands, sat down on a chair, and,

taking the boy in her lap, she spent the next few minutes answering his questions. After the child had left, I commented on her having interrupted her chores to answer the boy's question, saying, "Most mothers wouldn't have."

"I expect to be washing cream separators for the rest of my life," she told me, "but never again will my son ask me that question."

⌘

TO APPRECIATE "the inner meaning of another's experience" requires something not often considered part of the "strenuous mood" lauded by William James. But James did acknowledge the importance of the ability to listen truly and well, recognizing that all community begins in listening. "Spirituality," "wisdom," "that-which-all-seek" is initially transmitted from one person to another by *attending*, one of James's favorite verbs, which means to be present in a hearing way, to listen to others in such a way that we are willing to surrender our own worldview. Only by such "attending" can we discover the way of life that we really seek—a way of life that is more than mere "worldview" in the same way that wisdom is more than knowledge and love is more than acquaintance. What happens first, in any "community," is that those who would participate in it listen.

Attending: A man stood in a Metro station in Washington, DC, and started to play the violin; it was a cold January morning. He played six Bach pieces for about forty-five minutes. During that time, since it was rush hour, it was calculated that thousands of people went through the station, most of them on their way to work.

Three minutes went by and a middle-aged man noticed there was a musician playing. He slowed his pace and stopped for a few seconds and then hurried up to meet his schedule.

A minute later, the violinist received his first dollar tip: a woman threw the money in the till and without stopping continued to walk.

A few minutes later, someone leaned against the wall to listen to him, but the man looked at his watch and started to walk again. Clearly he was late for work.

The one who paid the most attention was a three-year-old boy. His mother dragged him along, hurrying, but the kid stopped to look at the violinist. Finally the mother pushed hard and the child continued to walk, turning his head all the time. This action was repeated by several other children. All the parents, without exception, forced them to move on.

In the forty-five minutes the musician played, only six people stopped and stayed for a while. About twenty gave him money but continued to walk their normal pace. He collected $32. When he finished playing and silence took over, no one noticed it. No one applauded, nor was there any recognition.

No one knew this, but the violinist was Joshua Bell, one of the best musicians in the world. He played one of the most intricate pieces ever written on a violin worth $3.5 million.

Two days before his playing in the subway, Joshua Bell sold out at a theater in Boston where the seats average $100.

This is a true story. Joshua Bell playing incognito in the Metro station was organized by the *Washington Post* as part of a social experiment about perception, taste, and the priorities of people.

❧

ATTENDING, PAYING attention, can be difficult in other situations. There are so many distractions. . . .

A young and successful executive was traveling down a neighborhood street, going a bit too fast in his new Jaguar. He was watching for kids darting out from between parked cars and slowed down when he thought he saw something.

As his car passed, no children appeared. Instead, a brick smashed into the Jag's side door! He slammed on the brakes and spun the Jag back to the spot where the brick had been thrown. He jumped out of the car, grabbed some kid, and pushed him up against a parked car, shouting, "What was that all about and who are you? Just what the heck are you doing?" Building up a head of steam, he went on, "That's a new car and that brick you threw is going to cost a lot of money. Why did you do it?"

"Please, mister, please, I'm sorry, I didn't know what else to do," pleaded the youngster. "I threw the brick because no one else would stop." Tears were dripping down the boy's chin as he pointed around the parked car. "It's my brother," he said. "He rolled off the curb and fell out of his wheelchair and I can't lift him up." Sobbing, the boy asked the executive, "Would you please help me get him back into his wheelchair? He's hurt and he's too heavy for me."

Moved, the driver tried to swallow the rapidly swelling lump in his throat. He lifted the young man back into the wheelchair and took out his handkerchief and wiped the scrapes and cuts, checking to see that everything was going to be okay.

"Thank you and may God bless you," the grateful child said to him. The man then watched the little boy push his brother down the sidewalk toward their home.

It was a long walk back to his Jaguar . . . a long, slow walk. He never did repair the side door. He kept the dent to remind him not to go through life so fast that someone had to throw a brick at him to get his attention.

∞

A FINAL thought, since in this book we rely so much on stories (and so little on pictures). As fantasy writer J.R.R. Tolkien noted:

However good they may be in themselves, pictures do little good in fairy-stories. All art that offers a visible presentation imposes one visible form. Literature, on the other hand, works from mind to mind and is thus at the same time more universal and more poignantly particular. If it speaks of bread or wine or stone or tree, it appeals to the whole of these things, to their ideas, but each hearer gives them a peculiar personal embodiment in an imagination derived from his or her unique history of experience.

And a final story:

It was high noon in Manhattan, and the streets were, as usual, buzzing with crowds, cars, taxis, horns blowing, brakes screeching, sirens wailing. Two men were making their way together through the crowd. One was a native New Yorker, and the other a farmer visiting from Kansas. Suddenly the farmer stopped in his tracks. "Hold on," he said, "I hear a cricket."

His friend replied, "Are you kidding? Even if there were a cricket around here, which isn't likely, you would never be able to hear it over all this noise."

The farmer remained quiet for a few moments then walked several paces to the corner, where a bush was growing in a large cement planter. He turned several leaves over and found the cricket. The city man was flabbergasted.

"What great ears you have," he said.

"No," the farmer replied, "it's a matter of what you've been conditioned to listen for. Look, I'll show you." With that, he pulled a handful of coins from his pocket and let them drop to the sidewalk. As if on signal, every head on the block turned.

"You see," said the farmer, "you hear what you want to hear. It's a matter of what you're listening for."

FORGIVENESS

Forgiveness is a funny thing; it warms
the heart and cools the sting.
WILLIAM ARTHUR WARD

Human forgiveness is not doing something but discovering
something—that I am more like those who have hurt me
than different from them. I am able to forgive when I
discover that I am in no position to forgive.
JOHN PATTON

There's a Spanish story of a father and son who had become estranged. The son ran away, and the father set off to find him. He searched for months to no avail. Finally, in a last desperate effort to find him, the father put an ad in a Madrid newspaper. The ad read: Dear Paco, meet me in front of this newspaper office at noon on Saturday. All is forgiven. I love you. Your Father. On Saturday eight hundred Pacos showed up, looking for forgiveness and love from their fathers.

Hannah Arendt has suggested that the concept of forgiveness is one of the two most original ideas in Western civilization. "Forgiving, in other words, is the only reaction which does not merely react but acts anew and unexpectedly, unconditioned by the act which provoked it and therefore freeing from its consequences both the one who forgives and the one who is forgiven."

Dag Hammarskjöld lauded forgiveness as "the answer to the child's dream of a miracle by which what is broken is made whole again, what is soiled is again made clean."

Theologian Paul Tillich called the experience of forgiveness the greatest experience anyone can have, "the fundamental experience in any encounter with God."

Such high praise has led many to urge forgiveness, some to claim forgiveness, and perhaps a few to actually forgive. But lip service, even by renowned figures, is not action. One large reason for the many failures of forgiveness would seem to be the many misunderstandings of its nature. For there are several things that forgiveness is NOT.

As William R. Miller has pointed out: "Forgiveness is not amnesia. Forgiving and forgetting may be akin, but they are two different acts. Forgiveness does not require forgetting, nor *can* one forgive that which has been forgotten. Forgiveness is a gift given with full memory of what has happened."

Abbot Anastasius had a book of very fine parchment, which was worth twenty drachmas. It contained both the Old and the New Testaments in full. Once a certain monk came to visit him and, seeing the book, made off with it. So that day when Anastasius went to his Scripture reading, he found the book gone and knew at once that the monk had taken it. But he did not send after him, for fear that he might add the sin of perjury to that of theft.

Now the monk went into the city to sell the book. He asked eighteen drachmas for it. A buyer said, "Give me the book so that I may find out if it is worth that much money." He took the book to Anastasius and said, "Father, take a look at this and tell me if you think it is worth eighteen drachmas." Anastasius said, "Yes, it is a fine book. At eighteen drachmas it is a bargain."

So the buyer went back to the monk and said, "Here is your money. I showed the book to Father Anastasius and he said it is worth eighteen drachmas."

The monk was stunned. "Was that all he said? Nothing else?"

"No, he did not say a word more than that."

"Well, I have changed my mind and don't want to sell the book after all."

Then the monk went back to Anastasius, begging him with many tears to take the book back, but Anastasius said gently, "No, brother, keep it. It is my gift to you." The monk said, "If you do not take it back, I shall have no peace."

After that the monk dwelt with Anastasius for the rest of his life.

※

NOR IS forgiveness acquittal, finding a person to be guiltless, blameless, without responsibility for what happened.

An atheist was taking a walk through the woods, admiring all that the "accident of evolution" had created. "What majestic trees! What powerful rivers!" he said to himself.

As he was walking alongside the river he heard a rustling in the bushes behind him. He turned to look and saw a seven-foot grizzly charging toward him.

He ran as fast as he could up the path. Looking over his shoulder, he saw that the bear was closing. He ran even faster, so scared that tears were coming to his eyes. He looked over his shoulder again, and the bear was even closer. His heart was pumping frantically and he tried to run even faster. He tripped and fell on the ground. He rolled over to pick himself up but saw the bear right on top of him, reaching for him with his left paw and raising his right paw to strike him.

At that instant the atheist cried out, "Oh my God! . . ."

Time stopped.

The bear froze.

The forest was silent.

Even the river stopped moving.

A bright light shone upon the man, and a voice came out of the sky: "You deny my existence for all of these years, teach others I don't exist, and even credit creation to a cosmic accident. Do you expect me to help you out of this predicament? Am I to count you as a believer?"

The atheist looked directly into the light: "It would be hypocritical to ask ME to be a Christian after all these years, but perhaps could you make the bear a Christian?"

"Very well," said the voice.

The light went out.

The river ran again.

And the sounds of the forest resumed.

And the bear dropped his right paw . . . brought both paws

together . . . bowed his head, and spoke: "Lord, for this food that I am about to receive, I am truly thankful."

❦

AND FORGIVENESS is not an achievement, an award given to the most deserving. It is not earned, nor can it be. Forgiveness is an unearned gift, freely given, without regard to merit.

There was once a man and woman who had been married for more than sixty years. They had shared everything. They had talked about everything. They had kept no secrets from each other except that the old woman had a shoebox in the top of her closet that she had cautioned her husband never to open or ask her about. For all these years, he had never thought about the box, but one day, the old woman got very sick, and the doctor said she would not recover.

In trying to sort out their affairs, the man took down the shoebox and took it to his wife's bedside. She agreed that it was time that he should know what was in the box.

When he opened it, he found two crocheted doilies and a stack of money totaling $25,000. He asked her about the contents.

"When we were to be married," she said, "my grandmother told me the secret of a happy marriage was to never argue. She told me that if I ever got angry with you I should just keep quiet and crochet a doily."

The old man was so moved he had to fight back tears. Only two precious doilies were in the box. She had been angry with him only two times in all those years of living and loving! He almost burst with happiness.

"Honey," he said, "that explains the doilies, but what about all of this money? Where did it come from?"

"Oh," she said, "that's the money I made from selling the doilies."

❧

NOR IS forgiveness approval. To forgive another's action is not to condone the act.

There was an old Sufi who earned his living by selling all sorts of odds and ends. It seemed as if the man had no judgment because people would frequently pay him in bad coins and he would accept them without a word of protest; or people would claim they had paid him when they hadn't and he accepted their word for it.

When it was time for him to die, he raised his eyes to heaven and said, "Oh, Allah! I have accepted many bad coins from people, but never once did I judge them in my heart. I just assumed that they were not aware of what they did. I am a bad coin, too. Please do not judge me."

And a Voice was heard that said, "How is it possible to judge someone who has not judged others?"

❧

AND FORGIVENESS is not understanding.

*There is a saying that to understand is to forgive, but that
is an error. You must forgive in order to understand.
Until you forgive, you defend yourself against the possibility*

> *of understanding. . . . If you forgive, you may indeed*
> *still not understand, but you will be ready to*
> *understand, and that is the posture of grace.*
>
> MARILYNNE ROBINSON

Nor, finally, is forgiveness acquiescence. It is not a license that reads: "Do whatever you like in the future, and it will be okay."

In his books on African and Afro-American tales, Roger Abrahams presents a story from Surinam and one from the Amakosa people of South Africa. In both stories, a hunter encounters a snake. In one case, it cannot get out of a hole it has fallen into; in the other, it cannot get out from under a stone that has fallen onto its back. The snake begs the hunter to rescue it. The hunter is reluctant to do so, believing that the snake will bite him when freed. The snake promises it will not. The hunter frees the snake, and, of course, the snake attempts to bite him.

Jackie Torrence, an African-American woman born in Chicago and raised in a North Carolina family steeped in oral tradition, tells a similar story wherein the snake is in a hole and has a stone upon his back. An opossum is the rescuer. The Afro-American tales are close enough to the African that one can readily see the connection.

These three stories have similar endings. In all of them, the rescuers ask a judge to decide whether it is right that the snake should bite the hand that freed it. And here again we see African influence. In West Africa it is common for a judge to ask for a reenactment of the circumstances of the case. The judges in all the stories ask the snake and the rescuer to re-create the snake's dilemma. Once the snake is again imprisoned, the judge advises the rescuer to leave the snake as he found it.

❧

WHAT, THEN, is forgiveness? To return to the thought of William Miller, "Forgiveness is knowing acceptance of the person, an acceptance that inspires change rather than waiting for it to happen." Forgiveness *inspires* change rather than waiting for it to happen.

More profoundly, Denis Donoghue has reminded:

> *The word forgiveness belongs to the divine. It is God's act: something other, something that is not ours; and unless we can acknowledge this, the word is only "a noise we make with our mouths." Its otherness is in its very name: "Forgiveness" is "given"—and not only in English and its kindred languages; the French say par-donner, the Spanish per-donar. It is not ours to give, but to receive; the human being cannot create it. We can be certain only that it is beyond us.*

Forgiveness, not tolerance, furnishes the proper corrective to the egoism and self-righteousness of groups, theologian Reinhold Niebuhr argued: "The religious ideal of forgiveness is more profound and more difficult than the rational virtue of tolerance." Tolerance too easily becomes an attitude of not believing in anything. Forgiveness, on the other hand, makes it possible for contending groups to fight without denying each other's humanity. Since the sources of social conflict cannot be eradicated, it is "more important to preserve the spirit of forgiveness amidst the struggles than to seek islands of neutrality."

∾

IN 1992, Seattle University researchers Steen Halling, Jan O. Rowe, and colleagues asked, "Why is forgiveness a neglected topic?" That could hardly be a question today with the plethora of forgiveness books bulging bookstore shelves—*Forgive to Win, Forgive for Good, Don't Forgive Too Soon, How to Forgive . . . When You Don't Feel Like It*— to name just a few. The Seattle University researchers focused on *self*-forgiveness, which must come before any genuine forgiveness of an-other is possible. What they discovered merits meditation. To summarize their findings:

> *The term self-forgiveness implies that this is a solitary act completed in isolation from others. On the contrary, the process described in this research is a long one, not entirely of one's own doing, which involves a radical shift in one's way of moving in the world. The initial experience is an emerging awareness that something is fundamentally wrong about one's life, and a feeling of estrangement from self and others. As forgiveness is gradually embodied, one moves toward feeling at home in the world.*
>
> *. . . "self"-forgiveness always takes place in the context of some variation of loving relationships with others.*

In this openness there is a kind of letting go—letting go of one's old identity, expectations, and beliefs, especially the belief that one can heal oneself. This may be combined with a sense that "life is too short" to hang on to old grudges, to punish oneself.

*. . . forgiveness is the letting go of one's
justified feelings of resentment.*
BISHOP JOSEPH BUTLER

We forgive once we give up attachment to our wounds.
LEWIS HYDE

And perhaps most incisively:

Forgiveness is giving up all hope of having had a better past.
ANNE LAMOTT

Such "letting go," however, is not an intellectual, conscious act that
we can engage in at will. There is a kind of trap here. People think
that they've forgiven themselves or somebody else when they've
just figured out why they did what they did. But that is not forgiveness. Understanding is in the head; forgiveness is a surrender of
the heart.

I heard a Padshah giving orders to kill a prisoner. The helpless
fellow began to insult the King on that occasion of despair, and
to use foul expressions according to the saying: "Who washes
his hands of life, says whatever he has in his heart." When a man
is in despair his tongue becomes long, and he is like a van-
quished cat assailing a dog.

When the King asked what he was saying, a good-natured
vizier replied: "My Lord, he says, 'Praise those who bridle their
anger and forgive men; for Allah loveth the beneficent.'"

The King, moved with pity, forbore taking his life; but another vizier, the antagonist of the former, said: "Men of our rank

ought to speak nothing but the truth in the presence of Pad-shahs. This fellow has insulted the King and spoken un-becomingly."

The King, being displeased with these words, said: "That lie was more acceptable to me than this truth thou hast uttered, be-cause the former proceeded from a conciliatory disposition, and the latter from malignity; and wise men have said, 'a falsehood resulting in conciliation is better than a truth producing trouble.'"

He whom the Shah follows in what he says, it is a pity if he speaks anything but what is good.

⬥

FORGIVENESS AND MERCY are not the same...or are they? Christians, among others, pray to be forgiven as they forgive others. But what does that "as" mean? William R. Miller, whose an-alysis of forgiveness opened this segment, suggested that "as" means *when, while*: We find our forgiveness only *in* forgiving others. Miller, a psychologist, suggests that "there is a direct relationship between the experience of accepting ourselves and our ability to accept others unconditionally. *As* we forgive, we become forgiven." Self-acceptance is no small gift.

⬥

IN THE current age of popular "spirituality" and psychology, some practitioners urge forgiving one's self—self-forgiveness—as if it were some easy exercise to be practiced almost "by the way." But thoughtful philosophical and theological writers challenge that possibility. Gordon Marino points out, for example, that "the idea that we can forgive ourselves our own trespasses violates all traditional conceptions of forgiveness. Forgiveness is a relational act and as such cannot be carried out alone."

Forgiveness of self can occur only in the context of forgiving relations with others. Forgiveness is not act nor attitude, but *discovery*. That discovery can take place only in a forgiving environment. Self-forgiveness involves a shift from self-estrangement to a feeling of being at home with the self, a shift that can take place and indeed be facilitated only in such an environment. This is thus another benefit of small communities such as twelve-step groups. Members get to know one another's lives well enough that they are able to participate in one another's stories of forgiving and of being forgiven. Such practice does not "make perfect," but it can move toward the peace that makes true forgiveness—both giving it and receiving it—possible.

One large importance of any forgiveness is that it ends the corrosion of the soul that is resentment. In any genuine forgiveness there is a true *repentance* in the original sense of that word, a *metanoia* which means a rethinking, a change of mind, transforming one's understanding, a "turn around." That which has seemed clear and stable becomes unclear and uncertain. To repent is to be troubled, precisely what the person holding a grudge or resentment does not want. The unforgiving and unforgiven individual is like the man who fell into a cesspool, and when someone lowered a rope refused it, demanding instead, "Teach me how to swim without making waves."

❧

AN IMPORTANT aspect of the self-forgiveness process is experiencing the grief that comes with letting go—grieving for what might have been, feeling regret for what was, accepting who one *is*.

*In general, the structure of self-forgiveness, or more accurately that
"of experiencing forgiveness," involves a shift from fundamental
estrangement from self and the world to being-at-home with self
and the world. This at-home-ness involves a change in one's
identity which simultaneously feels very new and very familiar,
as if recognizing for the first time someone who had always been
there: That which one has avoided accepting fully about oneself,
for example, the capacity to be enraged or hurtful, is now
acknowledged as part of who one is.*

STEEN HALLING

One also comes to a new understanding of responsibility. Where
before one was primarily in a denying or blaming stance toward
self, now there is the honest acknowledgment of participation in
the event. This awareness of responsibility frees one to move into a
more accepting relationship with self. Thus, self-forgiveness involves a shift from estrangement to being at home with one's self
and others. It involves accepting one's own humanness.

Not until 1966 was there a separate entry in The Readers' Guide to
Periodical Literature *under the word "Failure." Up to that time, anyone searching for "Failure" would find "Failure—see Success."*

A preoccupation with success—striving for it, attaining it, preserv-
ing it—obfuscates the reality of failure in human life and obscures
the need for forgiveness, too, because forgiveness presupposes failure and attempts to be creative about it.

In both relational and self-forgiveness, at some point we realize
that we have experienced forgiveness. What we had previously
negated or tried to change in self is now accepted as a part of who

we are. This acceptance leads to a new relationship with self that has the quality of "being at home," a sense of ease about oneself and one's place in the world. This is a gradual, subtle change—not a case of "before I was a stranger in a strange land but now I'm home for good"; instead there dawns a growing sense of ease about our identity and a lessening of self-recrimination and anguish over our relationship with the world.

One of my teachers had each one of us bring a clear plastic bag and a sack of potatoes to class. For every person we had refused to forgive in our lives, we were told to choose a potato, write on it the name and date, and put it in the plastic bag. Some of our bags, as you can imagine, were quite heavy. We were then told to carry this bag with us everywhere for one week, putting it beside our bed at night, on the car seat when driving, next to our desk at work.

The hassle of lugging this around with us made it clear what a weight we were carrying spiritually, and how we had to pay attention to it all the time to not forget and keep leaving it in embarrassing places.

Naturally, the condition of the potatoes deteriorated to a nasty, smelly slime.

This was a great metaphor for the price we pay for keeping our pain and heavy negativity! Too often we think of forgiveness as a gift to the other person, and while that's true, it clearly is also a gift for ourselves!

❧

RIGHTLY, AND for more than alcoholics, does the "Big Book" of Alcoholics Anonymous suggest that "Resentment is the number one offender" that destroys more of its victims than does anything else. To refuse forgiveness is to refuse the fresh air without which the spiritual life cannot flourish—in the absence of forgiveness, gratitude is necessarily stunted. Both forgiveness and gratitude are basic to our relationships with others.

To attain self-forgiveness requires seeking out settings where forgiveness flourishes, situations in which participants are honestly open about their faults and failings. These may be religious, they may be professional, or they may be some informal but regular gathering. But here again, as so often when dealing with "the spiritual," we need others in order to become our truest selves.

❧

FOR MANY there is another aspect to forgiveness, and it is perhaps the most important. As noted briefly in passing after our treatment of what forgiveness is "not," the God of the Abrahamic religions—Judaism, Christianity, Islam—is portrayed as a merciful God, a forgiving God. For believers in such a God, it is only in forgiving others that they lay hold of—really *believe*—in that God's forgiveness in a way that makes it real. Rather than attempting to speak to this directly, we conclude this segment by telling a few telling stories.

On the day before Yom Kippur, the "Day of Atonement," many women brought food to Rabbi Abiah for a decision whether it conformed to the dietary laws. In every instance he pronounced the food kosher.

A court official asked him: "Is it not fitting that we be more strict than usual on the eve of Yom Kippur?"

Rabbi Abiah replied: "On the contrary. If I should pronounce a questionable fowl unclean, I would be guilty of a sin against men, by depriving them of their meal before the Fast. And a sin against men is not forgiven on Yom Kippur. But when I pronounce the fowl kosher, even though there may be doubt involved, I sin only against God. And we are taught that Yom Kippur brings forgiveness of sins against God."

❧

FOR DEVOUT MUSLIMS, the first of the divine names is the All-Merciful—the All-Compassionate.

A Sufi saint, on pilgrimage to Mecca, having completed the prescribed religious practices, knelt down and touched his forehead to the ground and prayed: "Allah! I have only one desire in life. Give me the grace of never offending you again."

When the All-Merciful heard this he laughed aloud and said, "That's what they all ask for. But if I granted everyone this grace, tell me, whom would I forgive?"

❧

A MODERN RABBI, Benjamin Blech, in his anniversary exploration "Forgive the Terrorists?", begins by reminding:

Forgiveness is a divine trait. It defines the goodness of G-d. Without it human beings probably couldn't survive. Because G-d forgives, there's still hope for sinners. When we do wrong, G-d reassures us that he won't abandon us as a result of our transgressions. Divine forgiveness is the quality that most clearly proves G-d's love for us.

But one cannot presume on God's forgiveness:

Rabbi Levi Yitzhak said to G-d: "I want to propose a deal. We have many sins and misdeeds, and you an abundance of forgiveness and atonement. Let us exchange! Perhaps you will say: 'Like for like!' My answer is: Had we no sins, what would you do with your forgiveness? So you must balance the deal by giving us life and children and food besides."

HUMOR

The famous Rabbi Zevi Elimelech of Dinov had a son, Dovidl, who was himself a Hasidic rabbi and had many ardent disciples. On every Sabbath and also on Holy Days, Rabbi Dovidl refrained from the time-honored custom of expounding the Torah as he sat in the midst of his disciples. Instead, he diverted them with merry tales and jokes, and everybody, even the graybeards, would laugh heartily.

Once, Rabbi Yichezkel Halberstam was paying him a visit, and he was amazed at Rabbi Dovidl's odd carryings-on. "Who ever heard," he began indignantly, "that a tzaddik and his disciples should behave in such an outrageous way? A fine thing indeed to celebrate God's Sabbath with nonsense, funny stories, and jests! Really, Rabbi Dovidl, you ought to feel ashamed of yourself! Come now expound a bit of Torah for us!"

"Torah!" exclaimed Rabbi Dovidl. "And what do you suppose I've been expounding all this time? Believe me, Rabbi, there's God's holy truth in all stories and jests!"

RABBI DOVIDL would have appreciated Reinhold Niebuhr's suggestion: "Humor is, in fact, a prelude to faith, and laughter is the
beginning of prayer"; and perhaps even more, writer Anne Lamott's vivid observation: "Laughter is carbonated holiness."

Narratives, drama, and stories: Whatever we tell, however we
tell, the intertwined masks of comedy and tragedy hang always
overhead. There are many provocative theories of tragedy, but on
the side of comedy-humor, most agree with E. B. White's analysis:
"Humor can be dissected as a frog can, but the thing dies in the
process and the innards are discouraging to any but the purely scientific mind." We can nevertheless observe that at a most naïve yet
also most profound level, comedy, like spirituality, concludes with
a happy ending, a denouement that conveys a kind of joy, an insight impossible to put into analytic words.

Thinkers uncowed by E. B. White have suggested that the essence of humor, in a self-reflecting definition, is the "juxtaposition
of incongruities"—putting together two items that do not belong
together. Characteristically, there is a twist at the end of a joke—
something unexpected. Humor and story thus go hand in hand. A
still life can be tragic; humor requires movement—a context that is
violated.

The story is told that once, when playwright George Bernard
Shaw was interviewing a young woman for the position of being his secretary, he cautioned her: "There are two words that
must never be spoken in my presence: one is 'nice,' and the other
is 'awful.'"

After a brief pause the candidate asked: "Yes, Mr. Shaw. Now what are those two words?"

❧

GREEK AND Russian Orthodoxy have their "Holy Fools," and in some Orthodox churches of the Christian East it is the custom on the morning of Easter Sunday or Easter Monday for the clergy to appear in the sanctuary and tell jokes, from pious to ribald. Why? Because the resurrection of Jesus Christ from the dead is the greatest joke ever played, played on the Devil himself, and so such laughter is ridicule of Satan—a bunch of happily innocent children making fun of the big bully who has just taken a pratfall in the mud puddle. The practice brings to perfection the prime principle of all humor: puncturing pomposity.

Similarly, students of Zen inform us, much of the humor of Zen is iconoclastic in character—for before true liberation can occur, all idols must be overturned, stood upside down.

One of Thomas Merton's favorite figures was Tan-hsia, a ninth-century master who often is pictured warming his bare backsides at a fire which he had made with a wooden image of the Buddha. In the Zen tradition, it is understood that idols of every sort are to be relentlessly smashed—whether they be one's dependence upon the ego, doctrine, scriptures, or even the Buddha.

❧

ANYTHING, HOWEVER holy, is potentially an idol; therefore, anything is a legitimate object of laughter. No aspect of one's existence is to be elevated beyond the requirements of humor, including one's existence itself. To take things too seriously, let alone absolutely, however significant they might otherwise seem, is to be dependent upon them and therefore caught in the wheel (the vicious cycle) of attachment, desire, and bondage.

Nor is this a lonely insight of Buddhism. There is no better way than humor to take down idols—or pretty much anything else. Tyrants have always feared humor, and rightly. There can be few better proofs of this than what took place in central and Eastern Europe near the end of the twentieth century. A bit before those pregnant years that saw the dissolution of the Soviet Union and the birth of several new nations:

When Khrushchev pronounced his famous denunciation of Stalin, someone in the Congress Hall is reported to have said, "Where were you, Comrade Khrushchev, when all these innocent people were being slaughtered?"

Khrushchev paused, looked around the hall, and said, "Will the man who said that kindly stand up!"

Tension mounted in the hall. No one moved.

Then Khrushchev said, "Well, whoever you are, you have your answer now. I was in exactly the same position then as you are now."

❧

WHOEVER IT was may later have usefully pondered James Thurber's observation: "Humor is emotional chaos remembered in tranquility."

A bit less dramatically:

Children were lined up in the cafeteria of a Catholic school for lunch. At the head of the table was a large pile of apples.

The nun had written a note: "Take only one: God is watching."

Moving through the line, to the other end of the table, students found a large pile of chocolate chip cookies.

A boy wrote a note: "Take all you want: God is watching the apples."

⸎

"THE SPIRITUAL" involves *mystery*, that which eludes ready grasp. Genuine mystery brings about the collapse of categories—which is also the intent of the comic spirit. We find such a mystical integration of opposites in the body paint and costume worn by clowns: The "union of opposites" is symbolically achieved in the motley figure of the clown-fool. His is an ambiguity that represents an order of being and knowing that lies *beyond* all duality, all hierarchy, all intellection—it rests instead in the freedom and innocence and playful spontaneity lived only by little children and great sages. And there may be more here than meets the immediate eye: As student of myth Jan Knappert has suggested, "In a culture based on power, the true intellectual can only be a jester."

Bono is playing a U2 concert in Ireland when he asks the audience for quiet.

Then in the silence, he starts to slowly clap his hands, once every few seconds.

Holding the audience in total silence, he says into the microphone, "Every time I clap my hands, a child in Africa dies."

A voice from near the front of the crowd pierces the silence. . . .

"Fookin' stop doing it then!"

❧

FROM THE standpoint of Zen and the comic spirit, seriousness itself, however noble its motives and commendable its intentions, remains nevertheless a sign of attachment and bondage. Seriousness is a part of the same entanglements that seriousness hopes to overcome, for implicit in all seriousness is the inclination to take one's self and one's situation too seriously. Sometimes.

Barbara Walters, then of television's *20/20*, did a story on gender roles in Kabul, Afghanistan, several years before the Afghan conflict. She noted that women customarily walked five paces behind their husbands.

She later [2010] returned to Kabul and observed that women still walked behind their husbands. From Ms. Walters's vantage point, despite the overthrow of the oppressive Taliban regime, the women now seemed to walk even farther behind their husbands and were happy to maintain the old custom.

Ms. Walters approached one of the Afghani women and asked, "Why do you now seem happy with the old custom that you once tried so desperately to change?"

The woman looked Ms. Walters straight in the eyes and without hesitation said, "Land mines."

❧

BECAUSE ANYTHING that is classed as holy may become simply a new and more subtle basis of dependence instead of a vehicle for emancipation from the bondage of grasping and clinging, holy things of whatever kind must constantly be subjected to profanation of one kind or another.

A farmer got pulled over by a state trooper for speeding, and the trooper started to lecture the farmer about his speed, and in general began to throw his weight around to try to make the farmer uncomfortable. Finally, the trooper got around to writing out the ticket, and as he was doing that he kept swatting at some flies that were buzzing around his head. The farmer said, "Having some problems with circle flies there, are ya?"

The trooper stopped writing the ticket and said, "Well, yeah, if that's what they are—I never heard of circle flies."

So the farmer said, "Well, circle flies are common on farms. See, they're called circle flies because they're almost always found circling around the back end of a horse."

The trooper said, "Oh," and went back to writing the ticket. Then after a minute he stopped and said, "Hey . . . wait a minute, are you trying to call me a horse's ass?"

The farmer said, "Oh no, Officer. I have too much respect for law enforcement and police officers to even think about calling you a horse's ass."

The trooper said, "Well, that's a good thing," and went back to writing the ticket.

After a long pause, the farmer said, "Hard to fool them flies though."

❧

SOMETIMES THE "profanation" is—perhaps—less consciously intended:

Joseph Chamberlain, at the time the prime minister of England, told this story about himself. He was guest of honor at a banquet. The mayor of the city presided and when coffee was being served, he leaned over and touched Mr. Chamberlain, saying, "Shall we let them enjoy themselves a little longer or had we better have your speech now?"

❧

HUMOR DELIVERS something that one does not expect—the comic surprise, so to speak. Zen humor relies on this comic surprise not just to be funny, but also to allow the reader to experience certain truths. The same is true of much non-Zen humor.

A young family moved into their new home, which was next to a vacant lot. One day, a construction crew turned up to start building a house on the empty lot.

The young family's five-year-old daughter naturally took an interest in all the activity going on next door and spent much of each day watching the workers.

Eventually the construction crew, all of them "gems in the rough" more or less, adopted her as a kind of project mascot. They chatted with her, let her sit with them while they had coffee breaks, and gave her little jobs to do to make her feel important.

At the end of the first week, they even presented her with a pay envelope containing $10. The little girl took this home to her mother, who suggested that she take her "pay" to the bank to start a savings account.

When the girl and her mom got to the bank, the teller was impressed and asked the little girl how she had come by her very own paycheck at such a young age. The little girl proudly replied, "I worked last week with a real construction crew building the new house next door to us."

"Oh, my goodness gracious," said the teller, "and will you be working on the house again this week, too?"

The little girl replied, "I will, if those assholes at Lowe's ever deliver the damn Sheetrock."

❧

THE "OPPOSITES" whose unreconciled status seems so much a part of Zen humor can be of many different kinds.

Smith, seated in a movie house, could not help being aware that the man sitting right in front of him had his arm around the neck of a rather large dog that sat on the seat next to him. The dog clearly was taking in the picture with understanding. He snarled at the villain, yelped happily at the funny remarks, and so on.

Smith leaned forward and tapped the man in front of him on the shoulder. He whispered, "Pardon me, sir, but I can't get over your dog's behavior."

The man turned and whispered back, "Frankly, it surprises me, too. He hated the book."

❧

THE BREAKING DOWN of boundaries reveals how one should not discriminate against, but rather move toward, a doctrine of unification and non-duality. Of course, that insight works also in places other than Zen. Much depends on how one understands "boundaries."

Isaac and Sarah got married and left on their honeymoon. When they got back, Sarah immediately telephoned her mother, Leah.

"Well," said Leah, "how was the honeymoon, darling?"

"Oh, Mum," Sarah replied, "the honeymoon was fantastic. It was so romantic, and . . . and . . ."

Then Sarah started to cry. "Oh, Mum, as soon as we got back, Isaac started using terrible language. He said things I'd never hoped to hear, all those four-letter words. Please, Mum, get into your car now and come and take me home."

"Calm down, darling," said Leah, "tell your mother what could be that awful. Don't be shy, tell me what four-letter words Isaac used."

"Please, Mum, I'm too embarrassed to tell you, they're terrible words. Just come and take me away," said Sarah.

"But, bubeleh, you must tell me, you must tell me what the four-letter words were."

Still crying, Sarah replied, "Oh, Mum, he used words like WASH, COOK, IRON, DUST . . ."

❧

OTHER FORMS of misunderstanding undergird other, diverse examples of humor. Sometimes the problem is not so much one of misunderstanding as the failure of an assumption, some too blithe a disregard of the complexity of human beings.

Lawyers should never ask a Mississippi grandma a question if they aren't prepared for the answer.

In a trial, a Southern small-town prosecuting attorney called his first witness, a matronly woman, to the stand. He approached her and asked, "Mrs. Jones, do you know me?"

She responded, "Why, yes, I do know you, I've known you since you were a young boy, and frankly, you've been a big disappointment to me. You lie, you cheat on your wife, and you manipulate people and talk about them behind their backs. You think you're a big shot when you haven't the brains to realize you never will amount to anything more than a two-bit paper pusher. Yes, I know you."

The lawyer was stunned! Not knowing what else to do, he pointed across the room and asked, "Mrs. Jones, do you know the defense attorney?"

She again replied, "Why, yes, I do. I've known him since he was a youngster, too. He's lazy, bigoted, and he has a drinking problem. He can't build a normal relationship with anyone and his law practice is one of the worst in the entire state. Not to mention he cheated on his wife with three different women. One of them was your wife. Yes, I know him."

The defense attorney almost died. The judge asked both counselors to approach the bench and, in a very quiet voice, said, "If either of you idiots asks her if she knows me, I'll send you to the electric chair."

∽∾

CONTEXT IS important, both to understanding and to assumptions. Almost always in such stories, as in most of life, the breaking of context comes in the final brief phrase. Two short examples, featuring children, then one a bit longer, featuring children of a different age:

A woman was trying hard to get the ketchup to come out of the jar. During her struggle the phone rang so she asked her four-year-old daughter to answer it.

"It's the minister, Mommy," the child said to her mother. Then she added, into the phone, "Mommy can't come to the phone to talk to you right now. She's hitting the bottle."

❧

A Sunday school teacher was discussing the Ten Commandments with her five- and six-year-olds.

After explaining the commandment to "honor" thy Father and thy Mother, she asked, "Is there a commandment that teaches us how to treat our brothers and sisters?"

Without missing a beat one little boy (the oldest in his family) answered, "Thou shall not kill."

❧

Arthur Miller takes his new wife, Marilyn Monroe, to his mother's apartment for her first seder. On the way home, Miller asks Marilyn if she enjoyed it.

"Darling, I loved it all," she says, "all your family together, the ritual, the prayers, the food—especially the food."

"I'm delighted," says Miller, "but tell me, sweetheart, what dish did you like best?"

"I loved your mother's chicken soup," Marilyn says. "So clear, so golden, so flavorful."

"And the matzo balls?" he asks. "What did you think of my mother's matzo balls?"

"Oh, Arthur, I especially loved those matzo balls. However did your mother get them to be so light, so perfectly round, so tasty? They were absolutely scrumptious."

"My mother will be pleased to hear it," Miller says.

"In fact, I'll write your mother a note tomorrow about her fabulous matzo balls. I just loved those matzo balls to death. But tell me, Arthur, what do you Jews do with the rest of the matzo?"

≈

IS JEWISH humor different, or are Jews different? We suspect both. The long, often sad, and even tragic history of the Jewish people shaped a resilient sensibility that can appreciate ambiguity in just about any situation, but food seems a favorite. First, then, another dinner story, then one more about a snack:

The Goldberg family was having Friday night dinner at their grandmother's house—Bubbie Adella. Seated at the table, little Moishe Goldberg dug into the food immediately.

"Moishe!" his mother exclaimed. "You have to wait until we make the blessing."

"No, I don't," the little boy replied.

"Of course you do," his mother insisted, "we always say a blessing before eating at our house."

"That's at our house," Moishe explained, "but this is Bubbie's house and she knows how to cook."

≈

Mrs. Moskowitz was having her house painted, and between the smell of the paint and the hassle she found life hard. It was the last straw when Mr. Moskowitz forgot himself and leaned against the bedroom wall, leaving a distinct hand mark on the fresh paint. The Mrs. made her feelings clearly known and the husband tried to calm her down. "What's the fuss?" he said. "The painter's returning tomorrow so he'll paint it over."

Nevertheless Mrs. Moskowitz found it difficult to sleep all night. The thought of that hand mark bothered her. The next morning, then, the painter had barely stepped over the threshold when she was upon him, saying, "Oh, I'm so glad you're here. All night long I've been thinking of you and waiting for you. Come with me to the bedroom. I want to show you where my husband put his hand."

The painter blanched and stepped back, aghast. "Please," he said, "I'm an old man. A glass of tea, and maybe a cookie, is all I want."

❦

SOME HUMOR works especially well because of the names attached to the incident.

George Bernard Shaw to Winston Churchill: "I enclose two tickets to the first night of my new play, bring a friend . . . if you have one."

Winston Churchill, in response: "Cannot possibly attend first night; will attend second, if there is one."

❦

TOO MANY stories? How about viewing them as anecdotes? For although your authors are not Zen scholars, we find a certain resonance in this observation—humorous tales are, after all, one form of "anecdotal material":

Anecdotal materials, to be sure, may be found in any tradition. But in Zen the role of the anecdote is much more central to the "communication" of the teaching, and much closer to the "point" of the teaching. The Zen tradition is not disseminated through a heavily symbolic ritual, or creed and confession, or scriptural canon, or catechetical indoctrination, or theological and philosophical disputation all so familiar in Western religion.

In the West the anecdote stands far more toward the periphery of the tradition, as a matter of popular discourse, sermonic illustration, anteroom banter, and the like. It is not at the heart of the teaching, either in terms of method or content, but is a kind of concession to those unable to ascend the lofty heights of theological, philosophical and ethical discourse, or unable to sustain such a level indefinitely without reprieve.

In Zen, however, the reverse is closer to its peculiar genius. Without a focus on scripture, liturgy, myth, doctrine or metaphysics, the anecdote is more an official organ than an appendage. Rather than being a vehicle for popularization, it points instead to that level of understanding and awareness that lies beyond all symbol, gesture and word, all reason and belief, even the most sophisticated.

M. CONRAD HYERS

Some Zen-like not-Zen:

A priest who worked for a local home health care agency was out making his rounds caring for the sick when his car ran out of gas. As luck would have it there was a gas station just up the street. He walked to the station to borrow a can with enough gas to start the car and drive to the station for a fill-up.

The attendant regretfully told him that the only gas can he owned had been loaned out, but if he would care to wait he was sure it would be back shortly.

Since the priest was on the way to see a sick patient he decided not to wait and walked back to his car. Looking through his car for something to carry to the station to fill with gas, he spotted a bedpan that he was planning on taking to a patient. Always resourceful, he carried it to the station, filled it with gasoline, and carried it back to his car.

As he was pouring the gas into the tank of his car two men walked by. One of them turned to the other and said: "Now that is what I call faith!"

⊱⊰

SOMETIMES, FOR whatever reason, the most stale old stories can take on a new life—and yet retain their deep meaning—if given the kind of shift that conceals them from the too-knowledgable. We conclude this segment with two stories that in different ways bear this out.

An Arab was walking through the Sahara Desert, desperate for water, when he saw something, far off in the distance. Hoping to find water, he walked toward the image, only to find Hymie sitting at a card table with a bunch of ties laid out on it.

The Arab asked, "Please, I'm dying of thirst, can I have some water?" Hymie replied, "I don't have any water, but why don't you buy a tie? Here's one that goes nicely with your robes."

The Arab replied, "I don't want a tie, I need water."

"Okay, don't buy a tie. But to show you what a nice guy I am, I'll tell you that over that hill, about four miles, is a nice restaurant. My brother owns it. Walk that way, they'll give you all the water you want."

The Arab thanked him and walked away toward the hill and eventually disappeared. Three hours later the Arab came crawling back to where Hymie was sitting behind his card table.

Hymie said, "I told you, about four miles over that hill. Couldn't you find it?"

The Arab rasped, "I found it all right. But they wouldn't let me in without a tie."

⤫

WANTING MORE than water—

A Scotsman, an Englishman, an Irishman, a Welshman, a Latvian, a Turk, an Aussie, a Yank, a Canadian, a Brazilian, an Egyptian, a Japanese, a Vietnamese, a Mexican, a Spaniard, a Greek, a Russian, an Estonian, a German, an Italian, a Pole, a Lithuanian, a Swede, a Finn, a Norwegian, an Israeli, a Romanian, a Bulgarian, a Serb, a Czech, a Cambodian, and a Swiss all went to a nightclub. . . .

The doorman said: "Sorry, I can't let you in without a Thai."

GRAY

*Paradise on this earth, we have learned, is beyond our capacities.
But we can, if we are modest and hopeful, possibly establish a
reasonably livable purgatory and escape the inferno.*

ROBERT BELLAH

*Mortality makes us all alike: it makes us kin and can
make us kind. Death is at once certain and unknown. We may
feel confident that when we're dead we're dead, but we have
no conclusive evidence. We assume that we are closer to the
truth than earlier ages, but death, like the sacred,
remains beyond our knowledge.*

MICHAEL ROEMER

*The true theology, [Luther] said, is one that discerns the
omnipotent God not in manifestations of power and
glory but in the midst of peril and suffering.*

FRANK SENN

There is sadness, there is sorrow, there is grief, there is desperation . . . there is much more. But not all "down" occasions are Dark. Some are less tragic and may even have lighter aspects, and so we add this segment and call it *Gray*.

A disciple asks the rebbe, "Why does Torah tell us to 'place these holy words *upon* your hearts'? Why does it not tell us to place these holy words *in* our hearts?"

The rebbe answers, "It is because as we are, our hearts are closed, and we cannot place the holy words in our hearts. So we place them on top of our hearts. And there they stay until, one day, the heart breaks and the words fall in."

⚮

No one is as whole as he who has a broken heart.
RABBI MOSHE LEIB OF SASOV

Pain hurts. But some—great artists, for example—see beyond pain.

As a young man, the painter Henri Matisse paid weekly visits to the great Renoir, twenty-eight years his senior. When Renoir was stricken with arthritis, Matisse visited him daily, bringing him paints, brushes, food, and other gifts. Concerned that Renoir was working too hard, Matisse often tried to persuade him to rest a little.

One day as Matisse watched the great master work, he noticed that with each brushstroke Renoir winced in pain. Unable to contain himself any longer, he implored his friend to set his brushes aside for a moment.

"Master, you have already created an immense and distinguished body of work. Why do you continue to torment yourself in this way?"

"Very simple," Renoir responded. "Beauty remains, but pain passes."

&

BUT PAIN is also a singular foundation of community, as Rabbi David Wolpe explores in his autobiographical book *In Speech and in Silence:*

> *When one suffers a tragedy, the population of fellow sufferers suddenly opens up. The world is filled with those who have undergone the same trauma, but one never knew it. Suddenly everyone was close to or acquainted with someone who had had the same experience. . . . There is no nationality so abrupt, so unseen, and so ready to spring into action as the nation of those who have suffered loss—the vast, wounded totality of the human race. We were now part of the great tribe of pain.*
>
> *. . . Help is accepted, if at all, with slightly mixed feelings. Each tragedy is a private one, and part of the hubris of grief is that no one else truly understands, can fully share. But sickness strips away pride. It is humbling. It speaks in gigantic terms of our helplessness. The feebleness is not whispered, it is written across the sky. Everyone can see it, and you feel the notice especially keenly in those who avert their eyes and pretend not to look.*

Wolpe echoes the classic unchanging lament about pain, about profound suffering and brokenness. But he also hints at a grasp of its anodyne. The lament was first and most memorably set forth by the Greek lyric poet Sappho in the sixth century BCE:

Mother, I cannot mind my wheel;
My fingers ache, my lips are dry;
Oh! if you felt the pain I feel!
But oh! who ever felt as I!

Thus Sappho—and later Emily Dickinson—remind us of a too often overlooked aspect of suffering and pain: the sufferer's loneliness, the feeling of complete isolation from others. But as classics scholar Henry Alonzo Myers reminds us in his study *Tragedy: A View of Life*:

The answer [to the question "But oh! who ever felt as I!"] is, of course, everyone—without exception. To an actual sufferer, however, we offer that answer as convincingly and gently as possible. But we offer the consolation and relief that come to the sufferer who knows that suffering is a meaningful bond uniting him with others, not a void separating him from them.

⁂

DO PAIN and suffering separate and isolate? Or do they connect and bond? The only answer is, of course, "Both!" But only if each is embraced, owned.

Rabbi Moshe Leib of Sasov learned to love when he went to an inn and heard one drunken peasant ask another, "Do you love me?"

"Certainly I love you," replied the second. "I love you like a brother."

But the first shook his head and insisted, "You don't love me. You don't know what I lack. You don't know what I need."

The second peasant fell into sullen silence, but Rabbi Moshe Leib understood: "To know the need of men and to bear the burden of their sorrow, that is the true love of men."

> *Joy and sorrow are not opposites. The opposite*
> *of joy is cynicism; the opposite of sorrow is*
> *callousness—inability to be touched, to feel.*
> BONNIE BRANDEL

Many sources optimistically encourage "thinking positive" and "looking at the lighter side" or "attending to the doughnut rather than the hole." Useful guidance, perhaps, at times, for all of us. But then there are those moments when any "lighter side" gets obscured, when nibbles—necessary or not—make the hole the dominant part of the doughnut.

As many alcoholics and addicts discover in recovery, it is not the "big things," the major disappointments and hurts that threaten their progress—it is "the little things," the offhand, uncaring remark by a supposed friend, the traffic tie-up that impedes reaching a destination, the carelessness of someone who is supposed to be helping. Anyone with a bit of self-awareness and gumption can handle the large upsets, which often come quite clearly tagged as threats to serenity. But oh, those little piddly nudges! They are too small to get upset over, which adds to our upset, for we all—addicts or not—tell ourselves, "This shouldn't bother me like that!"

> *Any idiot can face a crisis—it's the day-to-day*
> *living that wears you out!*
> ANTON CHEKHOV

Never mind the *should*: We all have them. The undertone is more interesting. "I am too big, too spiritually advanced, to be bothered like this!" "Sure," a mocking under-voice intones, sniggering up its sleeve. Now our humility is being challenged—by ourselves! Why am I bothered? Because I am not as spiritually advanced as I would like to think. This is unwelcome knowledge.

Some people—perhaps this is why and how they become politicians—have no problem at all with even public "shoulds":

During one of his presidential campaigns, William Jennings Bryan spoke in a city in one of the northwestern states. The chairman, in presenting the speaker, made an embarrassingly fulsome and eulogistic introduction of Bryan, in such bad taste that many wondered how Bryan would succeed in overcoming the unfortunate effect of it.

Bryan, however, was not easily dismayed: "The very kind observations of the chairman," said he, "bring to mind the case of the man at a formal banquet table who impulsively put into his mouth a large forkful of steaming hot baked potato, which he instantly spat out upon his plate. Looking about at the disconcerted fellow guests and at his hostess, he remarked blandly, 'Some damn fools would have swallowed that.'"

❦

SOMETIMES OUR very flaws, our defects of character, can be manipulated to some larger good.

Once upon a time there was an inn called the Silver Star. The innkeeper was unable to make ends meet even though he did his very best to draw customers by making the service cordial and the prices reasonable. In despair, he consulted a Sage.

After listening to his tale the Sage said, "It is very simple. You must change the name of your inn."

"Impossible!" said the innkeeper. "It has been the Silver Star for generations and is well known by that name."

"No," said the Sage firmly. "You must now call it the Five Bells and have a row of six bells hanging at the entrance."

"Six bells? But that's absurd. What good will that do?"

"Try it and see," said the Sage. The innkeeper gave it a try. And this is what happened: Just about every traveler who passed by the inn walked in to point out the mistake, each believing that no one else had noticed it. Once inside, they were impressed by the cordiality of the service and stayed on to refresh themselves, soon providing the innkeeper with the success that he had been seeking for so long.

There are few things the ego delights in more than correcting other people's mistakes.

❦

BUT THERE are, of course, some "mistakes" that may be more difficult to correct.

Wee Hughie was dying.

Tenderly, his wife, Maggie, knelt by his bedside and asked, "Anything I can get you, Hughie?"

"No," he replied.

"You must have a last wish, Hughie?" asked his wife.

Faintly came the answer, "A wee bit of that boiled ham over yonder would be nice."

"Ach, man . . . you can't have that," said Maggie. "You know it's for your funeral."

❧

FILM DIRECTOR Michael Roemer, exiled as a child from Nazi Germany, has noted how "the refusal to acknowledge suffering has contributed directly to the invalidation of narrative, for it can no longer report what we know to be true, and must instead purvey illusions few of us believe."

This may be true of some narratives, but there are others.

A Bedouin set out one day with his young son to graze his she-camel and look for wild herbs and roots to take back for his wife to cook. When they had loaded the camel and were heading toward home, a herd of magnificent gazelles suddenly appeared across their path. Silently and quickly the father made the camel lower herself onto her knees, and he slid from her back. Warning the boy not to stray until he returned, he hurried after the gazelles. The wild things leaped into the air and streaked off as soon as he stepped toward them, but the Bedouin was a keen hunter and loved nothing better than the chase. Eagerly he followed on their trail.

Meanwhile the tender child waited alone. From destiny there is no escape. It was his fate that a She-Ghoul, that monster of the wilderness who loves to feed on human flesh, should spy him as he stood unprotected. With one leap she sprang upon him and greedily devoured him.

The father hunted long and far but could not catch a single deer. At last he resigned himself and returned without the game. Though the camel was kneeling where he had left it, he could not see his son. He looked on every side, but the boy was gone. Then on the ground he found dark drops of blood. "My son! My son is killed! My son is dead!" he shrieked. Yet what could he do but lead his camel home?

On the way he rode past a cave, and there he saw the She-Ghoul dancing, fresh from her feast. The Bedouin took careful aim and shot the She-Ghoul dead. He slashed open her belly, and in it he found his son. He laid the boy upon his cloak, pulled the woolen cloth around him tight, and so carried him home.

When he reached his tent the Bedouin called his wife and said, "I have brought you back a gazelle, dear wife, but as God is my witness, it can be cooked only in a cauldron that has never been used for a meal of sorrow."

The woman went from tent to tent for the loan of such a pot. But one neighbor said, "Sister, we used the large cauldron to cook the rice for the people who came to weep with us when my husband died." And another told her, "We last heated our big cooking pot on the day of my son's funeral." She knocked at every door but did not find what she sought. So she returned to her husband empty-handed.

"Haven't you found the right kind of cauldron?" asked the Bedouin.

"There is no household but has seen misfortune," she answered. "There is no cauldron but has cooked a meal of mourning."

Only then did the Bedouin fold back his woolen cloak and say to her, "They have all tasted their share of sorrow. Today the turn is ours. This is my gazelle."

※

WHAT IS the relationship between narrative and myth? Myth often presents itself as narrative, as in the Bedouin story. Does that somehow invalidate it? Perhaps, for some individuals. But if we remember that "a myth is something that never happened because it is always happening," the narrative wrapping may be deep truth's best alias. There is something about how people hear such stories. Here is another one:

High in the hills of Haiti there lived a poor farmer and his good wife. Every day he went out to his field to tend the crop that grew between the stones so that his wife and twelve children might eat.

Then, one day, the poor farmer came in from his fields just as the sun was setting. There was his wife blocking the passageway. She held the baby in one arm and a cooking spoon in the other. And she knit her brow, looked him straight in the eye, and said, "My Good Man!"

Now, the farmer knew what that meant. But his worry was not how they would feed a thirteenth child, but how they would find someone to be Godparent. For a Godparent would bring gifts at the Baptism. And they had already asked all their neighbors for their other children. And their neighbors were as poor as they were.

The next morning the farmer walked slowly to his field, still wondering who to ask. He worked for a couple of hours, and then saw someone walking over the hill toward him.

The stranger was a heavyset man with a full white beard. He wore a white linen suit topped with a fine white Panama hat. He tipped his hat to the farmer, and they struck up a conversation. Suddenly the man said, "I'll be Godparent."

Now the farmer was surprised. How did this man know about the child? And now that he had someone to be Godparent, the farmer was no longer so desperate. Why, just who was the stranger, anyway?

"I am God," said the white-bearded man. But the farmer said, "I don't want you as Godparent. You give much to the rich, and little to the poor." So God tipped his hat, smiled, and walked away.

The poor farmer worked until the sun blazed hot and bright at noonday. Then he saw a second traveler walking through his field: A tall man in a black suit with a neatly trimmed beard. He said, "I'll be Godparent." The farmer was quick to ask: "And who are you?"

With a wicked laugh the man said, "You know who I am." And indeed the poor farmer did. But to his own surprise, he said, "I don't want you, either: You're always making promises of happiness, pleasure, and wealth. And in the end, you never deliver." The stranger snarled, there was a puff of smoke, and he was gone.

Just as the sun began to set, a tall, skinny man came over the crest. He had no beard, and no hair. He grinned a toothless grin and said, "I'll be Godparent. And don't bother asking who I am. For I am Death."

The poor farmer trembled and said, "Yes, you may be Godparent to my child. For you treat the rich and poor equally. And in the end, you always keep your promise."

⋙⋘

THE ENGLISH essayist Gilbert Keith Chesterton observed: "For some strange reason man must always plant his fruit trees in a graveyard.... He can make the future luxuriant and gigantic, so long as he is thinking about the past."

And perhaps also about the future. As Abraham Maslow remarked after his heart attack: "I wonder if we humans could love—love passionately—if we knew we'd never die." Rollo May, who tells this story, continues: "This is another asset of mortality: We learn to love each other. *We are able to love passionately because we die.*"

> *The opposite of love is not hate, it's indifference.... And*
> *the opposite of life is not death, it's indifference.*
>
> ELIE WIESEL

⋙⋘

Dr. George Vaillant, principal investigator on a sixty-eight-year longitudinal study that followed a cohort of 237 physically and mentally healthy Harvard college sophomores from the classes of 1939 to 1944, told this story about one of the men, a physician and well-loved husband:

On his seventieth birthday, when he retired from the faculty of medicine, his wife got hold of his patient list and secretly wrote to many of his longest-running patients, "Would you write a letter of appreciation?"

And back came one hundred single-spaced, desperately loving letters—often with pictures attached. And she put them in a lovely presentation box covered with Thai silk, and gave it to him.

Eight years later, Vaillant interviewed the man, who proudly pulled the box down from his shelf. "George, I don't know what you're going to make of this," the man said, as he began to cry, "but I've never read it."

"It's very hard," Vaillant said, "for most of us to tolerate being loved."

∞

LOVE . . . AND INDIFFERENCE. Death . . . and indifference. But what is "indifference"? A mythical statement reaches to blend our understandings.

Once upon a time a man captured a herd of cattle. Tenderly he cared for them, for he loved them very much. One morning he went to the shelter to milk the cows and found that their udders were dry. Perhaps they needed a new area to graze, he thought, and so he moved them that day to a new field where they ate their fill. But the next morning he discovered that their udders were again dry and wrinkled, and he knew then that someone had come in the night to milk them.

"I will watch tonight to see who has milked them," he decided. The stars were bright in the late night sky when he saw a rope coming down from the heavens. He watched in wonder as the beautiful young women of the people of the stars climbed down the rope. Carrying their baskets and gourds and speaking softly to each other, they stepped lightly across the field and began to milk the cows. The man followed them and watched in amazement, for he had heard only of the star women in legends and stories.

When they saw him, they quickly sped away to the rope and climbed back to the stars. One woman—the loveliest of all—was slower than the rest and when he caught up to her, he asked if she would stay and live with him. She agreed, but with one condition. He must never look in her basket with the lovely lid—the star basket. He promised her that he would never look in the basket—unless she gave her permission—and they lived many happy, peaceful days tending the cattle and gathering herbs and plants in the field.

He forgot about the basket, but one day he came home early and something drew him to it. He could not take his eyes off the beautiful basket. Feeling compelled to open it, he laughed when he looked inside.

That evening the star-woman knew immediately what happened. Gently, she said, "You have looked in the basket." "Yes," he said, laughing softly. "Silly woman, there is nothing inside!"

Sadly, she said, "You saw nothing in the basket?"

"No," he replied. "Nothing."

She turned away from him, then, and that evening as the sun set behind the golden fields, she vanished.

❧

WHAT IS your reaction to the stories we have been telling in this segment? Perhaps they are too closely spaced, but one overall impression reminded us of another observation by Michael Roemer: "Not feeling is a feeling and may be the only way some of us can connect with the work of art."

In his youth, Rabbi Moshe Teitelbaum had been an enemy of the Hasidic teachings, for he regarded them as rank heresy. Once he was staying with his friend Rabbi Joseph Asher, who was also opposed to these innovators. At just about this time, the prayer book of the holy Rabbi Isaac Luria had appeared in print. When the volume was brought to the two friends, Rabbi Moshe snatched the heavy tome from the messenger and threw it on the floor. But Rabbi Joseph Asher picked it up and said: "After all, it is a prayer book, and we must not treat it disrespectfully."

When the rabbi of Lublin was told of the incident, he said: "Rabbi Moshe will become a Hasid; Rabbi Joseph Asher will remain an opponent of the Hasidic way. For he who can burn with enmity can also burn with love for God, but he who is coldly hostile will always find the way closed."

And so it was.

❧

WORKS OF art come in many forms. In some ways, all of life is an art. And in some cases that may include more than human life.

There was a young Nigerian boy named Olu who had a pet white chicken. They became great friends and inseparable companions. One day the hen disappeared and Olu cried and cried. Then after three weeks the white hen returned to the compound with seven beautiful white chicks. The Nigerian boy was overjoyed. The mother took very good care of her chicks.

One day late in the dry season the older boys set a ring of fire to the bush area outside the village. Everyone stood outside the ring as the fire burned toward the center. The purpose was to drive little animals such as rabbits and small antelopes out of the circle. Then the waiting cutlasses claimed their prey. When the slaughter and the fire were over, Olu and his friends walked through the smoldering embers. The boy noticed a heap of charred feathers and smelled burned flesh. It looked like the remains of a bird that had not escaped from the fire. Then Olu realized in horror: it was his beloved friend the white hen all black and burned to death. But then came the sounds of chicks. The mother hen had covered them with her body and they were still alive and well. The mother had given her life for her children.

She died that they may live.

∽

THERE IS, of course, gray ... and then there is grey: Much depends on our perception, more on our naming. Some stories, as we have seen in this segment, stretch literal truth in their effort to become mythical. The next story, the final one in this segment, does not do so. It is to be taken at face value.

Rabbi Eliezer Silver was a leader and activist who saved thousands of Jewish lives during the Holocaust. After the liberation of the Nazi death camps, he tried to revive the spirit of Judaism among the survivors.

One of his many activities was organizing prayer services. A certain refugee refused to participate, explaining that he'd been turned off to Judaism forever. He said that there had been a religious Jew in this refugee's camp who had smuggled in a Siddur (prayer book), and he would charge people half their bread ration to use his Siddur for ten minutes. After witnessing such cruelty, the refugee refused to have anything to do with Siddurim, prayer services, or anything Jewish.

Rabbi Silver approached him with great compassion and understanding, but offered him a new perspective. "You only see the Jew who was so cruel," he said. "What about the holy Jews who were willing to give up half their meager rations for just ten minutes with a Siddur?"

MEMORY

Memory is the connections. Meaning comes from what something is connected to. Something unconnected, unassociated with, unrelated to anything is literally meaningless. Conversely something connected, associated, linked with many things is supercharged with meaning. And the farther back in time the connections go, the greater the meaning. By joining the pieces of our lives together we create ourselves, free ourselves. It's all in the order and the sequence. For this reason, memory may be more in the way things are stored, rather than what is stored.

LAWRENCE KUSHNER

During the late 2012 "superstorm" Sandy, which ravaged coastal Long Island and New Jersey, many residents fleeing their homes grabbed first for irreplaceable photo albums and scrapbooks, deeming souvenirs of memorable moments more valuable than jewelry. Later, when those who had barely escaped with their lives returned to pick through the shattered debris of their now uninhabitable homes, they searched first for those same memories.

J. M. Barrie wrote: "God gave us memories that we might have roses in December." Rabbi Benjamin Blech, commenting on the Sandy disaster, observed: "Memories take precious moments and grant them eternity." He continued: "Whether it be for our families, our friends or the people with whom we interact in our lives, it is only through the memories of beautiful moments that we leave behind something of permanent value."

Without memory, life would consist of momentary experiences that have little relation to one another. Without memory we could not communicate with other people, for we could not remember the ideas we wished to express. Without memory, we would not have the sense of continuity even to know who we are. Memory is central to being human.

> *That which determines a person, that which makes him one*
> *person and not another, is the principle of unity and of*
> *continuity that is memory. Memory is the basis of individual*
> *personality. . . . We live in memory and by memory, and our*
> *spiritual life is at bottom simply the effort of our memory*
> *to persist, to transform itself into hope, the effort*
> *of our past to grow into our future.*
> MIGUEL DE UNAMUNO

Important as are photographs, it is story that is the most effective tool of memory, offering context as well as reminders, creating the connective tissue that joins the pieces of our lives—our memories, our history, the history of human beings, of being human—together. Indeed a main function of photographs is to remind of stories: "Remember when . . ."

Many centuries ago, a rich sultan gave a banquet in honor of the birth of his son. All the nobility who partook of the feast brought costly gifts, except a young sage who came empty-handed. He explained to the sultan, "Today the young prince will receive many precious gifts, jewels, and rare coins. My gift is different. From the time he is old enough to listen until manhood, I will come to the palace every day and tell him stories of our nation's heroes. When he becomes our ruler he will be just and honest."

The young sage kept his word. When the prince was at last made sultan, he became famous for his wisdom and honor. To this day, an inscription on a scroll in that ancient city reads, "It was because of the seed sown by the tales."

∞

WHY STORYTELLING? Why stories? Story is the vehicle of memory. Stories are the triggers of memory—or is memory the trigger of stories? An observation by art critic Paul Brockelman, commenting on the Goya masterpiece *The Third of May 1808*, sheds light on the human story at the heart of all art and all experience. "We don't look at the painting so much as we look at our lives through it. Through it we come to see and understand more about our lives than we understood before." Meditatively he continued: "The human story is the story of story itself. Nothing occurs but the human mind finds a way to fit it into a story."

"Fitting" our experiences into stories helps us to *be* human, for story locates those experiences within memory. Then, especially when life threatens to overwhelm us, when catastrophe looms and we seem to lose our way, we find in memory's stories a way of exploring the fundamental mysteries: *Who are we? Why are we? How are we to live?*

When the great Rabbi Israel Shem Tov saw misfortune threatening the Jews, it was his custom to go into a certain part of the forest to meditate. There he would light a fire, say a special prayer, and the miracle would be accomplished and the misfortune averted.

Later, when his disciple, the celebrated Maggid of Mezritch, had occasion, for the same reason, to intercede with heaven, he would go to the same place in the forest and say: "Master of the Universe, listen! I do not know how to light the fire, but I am still able to say the prayer," and again the miracle would be accomplished.

Still later, Rabbi Moshe Leib of Sasov, in order to save his people once more, would go into the forest and say, "I do not know how to light the fire. I do not know the prayer, but I know the place and this must be sufficient." It was sufficient and the miracle was accomplished.

Then it fell to Rabbi Israel of Rizhyn to overcome misfortune. Sitting in his armchair, his head in his hands, he spoke to God: "I am unable to light the fire, and I do not know the prayer, and I cannot even find the place in the forest. All I can do is to tell the story, and this must be sufficient."

And it was sufficient. For God made man because He loves stories.[*]

---

[*] Elie Wiesel, *The Gates of the Forest* (1966). In his retelling of this story in *Souls on Fire* (1972), Wiesel ends it differently: After "And it was sufficient," instead of "God made man because He loves stories," he wrote: "It no longer is. The proof is that the threat has not been averted. Perhaps we are no longer able to tell the story. Could all of us be guilty? Even the survivors? Especially the survivors."

"WHY STORIES?" Philosophers, psychologists, theologians, writers, and, of course, storytellers offer subtly different perspectives on this question, providing at the same time implicit insights into the usefulness of memory.

> *Human beings are, in their actions and practice,*
> *essentially storytelling animals. I can answer the*
> *question "What am I to do?" only if I can*
> *answer the prior question "Of what story or*
> *stories do I find myself a part?"*
>
> ALASDAIR MACINTYRE

> *Life must be lived forwards, but it can*
> *be understood only backwards.*
>
> SØREN KIERKEGAARD

> *Stories are habitations. We live in and through stories. They*
> *conjure worlds. We do not know the world other than as story*
> *world. Stories inform life. They hold us together and keep us*
> *apart. We inhabit the great stories of our culture. We live*
> *through stories. We are lived by the stories of our race and*
> *place. . . . We are, each of us, locations where the stories*
> *of our place and time become partially tellable.*
>
> GEORGE S. HOWARD

> *Why story? Why should "story" be fundamental?*
> *Because without storytelling, we lose contact with our basic*

realities in this world. We lose contact because only through
story can we fully recognize our existence in time.
To be human is to be in a story.
BRIAN SWIMME

Remember only this one thing. . . . The stories people tell have a
way of taking care of them. If stories come to you, care for them.
And learn to give them away where they are needed.
Sometimes a person needs a story more than food to stay alive.
That is why we put these stories in each other's memory.
This is how people care for themselves.
BARRY LOPEZ

"Why stories"?

Remembering is soul-making,
is its very basis. As such, remembering
needs itself to be remembered. . . .
EDWARD S. CASEY

Memory preserves, but its stories detail, and so help us understand, the subtleties of our relationships. Each of us connects with many different others in many different ways. We also relate to the same person in different ways, and to different people in similar ways. One of the oldest stories, first told by the first historian, Herodotus, and retold by Walter Benjamin in The Storyteller, memorably portrays both the significance of memory and the power of different understandings of the same story.

When the Egyptian king Psammenitus had been beaten and captured by the Persian king Cambyses, Cambyses was bent on humbling his prisoner. He gave orders to place Psammenitus on the road along which the Persian triumphal procession was to pass, and he further arranged that the prisoner should see his daughter pass by as a maid going to the well with her pitcher. While all the Egyptians were lamenting and bewailing this spectacle, Psammenitus stood alone, mute and motionless, his eyes fixed on the ground, and when presently he saw his son, who was being taken along in the procession to be executed, he likewise remained unmoved. But when afterwards he recognized one of his servants, an old, impoverished man, in the ranks of the prisoners, he beat his fists against his head and gave all the signs of deepest mourning.

From this story it may be seen what the nature of true storytelling is. The value of information does not survive the moment in which it was new. It lives only at that moment; it has to surrender to it completely and explain itself to it without losing any time. A story is different. It does not expend itself. It preserves and concentrates its strength and is capable of releasing it even after a long time. Thus Montaigne referred to this Egyptian king and asked himself why he mourned only when he caught sight of his servant. Montaigne answers: "Since he was already over-full of grief, it took only the smallest increase for it to burst through its dams." Thus Montaigne. But one could also say: The king is not moved by the fate of those of royal blood, for it is his own fate. Or: We are moved by much on the stage that does not move us in real life; to the king, this servant is only an actor. Or . . .

❦

STORIES CONCENTRATE and release their strength over time, each new remembering offering fresh perspectives and awareness. The idea of a mere or "pure" sequence of isolated events may be thinkable or conceivable, but it is not experience-able. An "event" is already something that takes time, has temporal thickness, a beginning and an end. Life is not a series of still-frames: If it exists, it flows—an observation as true of the spiritual life as of any other life-form. This is but one reason why story and memory are inseparable.

> *The present is only ever understandable through the past, with*
> *which it forms a living continuity; and it is also true that the past is*
> *always grasped from our own partial viewpoint within the present.*
> *Thus, the "understanding" that allows us to face the future*
> *hopefully—having something to look forward to—comes when our*
> *grasp of the present becomes one with our grasp of the past.*
>
> TERRY EAGLETON

❦

THE WORD *remembering* implicitly conveys a second meaning— *re-membering*, putting back together something that has been sundered, broken apart. "Memory is the sense of loss, and loss pulls us after it," observes author Marilynne Robinson in her provocative work of fiction, *Housekeeping*. And Edward Casey, in his phenomenological study, *Remembering*, reminds that "nostalgia" and "homesickness" both derive from the German *Heimweh*, a term coined in the late seventeenth century by neurologist Johannes Hofer to describe an "affliction that admits of no remedy other than a return to the homeland."

To remember, then, means more than just to recall. As Wendell Berry reminds in his novel Remembering, it also means to be re-membered (the opposite of being dis-membered), to be drawn into a group or a circle from which we had, for whatever reasons, found ourselves excluded. Remembering means entering the "member"-ship of a community.

We all want to be remembered—a desire so deep that it can take unusual forms.

The poet Rupert Brooke set out to travel by boat from England to America. Everyone on deck had someone there to see him or her off—everyone except him. Rupert Brooke felt lonely, terribly lonely. Watching the hugging and kissing and good-byes, he wished he had someone to miss him.

The poet saw a youngster and asked his name. "William," the boy answered.

"William," he asked, "would you like to earn a few shillings?"

"Sure I would! What do I have to do?"

"Just wave to me as I leave," the lonely man instructed.

It is said that money can't buy love, but for six shillings young William waved to Rupert Brooke as the boat pulled out. The poet writes: "Some people smiled and some cried, some waved white handkerchiefs and some waved straw hats. And I? I had William, who waved at me with his red bandana for six shillings and kept me from feeling completely alone."

❦

THE DEPTH of memory is attested by the word's origin. *Memor,* the Latin for "mindful," and the Old English *murnan,* "to grieve," both trace to the Sanskrit *smárati,* "He remembers." Further linguistic study suggests that the deepest Indo-European root, *meror smer,* implies that "mourning" is even more ancient than "remembering." We are made of our memories: We are what we remember ourselves to be. We cannot dissociate the remembering of our personal past from our present identity. And memory unbridled may well be of mourning. Perhaps the first human memories were those of mourning? Cognitive scientist David Eagleman has suggested that "There are three deaths . . . when the body ceases to function . . . when the body is consigned to the grave . . . when your name is spoken for the last time."

Theodor Adorno has said that we dishonor sufferers by not telling their story; we increase our humanity by hearing and repeating it.

> *"Memory" is the key word. To remember is to create links between past and present, between past and future. To remember is to affirm man's faith in humanity and to convey meaning on our fleeting endeavors. The aim of memory is to restore its dignity to justice.*
>
> *. . . But you may ask: Isn't there a danger that memory may perpetuate hatred? No, there is no such danger. Memory and hatred are incompatible, for hatred distorts memory. The reverse is true: Memory may serve as a powerful remedy against hatred.*
>
> ELIE WIESEL

❧

ONE OF the most important features of lived time, of narrative and history, is that only from the perspective of the end do the beginning and middle make sense. In the service of memory, of re-collection, stories perform many tasks. They convey knowledge. They invite identification or detail difference. Stories *awaken* memory. They preserve and convey history. Some stories have implicit themes. Conversion narratives portraying "what I used to be like, what happened, what I am like now" are one familiar form. Many other stories at least implicitly convey a very similar message, in the format "This is how I used to think, then I heard this story, and this is how I think now." Such tales detail a very real shift in standpoint and perspective. The person who undergoes such a change does not "see different things" but rather *sees everything differently*.

One of the most respected of the Desert Fathers was Moses the Black. A story suggests one foundation of his greatness:

A brother at Scetis committed a fault. A council was called to which Abba Moses was invited, but he refused to go. Then the priest sent someone to say to him, "Come, for everyone is waiting for you."

So he got up and went, taking a leaking jug filled with water and carrying it with him. The other monks came out to meet him and said, "What is this, Father?"

The old man replied: "My sins run out behind me and I do not see them, and today I am coming to judge the faults of another." When they heard that, they said no more to the brother but forgave him.

❦

A HUMOROUS story from more modern times sheds light on the shift in perspective that may help us "see everything differently."

One day a Catholic, a Baptist, and a Methodist decided to go fishing.

They got in their boat and pushed their way out to the middle of the lake.

The Catholic said, "I forgot my hat," so he got up, got out of the boat, and walked across the water.

He came back, and the Baptist said, "I forgot the fishing bait," so he got up, got out of the boat, and walked across the water.

He came back, and the Methodist said, "I forgot the beer," so he got up, got out of the boat, tried standing in the water but quickly sank.

About that time the Baptist said, "Do you think it's time to tell him where the stepping-stones are?"

❦

"SEEING EVERYTHING differently" usually involves a revision of memories. "If we change the way we think about the world," explained Jean Piaget and Bärbel Inhelder, "we automatically update memories to reflect our new understanding." True healing implies not a wholeness that does not know brokenness, but the wholeness that repairs a recognized brokenness. The ability to endure and even flourish in the midst of ambiguity and confusion is the very nature of wisdom; in fact, it may perhaps even be the chief difference between wisdom and ideology. Ideology needs to be sure: It rejects the ambiguity of "both/and" for the certainty of "either-or." Story, aided by memory, understands that life offers both joy and suffering, good and evil, black and white and gray. Story is a tool that helps us—the tool that best helps us—to live with ambiguity, with uncertainty, with the inconsistency that flows from our own brokenness.

Rabbi Wolf's wife had a quarrel with her servant. She accused the girl of having broken a dish and wanted her to pay for the damage. The girl, on the other hand, denied having done what she was accused of, and refused to replace the article.

The quarrel became more and more heated. Finally the wife of Rabbi Wolf decided to refer the matter to the court of arbitration of the Torah, and quickly dressed for a visit to the rav of the town.

When Rabbi Wolf saw this, he, too, put on his Sabbath clothes. When his wife asked him why, he told her that he intended to accompany her. She objected to this on the grounds that this was not fitting for him, and that besides, she knew very well what to say to the court. "You know it very well," the zaddik replied. "But the poor orphan, your servant, in whose behalf I am coming, does not know it, and who except me is there to defend her cause?"

⌘

THE PRACTICE of telling stories does in some way "heal"—make whole. Perhaps the most important task of stories is the *healing of identity*, the *making whole* that comes by connecting our present with our memory. As Morris Berman pointed out in his study titled *The Reenchantment of the World*:

We are "whole" to almost no one, least of all to ourselves. Instead we move as in a world of social roles, interaction rituals, and elaborate game-playing that forces us to try to protect the self by developing what R. D. Laing calls a "false-self system."

Others have agreed:

> *Finding oneself means, among other things, finding the story or narrative in terms of which one's life makes sense.*
>
> ROBERT BELLAH

> *Recounting of a life story . . . leads one inevitably to the consideration of problems which are no longer psychological but spiritual.*
>
> PAUL TOURNIER

> *I need to remember my stories not because I need to "find out" about myself but because I need to found myself in a story I can hold to be "mine."*
>
> JAMES HILLMAN

> *One's self identity is the story one tells one's self of who one is.*
>
> R. D. LAING

And that is why we need to tell our own story AND why we need to own the story that we tell. However, as in any discussion concerning spirituality, we often discover more about what something *is* by recognizing also what it is *not*.

Story—the story that heals identity because it links with

memory—is not "untrue"; it requires the self-disclosure of actual events (although its truth is not in the "events").

Story is not mere nostalgia, a wallowing in the past as in a "drunkalog" or "war story"—for story requires actual movement, emplotment.

Story is not a "science," which claims to separate understanding and interpretation in a demand for "clear and distinct" ideas; the realities of self-disclosure and plot necessarily manifest and so require accepting the ambiguity of reality-as-it-is. Memory always affords context.

A final and, perhaps, the most important "NOT": The storytelling that taps memory is not "just a form of therapy"; it seems more accurate, indeed, to view some forms of therapy as attempts to make a particular use of the far longer and wider and deeper and richer tradition of storytelling and story-listening.

In addition to those "nots" there are other misunderstandings of the nature of healing story. Story does not use a specific language but uses language in a specific way: The difference between the language of the social scientist and the language of the storyteller is not in their "objectivity" or in the access to truth they respectively provide or fail to provide. They serve different purposes—the former is appropriate for manipulating human lives, the latter for making them intelligible, for understanding rather than prediction and control.

Stories do not give us facts nor do they give us proofs for anything—that is not their purpose. Instead, they do what they are meant to do: provide us with images and ways of thinking about life's imponderables.

Stories have a way of emerging out of nowhere. Rather than

making them up, we seem, instead, to find them; it may even be more accurate to say they find us.

❧

A person has an immensely powerful computer into which has been fed vast amounts of information.

She asks it, "Do you compute whether you will ever think like a human being?" Whirring away, the machine goes through its computations.

Finally, it prints out its answer:

"THAT REMINDS ME OF A STORY."

Does that little story frighten you or hearten you? As the "whirring away" and the IBM-ish caps in the computer's printout hint, this story was first told some four decades ago by the wide-ranging anthropologist Gregory Bateson. But the story is singularly appropriate here, for by highlighting the connection between story and memory, it reveals story as the tool that allows us to recognize time. Story sequences: It organizes "before" and "after" even if not recounted in strictly chronological order. In doing so, it anchors us in the temporality of "now." Some people claim to have a *carpe diem* seize-the-moment philosophy, but the wise have long recognized that to demand to "have it all now" is to have *no* "now."

A "computer story," of course, hints dissonance: As an art form, story is useful precisely because it is not straightforward. Good stories, as Christopher Lasch observed, like "lovemaking, artistic creation, and play do not provide 'straightforward' satisfaction. Instead, they become most deeply satisfying when they remind us of the tension that precedes release, the separation that precedes reconciliation, the loss underlying restoration, the unavoidable oth-erness of the other." The sense of wholeness does not come glibly: A basic lesson of all art, religion, and love (not to mention the experi-ence of alcoholism/addiction) is that there are no "shortcuts."

When asked if he was ever discouraged by the little fruit his ef-forts seemed to yield, the Master told the story of a snail that started to climb a cherry tree one cold, windy day in late spring.

The sparrows in a neighboring tree had a good laugh at his expense. Then one flew over and said, "Hey, stupid, don't you know there are no cherries on this tree?"

The little fellow did not stop as he replied, "Well, there will be when I get there."

❧

STORY IS many things, but its classic and, indeed, key image is that of mirror. A main function/task of "story" (as of all art) is to portray, to deepen awareness of, the human condition—to allow and invite us to know our-*selfs*. Story achieves this mainly and most directly by holding up a mirror to the ambiguity and incongruity that lie at the core of the human condition, a reality that we often forget. Underlying this understanding is the core ancient and clas-sic vision of "the human" as essentially mixed, middle: the strange combination of spirit and animal, "beast and angel," that which, although we all experience its reality, we cannot see directly. One basic function of all storytelling, whether written or spoken, is to invite the listener/reader to identify with the story, to see not only "self," but self-as-partaker-of-and-participant-in the human con-dition. All other functions flow from this foundational one.

Two final words on story . . . and memory:

There are two kinds of stories: Some tell how it was; others reveal how it is.

❦

Over the entrance to Yad Vashem, Israel's memorial to those who perished in the Holocaust, is inscribed into the stone an aphorism ascribed to the Baal Shem Tov: "Exile comes from forgetting. Memory is the source of our redemption."

VIRTUE

God loveth adverbs; and cares not how good, but how well.
JONATHAN GLOVER

The lions in front of the New York Public Library are named "Patience" and "Fortitude." They were named that by Mayor Fiorello LaGuardia, who concluded his radio addresses during the 1930s Great Depression with those two words, saying that was what New Yorkers needed.

Virtue: a word these days rarely heard and perhaps even less frequently thought. And that is a shame. For *virtue*, which derives proximately from the Latin *virtus*, means simply *strength*, the quality of *excellence*.

Over two thousand years ago, Aristotle explained the impossibility of setting up mechanical rules that could adequately define virtuous behavior. He pointed out that it is easy to describe extremely bad behavior, and to explain why bad behavior is so destructive. The reason why virtuous behavior is so difficult to define is because it is, in fact, simply the mean (the middle point) between two extremes of bad, destructive behavior. To lead the good life, to practice virtue, then, is quite simple in terms of its basic principle: We should seek the balance point between those two extremes. Perhaps because the Greek word for virtue, *aretē*, derives from the word *Arēs*, the name the ancient Greeks gave to the god of war, Aristotle chose the virtue of *courage* as an illustration of this basic principle of the mean. Courage, viewed from this perspective, is neither cowardice nor foolhardiness but rather stands between them.

In 1799, when the armies of Napoleon were sweeping over Europe, Massena's army of 18,000 suddenly appeared on the heights above the Austrian town of Feldkirch. It was Easter Sunday and the rising sun glittered on the weapons of the French army as they overlooked the village below.

A hasty town council meeting was called to decide what could be done. Resisting such an army was out of the question. Finally, the dean of the church arose and said, "It is Easter Day. Ring the bells and have services as usual, and leave the matter in God's hands." They agreed to do as he suggested and, from the towers of Feldkirch there rang out loud and joyous peals calling worshippers to gather.

The French heard the sudden clanging of the bells with surprise and alarm. They concluded that the Austrian army had arrived to defend the town. Massena broke up his camp, gave the order to march, and before the bells had ceased tolling, not a soldier was to be seen.

In the midst of fear and in the presence of danger, ringing the bells may be the most courageous act we can perform. For buried deep in courage we find the core serenity that allows us to accept what we cannot change.

Courage is not the absence of danger but the decision to go ahead despite the danger. To live. To ring the bells.

SEVERAL THINKERS have written wisely and well about the four cardinal virtues: prudence, justice, temperance, fortitude. Less often addressed are other qualities that the postmodern age tends to ignore, for example, *fidelity*.

Fidelity: The word signals a steadfastness, a faithfulness to some kind of promise, a loyalty to one's own story. Fidelity inspires and invites trust. But an ever-changing world that less invites than compels change can make *fidelity* seem old-fashioned, passé. Until, perhaps, we experience the desire and need for a friend. Basic to the deep meaning of friendship is the idea of faithfulness, a kind of presence—for a friend is in some way "there" and can be relied on.

As is the case with "benevolence" or "grace," defining some realities—especially when they concern qualities—is well nigh impossible. There are certain realities that we come to understand not by knowing what they *are*, but by observing what they *do*. This is one reason why stories *work*. They show us how *fidelity* and *loyalty*, for example, work. Fidelity has been explained in contrast to the concept of *covenant*, as not a legal bond or principle but a personal commitment to share in a common story with another person. For example:

A man died. When he awoke, he was walking with his dog along a dirt road across a beautiful prairie. After a time, the man came to a fenced area and he could see a large house set back from the road.

As the man drew near the gate, he saw the apparent keeper of the property, who was standing idly in leisure clothes and appeared to be enjoying the beautiful day. "Hi there," the walker said. "Could this by any chance be Heaven?"

"Sho' nuff is," the other replied. "And you are welcome to come in and join us."

Well, the man thought, this is not what I expected but it sure looks cozy.

"Just one thing," the man barring the gate said. "You are perfectly welcome to come in, but we do not allow animals here, so I'm afraid your dog cannot come with you."

The walker looked at his dog, who was standing expectantly. He sure hated to give up Heaven, but he was pretty sure he would hate himself even more if he gave up his dog.

"Thanks anyway, stranger," he said. "But I think I'll stay with my dog and just keep moseying along for now." And the two, man and dog, walked on down the road.

A short time later they came to another fenced area. And again, they saw a big old house set back away from the road. This time, the man barring the gate was dressed in overalls and a plaid flannel shirt.

"Howdy!" exclaimed our walker. "Where am I and what is this place, please?"

"Well," the farmer replied, "this just happens to be Heaven, and you are most welcome here—in fact, we'd like to have both you and your dog join us."

"Hey, wait a minute," the walker exclaimed. "There's another place that looks a lot like this a bit back up the road, but they told me that I could not bring my dog in there."

"Ah, yes." The old man smiled as he opened the gate. "Well, y'see, that place is not really Heaven; in fact, it's the opposite place, if you get my meaning."

"Well, why do you put up with them doing that, pretending to be you?"

"Well, y'see, they're pretty handy for us 'cuz they screen out the people who don't know the meaning of loyalty and love."

❧

SO: "LOYALTY," but perhaps, again, a better term is *fidelity*—faithfulness to some reality that is largely behind us, fidelity to our own story as it really is. Despots have always attempted to destroy the stories of the peoples they conquer. And as so many generations of immigrants to the United States attest, those uprooted from *place* cling with all the more fervor to the *story* of their past, seeking ways to make it flow into and with their new present.

Or take another virtue, *gratitude*. People who receive good things that are truly *gifts*—realities given not because they are in any way "earned" or "due" but from the sheer goodness and generosity of the giver—usually wish to express their gratitude by saying "thank you." But that is often impossible. Some gifts are bestowed anonymously or, more commonly, given in a way that renders individual thanks inappropriate or even impossible.

In such situations the suggestion is frequently made, or the gift-receiver himself or herself comes up with the idea of "forward gratitude"—saying "thanks" not backward but forward, by giving some kind of gift to yet another. This practice of "passing it on" also expresses the virtue of reverence, respect, both forward and backward.

It is important to realize that gratitude is not a *feeling*; it is, rather, a *vision*—a vision that enables recognizing *gift*. Indeed, one key to the experience of spirituality is recognizing the difference between *feeling* and *vision*. A workshop presenter of our acquaintance suggests to his participants: "If you want a warm, tingly, shivery feeling . . . go pee in your pants!"

That suggestion invites a question—are feelings only "felt," as in some warm, tingly, shivery sensation? Are feelings only on the surface—visible, doable, touchable, smell-able? When we smell a rose or watch a sunset or sit by the ocean mesmerized by the surge and the retreat of the waves, have we moved from feeling to vision—the kind of vision that recognizes gift? There is nothing wrong with feelings, and experiencing good ones is often a bonus delight, but spirituality itself runs more deeply: It is a *way of seeing*. The experience of spirituality thus involves recognizing new and different realities, especially the *qualities* of the gift-experience, appreciating not only the gift itself but also the sheer freedom and generosity contained in a genuine "gift."

Such gratitude connects with story. There is a connectedness among "think," "thank," and "remember." "Think" and "thank" have kindred roots, and the German word *an-denken*—literally, "to think on"—means to remember; hence, think, thank, and remembrance are related notions. Real thinking, thinking that is rooted in *be*-ing, is at once an act of thanking and remembrance. Gratitude is the kind of vision that enables seeing many gifts.

A blind man was begging in a city park. Someone approached and asked him whether people were giving generously. The blind man shook a nearly empty tin.

His visitor said to him, "Let me write something on your card." The blind man agreed. That evening the visitor returned. "Well, how were things today?"

The blind man showed him a tin full of money and asked, "What on earth did you write on that card?"

"Oh," said the other, "I merely wrote 'Today is a spring day, and I am blind.'"

~⚬~

STILL ANOTHER virtue preserves the integrity of gratitude, safeguarding it from any sense of either condescension or entitlement—the quality of *humility*, rightly understood. "Rightly understood"?

> *Humility is just as much the opposite of self-abasement as*
> *it is of self-exaltation. To be humble is not to make comparisons.*
> *Secure in its reality, the self is neither better nor worse, bigger*
> *nor smaller, than anything else in the universe. It is—is*
> *nothing, yet at the same time is one with everything.*
>
> DAG HAMMARSKJÖLD

Once upon a time there was a proud man named Carl who loved to ride his horse through his vast estate and to congratulate himself on his enormous wealth. One day he came upon Hans, an old tenant farmer, who had sat down to eat his lunch in the shade of a great oak tree. Hans's head was bowed in prayer. When Hans looked up he said, "Oh, excuse me, sir, I didn't see you. I was giving thanks for my food."

"Humph!" snorted the rich man, noticing the coarse dark bread and cheese that made up the old man's lunch. "If that were all *I* had to eat," he sneered, "I don't think I'd feel like giving thanks."

"Oh," replied Hans, "it's quite sufficient. But it's remarkable that you should come here today because I had a strange dream just before awakening this morning."

"And what did you dream?" Carl asked with an amused smile.

The old man answered, "There was beauty and peace all around, and yet I could hear a voice saying, 'The richest man in the valley will die tonight.'"

"Ah, dreams!" cried Carl. "Nonsense!" He turned and galloped away and Hans prayed as he watched the horse and its rider disappear.

"Die tonight!" mused Carl. "It's ridiculous! No use going into a panic." The best thing to do, he decided, was to forget the old man's dream. And yet—yet he couldn't forget it. He had felt fine, as least till Hans described that crazy dream of his. Now he wasn't sure that he felt all that well. So that evening he called his doctor, who was a personal friend. He asked him to come over right away for he had to speak with him. When the doctor arrived, Carl told him of the old man's dream, how the richest man in the valley would die this very night.

"Ah," replied the doctor, "sounds like poppycock to me, but for your own peace of mind, let me examine you." A little later, the examination complete, the doctor was full of smiles and assurances. He said, "Carl, you're as strong and healthy as that horse you ride. There's no way you're going to die tonight." The doctor was just closing his bag when a messenger arrived out of breath at the manor door.

"Doctor, Doctor," he cried, "come quick! It's old Hans. He just died in his sleep!"

❦

THE MOST misunderstood virtue may be humility. This occurs, for example, in interpreting the meaning of a spiritual seeker asking the guidance of someone, perhaps a "guide" or a "sponsor."

"The quality of the reply given by a spiritual father does not depend on the competence or holiness of the father, but on the condition of the person seeking advice," writes Simon Tugwell. "The reason why it is essential for people to consult the elders is not necessarily that the elders are in themselves wiser or holier, but because it is a gesture of humility, which will win God's blessing on people's undertakings." The gesture itself may awaken that virtue.

Humility and obedience are two painfully misunderstood virtues that are really the arts of listening. Humility involves the refusal to coerce, the rejection of all attempts to control others.

There once lived a saint so good that the angels came from heaven to see how a man could be so godly. This saint went about his daily life diffusing virtue as the stars diffuse light and the flowers scent, without being aware of it. His day could be summed up by two words—he gave, he forgave—yet these words never passed his lips. They were expressed in his ready smile, his kindness, and his charity.

The angels said to God, "Lord, grant him the gift of miracles." God replied, "Ask what it is that he wishes."

They said to the saint, "Would you like the touch of your hands to heal the sick?"

"No," answered the saint. "I would rather God do that."

"Would you like to convert sinful souls and bring back wandering hearts to the right path?"

"No, that is the angels' mission. It is not for me to convert."

"Would you like to become a model of patience, attracting men by your virtue to glorifying God?"

"No," replied the saint. "If men should be attracted to me, they might ignore God."

"What is it that you desire, then?" asked the angels.

"What can I wish for?" asked the saint. "That God gives me his grace; with that I have everything"

The angels said, "You must ask for a miracle, or one will be forced upon you."

"Very well," said the saint. "That I may do good without ever knowing it."

The angels, perplexed, took counsel and resolved upon the following plan: every time the saint's shadow fell behind him or to the side where he could not see it, it would have the power to cure disease, soothe pain, and comfort sorrow.

And so when the saint walked along, his shadow, thrown on the ground on either side or behind him, made arid paths green, caused withered plants to bloom, gave clear water to dried-up brooks, brought fresh color to pale children and joy to unhappy men and women.

The saint simply went about his daily life diffusing virtue as the stars diffuse light and the flowers scent, without being aware of it. The people, respecting his humility, followed him silently, never speaking to him about the miracles. Soon they even forgot his name, and simply called him "the holy shadow."

ALTRUISM IS not very fashionable today. Those who practice it may in fact find themselves accused of "codependence." And yet a funny thing happens to many people who experience the freedom of recovery from addiction or other similar blessings. Happy to the point of being overjoyed at their own release from bondage, they yearn to make that freedom available to others. Sometimes their enthusiasm can be overwhelming, with the unfortunate result that the ancient honored quality of compassionate concern has come to be viewed as a vice.

Perhaps because of outmoded, even stodgy associations, those who have difficulty with the reality of *qualities*—those "things" that exist that aren't really "things"—tend to write off expressions of altruism and compassion as specific events or particular acts. But altruistic "acts of compassion" are not merely particular behaviors such as a large donation to a charity or a visit to the hospital or a mealtime volunteering at a soup kitchen. Underlying such behaviors is a more significant framework—the language we use to make sense of such behaviors, the cultural understandings that transform them from physical motions into an action of human *be*-ing. The discourse in which such behavior is inscribed and described is no less a part of the act than is the behavior itself. How do we think about and talk about such behaviors and the realities to which they are a response?

It is difficult to talk about—and to think about—altruism. A common story invites more than passing thought.

The story goes that Abraham Lincoln, at the time an Illinois attorney, once glanced through the window of his carriage to catch sight of a piglet wallowing helplessly in the mire. He called to the driver to stop, then waded out into the mud to extricate the unfortunate animal. When asked why he had put himself to such inconvenience for a pig, Mr. Lincoln answered that, had he not acted, he "should have had no peace of mind all day."

Altruism or selfishness? Instead of seeking to label or categorize such behavior, it might be wiser to ask what it tells us about Mr. Lincoln's character . . . and virtue.

There is a world of difference between genuine and false
humility. A truly humble man does not know that he is humble.
Was it the Ostrowtzer who asked: If humility is so important
a commandment, why isn't it mentioned in the Torah?
Maybe because if it were a biblical commandment,
people would compete with each other. . . . Yes, humility
must be part of a person's subconscious.

ELIE WIESEL

But subconscious humility can be difficult.

An old rabbi was lying ill in bed and his disciples were holding a whispered conversation at his bedside, extolling his unparalleled virtues.

"Not since Solomon has there been one as wise as he," said one of them. "And his faith! It equals that of our father Abraham," said another. "Surely his patience equals that of Job," added a third. "Only in Moses can we find someone who conversed so intimately with God," declared a fourth.

The rabbi seemed restless. When his disciples had left, his wife said to him, "Did you hear them sing your praises?"

"I did," said the rabbi.

"Then why are you so fretful?" asked his wife.

"My modesty," complained the rabbi. "No one mentioned my modesty."

MORE SUCCESSFUL at unaware humility, perhaps, were the sages of a different tradition:

Certain Greek fishermen once netted a magnificent golden tripod from the deep. Its ownership became a matter of intense international concern. The quarrel was referred to Delphi.

"Whoever is first of all in wisdom," hissed Pythia, "to him the tripod belongs."

So peace was declared and the tripod presented to Thales of Miletus, a philosopher who enjoyed everyone's respect. But Thales passed it on to a second sage, whom he considered wiser than himself. The second sage passed it to a third, and so forth, until finally the tripod circled back to Thales, who discreetly gave it to Delphi.

THIS IS why we need *stories*. The language of motive and intention *provides* as well as describes *connections*. It links us more tightly with the values we hold, and it tells others that we cherish these values. The ability to care may not depend on giving one account rather than another. But being able to give *some* account makes it possible to conceive of our behavior as caring. By linking it with broader values, we place it in a context. Our accounts—stories— define the cultural meaning of our caring; our caring, in turn, becomes a reflection of our broader values.

A rabbi gathered together his students and asked them: "How do we know the exact moment when night ends and day begins?"

"It's when, standing some way away, you can tell a sheep from a dog," said one boy.

The rabbi was not content with the answer.

Another student said: "No, it's when, standing some way away, you can tell an olive tree from a fig tree."

"No, that's not a good definition either."

"Well, what's the right answer?" asked the boys.

And the rabbi said: "When a stranger approaches and we think he is our brother, that is the moment when night ends and day begins."

WE LIVE in an era when all accounts of motives have become subject to doubt; in fact, we have social norms against sounding too charitable, too "good." Compassion, our culture tells us, must really arise from some selfish motive. Utilitarianism, sociobiology, and many therapeutic accounts explain it away, telling us that altruism is really self-interest. And so the message we hear again and again from volunteer agencies and fund-raisers is that "helping people makes you feel good." That may be, and probably is, true. But might it not be so because the most profound kind of "feeling good" flows from *being* good?

There was once a famous British actress who was known as Mrs. Kendal. She appears as a character in the striking movie *The Elephant Man*, the story of a man who was, you might recall, grotesquely and horribly disfigured with skin the color of an elephant.

There was a particular incident in the movie I recall very well. The famous actress went to see the elephant man, as he was called, and she held out her hand to take his hand. And he extended the less deformed of his two hands, the left. Mrs. Kendal stood there; this great actress stood there and looked him straight in the eye, and she shook her head, indicating that was not sufficient.

The elephant man waited a long time. Finally, after the pause, out from under his coat he brought his more horribly deformed right hand. Mrs. Kendal took his hand in hers and she smiled. The elephant man said that was the first time in his life that a woman had held his hand.

⚮

VIRTUE RESPONDS not to exposition but to story. Story connects memory and hope—and as both Dickens and Goethe demonstrated, those who lack memory, lack hope. But just as "nostalgia" is not the same as memory, hope is very different from "optimism." Near the end of his life, Martin Luther King Jr. told his old Montgomery congregation that he was no longer an optimist, although he still had hope. The phrasing seems borrowed from Reinhold Niebuhr, but the distinction between optimism and hope was implicit in many of King's earlier statements. He had, quite simply, seen too much suffering to embrace any doctrine of progress.

Hope is an underappreciated virtue, perhaps because it is founded in the past at least as much as it looks to a future.

Being a veterinarian, I had been called to examine a ten-year-old Irish wolfhound named Belker. The dog's owners, Ron, his wife, Lisa, and their little boy, Shane, were all very attached to Belker, and they were hoping for a miracle.

I examined Belker and found he was dying of cancer. I told the family we couldn't do anything for Belker and offered to perform the euthanasia procedure for the old dog in their home.

As we made arrangements, Ron and Lisa told me they thought it would be good for six-year-old Shane to observe the procedure. They felt as though Shane might learn something from the experience.

The next day, I felt the familiar catch in my throat as Belker's family surrounded him. Shane seemed so calm, petting the old dog for the last time, that I wondered if he understood what was going on. Within a few minutes, Belker slipped peacefully away.

The little boy seemed to accept Belker's transition without any difficulty or confusion. We sat together for a while after Belker's death, wondering aloud about the sad fact that animal lives are shorter than human lives. Shane, who had been listening quietly, piped up, "I know why."

Startled, we all turned to him. What came out of his mouth next stunned me. I'd never heard a more comforting explanation. It has changed the way I try to live.

He said, "People are born so that they can learn how to live a good life—like loving everybody all the time and being nice, right?" The six-year-old continued, "Well, dogs already know how to do that, so they don't have to stay as long."

☙

Hope is not the conviction that something will turn
out well, but the certainty that something makes
sense, regardless of how it turns out.
VÁCLAV HAVEL

☙

VIRTUE: DOES it make a difference? The postmodern world would seem to deny that. But a recent book by Susan Neiman, *Moral Clarity*, suggests otherwise. As reviewer Tim Black noted, Neiman argues against resignation and cynicism: There is always an alternative, she says. The disparity between how the world is and how we believe it ought to be is not to be willfully ignored; rather, it is to be seized upon, cultivated, pursued. "The distinction between *is* and *ought* is the most important one we ever draw.... Truth tells us how the world is; morality tells us how it ought to be. Ideals matter not because they exist, but because they don't."

> *Ideals are irreducible. They are not things in the world like tables or chairs; they are not reducable to self-preservation or, its more developed form, self-interest; and they cannot be explained away by some genetic urge to propagate the species. Rather, the idealistic impulse is precisely the transcendence of what is, be it our biology or our environment. Idealism defines our humanity.*

☙

Once when the man who would be called Saint Francis of Assisi fell ill during his last years, his guardian and companion obtained a fox skin to sew into his tunic as protection against the winter cold. Francis would permit the fox-skin liner only if a piece of the fur was also sewn on the outside of his tunic so that no one would be fooled by the garment's patched outer appearance into thinking Francis was being more ascetic than he was.

SIN

A man consulted his physician. "I have a terrible problem," he said. "Lately I've been carousing and misbehaving. It's been happening more and more frequently, and my conscience is beginning to trouble me very deeply. Can you give me something that will help?"

The doctor replied, "Oh, I see, you want me to give you something to strengthen your willpower?"

"No," the patient protested, "that's not it. I don't want to strengthen my willpower. I want you to give me something to weaken my conscience."

❦

WELL, WHAT should we call it—our virtually unerring instinct for what gets us into so many kinds of trouble, our eager falling for what all our experience should warn is not good for us? The word *sin* is so passé! And besides, who believes in *sin* anymore?

Having examined *virtue*, let's approach sin from that perspective. Virtue, recall, is the mean, the middle, between two extremes. Thus, *courage* stands between cowardice and foolhardiness. So perhaps an easy way to think of sin is as virtue carried to extremes.

The Greek term translated as "sin" is *hamartia—ἁμαρτία*, which signifies a falling short or going astray, as an arrow missing its target. Again, then, the middling idea: Hitting the target requires neither undershooting nor overshooting it. A slightly extended image presents sin as a *deviation*, a veering off the correct course whereas the correctly shot arrow flies directly to the target.

But as is true of many words, the meaning of *sin* changed over time. Medieval theology distinguished "actual sin," concrete offenses of action or omission, from "original sin," the recognition of what some in later generations would term the dark side of human nature. Another distinction lurked in the background—that between sin as act (or omission), and sin as a state, the condition of being separated, alienated from ultimate reality.

"The modern world is suffering increasingly from sexual anorexia," said the psychiatrist.

"What's that?" said the Master.

"A loss of appetite for sex."

"How terrible!" said the Master. "What's the cure for it?"

"We don't know. Do you?"

"I think I do."

"What?"

"Make sex a sin again," said the Master with an impish smile.

꧁꧂

THE SO-CALLED *capital sins* are aspects of living in or near that state of alienation: They are less actions than dispositions or inclinations to certain actions or attitudes. We thus best think of these "capital sins" as neither acts nor omissions, but as attitudinal traps leading into ways of thinking and choosing—seeing and wanting— that are destructive of our own humanity.

The snare inherent in these traps is that they lead us into ourselves, and so cut us off from looking outward to modes of connecting with others. Each raises barricades that shift attention from "we" to *me*. They are named capital from the Latin *caput*, "head," because they are the fountainhead, the source of just about all the evils that plague human beings in our quest for the true, the good, the beautiful.

The tradition of naming these conditions—for they are states of being rather than any sort of actions—began with Evagrius Ponticus, one of the most influential of the Desert Fathers and Mothers, those men and women who, beginning in the third century CE, sought a deeper understanding of themselves by re- treating from the distractions of Egyptian cities into the vast emp- tiness of the Sahara Desert. But the nature of these *logismoi*, these traps into destroying our own humanity, is such that they merit more than mere historical mention here, in a context ripe with stories.

There's this little, scrawny guy sitting in a bar, just looking at his drink.

He stays like that for a half hour.

Then, this big trouble-making truck driver steps up next to him, takes the drink from the guy, and just drinks it all down.

The poor man starts crying. The truck driver says: "Come on, man, I was just joking. Here, I'll buy you another drink. I just can't stand to see a man crying."

"No, it's not that. This day is the worst of my life. First, I over- sleep, and I go late to my office. My boss, outraged, fires me.

When I leave the building to go to my car, I find out it was stolen. The police, they say they can do nothing. I get a cab to return home, and when I leave it, I remember I left my wallet and credit cards in it. The cabdriver just drives away. I go home, and when I get there, I find my wife in bed with the gardener. I leave home, and come to this bar. And just when I was thinking about putting an end to my life, you show up and drink my poison. . . ."

❧

THE "CAPITAL SINS" are less trespass than traps. These are the snares laid in every age, however differently, that lead us to deny and destroy our very own humanity as well as that of others. These fatal flaws may also be usefully understood not so much as "defects" as uglinesses of vision—ways of seeing that lead us away from reality and into worlds of destructive fantasy, that lead us into seeing what is not there in ways that prevent true vision and understanding of what *is* there.

The names remain: Pride, Avarice, Lust, Envy, Gluttony, Wrath, and the untranslatable bored emptiness of *acedia*, a morass of self-pity that the usual translation—"sloth"—barely captures.

PRIDE

Most listings of the capital sins give Pride the pride of place— it comes first. Until very recently, most dictionary definitions of pride presented it as the *Oxford English Dictionary* still does (in early 2014) as "an excessively high opinion of one's own worth or importance . . . an inordinate self-esteem."

"Excessively," "inordinate": Pride denies boundaries, rebels against limitations of any kind, defies concepts such as *appropriate* or *fitting*. Pride insists on *more*, and especially when Envy hovers near, on *more than*. Pride entails the sense of superior, the comparison better than, higher than. The proud man sees himself as above, and so necessarily looks down upon. Dante in his *Purgatorio* describes proud persons as bent over almost double, unable to lift their eyes from the ground. Those who looked down on everyone are now unable to look up at anything.

Pride exalts the self, and such exaltation necessarily comes at the expense of others. Insofar as the proud person attends to others, that attention involves belittling comparison. In impeding identification because of that ever-present comparison, Pride renders compassion impossible. There can be no serenity in the midst of this kind of striving. Pride must be competitive, for it cannot bear to concede first place to anyone else. Necessarily, then, Pride's competitiveness separates people from one another.

In one way or another, in placing Pride at the head of the list of capital, deadly sins, classic thought recognized that Pride reflects the desire, the demand—even the claim—to be more than human, to be in some way a god. How else to understand the constant drive to control, the implicit insistence that all reality recognize that self is the center of the universe?

With the end of World War II Britain found herself financially bankrupt and materially destitute. A severe Austerity Program was enacted by Parliament and Sir Stafford Cripps appointed the Minister of Austerity with extensive powers.

Sir Stafford apparently was of Puritan principles, with a perpetually dour mien, and he continually irritated Winston Churchill to distraction. One day as the minister entered the House of Commons, Churchill was heard to remark, "There but for the grace of God goes God."

❧

"PLAYING GOD" can happen in small ways, for example in the ever-present temptation to seek an edge, gain some privilege:

A car accident occurred in a small town. A crowd surrounded the victim so a newspaper reporter couldn't get close enough to see him.

He hit upon an idea. "I'm the father of the victim!" he cried. "Please let me through."

The crowd let him pass so he was able to get right up to the scene of the accident and discover, to his embarrassment, that the victim was a donkey.

❧

POSTMODERN PRIDE remains competitive but masks its striving under a veneer of self-satisfaction that assumes superiority. This is evidenced by a not-so-subtle change that has taken place in some dictionary definitions of pride. In contrast with the classic primary definition as "inordinate," "excessive," we find that more recently published dictionaries offer a new first meaning for pride: "a feeling of deep pleasure or satisfaction derived from one's own achievements. . . . ," "pleasure or satisfaction taken in an achievement, possession, or association."

"Opinion" has become feeling; thinking and judgment have been displaced by emotion. More important, the sense of "excessively" and "inordinate" has been downplayed. For in the postmodern world, the ideal has become an assertion of self-sufficiency that involves a denial of one's need for others, except, perhaps, as adorers. This refusal of any need for true community is the essence of selfishness, now become virtue rather than vice.

I asked Mom if I was a gifted child.... She said they certainly wouldn't have paid for me.

∞

HUMILITY, PRIDE'S cure, comes by attending to one's lacks, one's deficiencies, one's areas of emptiness. The focus of humility is on not the *things* but the *qualities* that one lacks or falls short of living. Because to be human is to need others, to deny our need for persons as full persons is to invite entrapment in a need for things—material possessions or the recognition of "honors." It is to become mired in the inevitably frustrated effort to fill a spiritual hole with what are ultimately material realities. It does not work.

Rabbi Elimelekh had delivered a wonderful sermon and now he was returning to his native land. To honor him and to show their gratitude, the faithful decided to follow Elimelekh's carriage out of the city.

At one point, the rabbi stopped the carriage and asked the driver to go ahead without him while he joined the people.

"A fine example of humility," said one of the men beside him.

"Humility has nothing to do with it, just a little intelligence," replied Elimelekh. "You're all out here having a walk, singing, drinking wine, chatting with each other, making new friends, and all because of an old rabbi who came to talk to you about the art of living. So let's leave my theories in the carriage, I want to enjoy the party."

&

AVARICE

Avarice, the love of wealth, is usually listed as the second deadly sin. If Pride focuses directly on the self, Avarice or Covetousness or Greed is the driving, never-ending, insatiable need for more things. In its quest for material goods, it is incapable of fulfillment, for there will always be some material reality that is not possessed. Seeking fulfillment in material things, greed lures away from "the spiritual" in the sense that it focuses on things rather than attending to other human beings.

The problem with greed is that it is insatiable.

In the old film *Key Largo*, Edward G. Robinson, in the role that defined him, plays a gangster whose life is filled with violence and deceit. In the film he holds a family hostage. Someone asks him what makes him want to live this kind of life, but try as he might Robinson can't answer this question. So one of the hostages, played by Humphrey Bogart, suggests an answer: "I know what you want. You want more." Robinson's face brightens as he says, "Yeah! That's it! That's what I want. I want more."

&

AVARICE INVOLVES not only pure material greed but the principle of thinking about what does not yet exist, a preoccupation with hopes and fears, with imaginary or future things. Hoarding money (or anything else) precludes attention to other human beings.

> One day a rich but miserly Hasid came to a rabbi. The rabbi led him to the window. "Look out there," he said, "and tell me what you see."
>
> "People," answered the rich man.
>
> Then the rabbi led him to a mirror. "What do you see now?" he asked.
>
> "I see myself," answered the Hasid.
>
> The rabbi said, "Behold—in the window there is glass and in the mirror there is glass. But the glass of the mirror is covered with a little silver, and no sooner is a little silver added than you cease to see others and see only yourself."

⚬⚬⚬

GREED IS not "good." The constant quest for "more," whether of material things or power or honors or whatever, manifests another trap that leads to the betrayal of our true selves. For no piling up outside the self will ever fill the yawning hole that one experiences within one's very self. *Piling up:* The modern versions of Scrooge can be found poring over new objects to be lovingly counted and caressed—the abstract numbers that tell "how my investments are doing." Have those who praise their financial adviser, "Whatever he touches turns to gold," ever heard the story of poor rich King Midas?

> A fox said that he would provide worms for any bird that would share his feathers. One bird thought that this was a good idea, so it pulled a feather from one of its wings and gave it

to the fox and then received a worm in return. This was wonderful! The bird decided that this was a good way to get worms easily. But, after a while, the bird had plucked out so many feathers that it could not fly away, and so the fox jumped on it and ate it.

❧

AN INDIAN PROVERB: "An old monkey never puts his hand in the pot."

As the story goes, hunters hollow out a small hole in a coconut, place a banana inside, and bury the coconut. When a monkey happens upon the coconut, he forces his hand into the hole to grab the banana but then cannot pull his clenched fist out through the narrow opening, no matter how hard he struggles. Rather than let go of the banana, the panicked monkey continues to wrestle with the coconut, hoping to claim his prize. Soon the hunters come and he is caught. For all his cleverness, the monkey's fate is sealed.

❧

AND SO it is with us, in our own lives.

The need to hold on to a particular object or possession—often something trivial and insignificant—ends up making us prisoners of that need.

LUST

The word *lust* is derived from the High German *lust*, where the word denotes simply "desire." The Greek word that translates as lust is *epithymia* (επιθυμια), which is translated into English as "to covet." Thus, the wider meaning of Lust is any intense desire or craving for self-gratification and excitement, and so we speak of "lust for blood" or a "lust for power."

Excessive craving, unbounded desire, is, of course, at the root of each of the capital sins. But Evagrius specified Lust as excessive love of sexual gratification. The problem here is not so much sexuality as the reality that Lust dehumanizes. Real human relationships with real human people are not the problem; Evagrius warned of imaginary entanglements, thoughts of "a variety of bodies," and a focusing on parts of bodies. Each leads to an obsession with the unreal rather than an attempt to cope with what is really there.

A visitor to an insane asylum found one of the inmates rocking back and forth in a chair cooing repeatedly in a soft, contented manner, "Lulu, Lulu. . . ."

"What's this man's problem?" he asked the doctor.

"Lulu. She was the woman who jilted him," was the doctor's reply.

As they proceeded on the tour they came to a padded cell whose occupant was banging his head repeatedly against the wall and moaning, "Lulu, Lulu. . . ."

"Is Lulu this man's problem too?" asked the visitor.

"Yes," said the doctor. "He's the one Lulu finally married."

∞

One afternoon the Indiana humorist George Ade was sitting with a little girl of eight at a friend's house.

"Mr. Ade," she said, looking up from her storybook, "does m-i-r-a-g-e spell marriage?"

"Yes, my child," Ade softly replied.

⚬⚭

LUST'S FOCUS on bodies means, first, attending only to the body rather than the spiritual reality of an-other. This exclusive attention to the physical already looks at only a part, but that dehumanization is compounded when one attends only to parts of bodies, a fixation that goes beyond feminist humor about the male fascination with "boobs."

There was once an ascetic who lived a celibate life and had as his life's mission to fight against sex in himself and others.

In due course he died. And his most faithful disciple died a short time later. When the disciple reached the other world, he couldn't believe what he saw: his beloved master held on his lap the most extraordinarily beautiful woman! The disciple's shock faded when it occurred to him that his master was being rewarded for his sexual abstinence on Earth. Going up to him he said, "Beloved master, now I know that God is just, for you are being rewarded in heaven for your austerities on Earth."

The master seemed annoyed. "Idiot!" he said. "This isn't heaven and I'm not being rewarded—she's being punished."

⚬⚭

BECAUSE "SEX SELLS," invitations to Lust abound, surrounding us with images that virtually impose continual thoughts and imaginings of sexual congress with parts of persons and bodies. A culture preoccupied with self-enhancement tends to overlook the merits of the unassuming virtues of humility and modesty, viewing them as signs of weakness or negativity.

Humility moderates, suggesting an evenhanded view of the self, one without an unjustified sense of entitlement. Modesty is a related virtue, helping one resist the temptation either to inflate or to depreciate the self. Lust destroys not because it has to do with sex but because it focuses on merely the bodily part of another person, indeed, usually only on parts of another person's body. Another's whole personhood is thus diminished, as is one's own in the deformed quest to somehow be made whole by attending only to a part.

Once there was an elderly man, and one evening he was taking his usual walk. He was enjoying the crisp night air and the wind blowing gently. But suddenly he heard a voice crying out, "Help me! Help me!"

The man looked around and saw no one and so he continued his walk. Again he heard a tiny voice, "Help me! Help me!" This time he looked down and saw a small frog. He gently lifted up the frog and looked at it intently.

The frog spoke. "I am really a very beautiful princess. If you will kiss me, I will turn back into a princess and I will hug you and kiss you and fulfill your every sensual dream."

The man thought for a moment, placed the frog in his top pocket, and continued walking. The little frog looked up out of the pocket and asked, "Why don't you kiss me?"

The man responded, "Frankly, at this stage of my life, I'd rather have a talking frog."

ENVY

Envy: not only wishing to have the good of another (without working for it), but with an aspect of "if I cannot, then neither should she," thereby wanting the destruction of another's story. The constant imagery of envy is that of a worm gnawing at one's very vitals.

Rarely has interpersonal Envy been portrayed as vividly as by Shakespeare in his creation of Iago, whose envy of the Black Moor Othello's possession of the beautiful Desdemona leads him to destroy what he cannot possess and to do so in the most vile way by deceiving Othello into murdering his beloved wife. Not able to have Desdemona, Iago destroys both her and Othello.

Envy involves not merely a grieving on account of another's good, but a grieving that views that good as somehow diminishing one's own. Modernity would turn this grief into a gnawing fear—if someone else is gaining something, that must mean I am losing something, even by only standing still. For the imperative of growth implies that there is no "standing still": who does not advance is falling behind.

Modernity: the economy of the market and the politics of democracy. Aristotle long ago observed that envy grows naturally in relationships between equals. For though Envy takes many forms and has varied proximate causes, one of the most destructive spurs to this unholy trait is the widespread assumption that everyone should be able to do and experience and enjoy everything that everyone else can do and experience and enjoy.

A man took his new hunting dog out on a trial hunt. Presently he shot a duck that fell into the lake. The dog walked over the water, picked up the duck, and brought it back to his master.

The man was flabbergasted! He shot another duck. Once again, he rubbed his eyes in disbelief as the dog walked over the water and retrieved the duck.

Hardly daring to believe what he had seen, he called his neighbor for a shoot the following day. Once again, each time he or his neighbor hit a bird, the dog would walk over the water and bring the bird back in. The man said nothing. Neither did his neighbor. Finally, unable to contain himself any longer, he blurted out, "Did you notice anything strange about that dog?"

The neighbor rubbed his chin thoughtfully. "Yes," he finally said. "Come to think of it, I did! The son of a gun can't swim!"

❦

ENVY IS the engine that drives the economy that is the essence of modernity. One of the most uncomfortable facts about our economic system is that it is bound to excite envy in those to whom it must sell. It must persuade everyone to want what everyone else has. People who have been wholly content in their own natures, and in their expression of them, are suddenly or slowly persuaded that they have been missing something.

An Amish boy and his father were in a mall. They were amazed by almost everything they saw, but especially by two shiny, silver walls that could move apart and then slide back together again.

The boy asked, "What is this, Father?"

The father (never having seen an elevator) responded, "Son, I have never seen anything like this in my life. I don't know what it is."

While the boy and his father were watching with amazement, a fat old lady in a wheelchair moved up to the moving walls and pressed a button.

The walls opened and the lady rolled between them into a small room. The walls closed and the boy and his father watched the small circular numbers above the walls light up sequentially.

They continued to watch until it reached the last number and then the numbers began to light in the reverse order. Finally the walls opened up again and a gorgeous twenty-four-year-old blonde stepped out.

The father said quietly to his son, "Go get your mother."

DANTE'S IMAGE of the envious in Purgatory is of people whose eyes have been closed by drawing threads of iron wire through the lids. The eyes of the envious could not bear to look upon joy, so now their eyes are wired shut so that they cannot see anything that might be good. The root evil of Envy, according to Aquinas, is that we grieve over what should make us rejoice, namely over our neighbor's good. Again, we see the refusal of shared community that underlies each capital sin. The "deadly sin" is that which wounds relationships among people, which destroys community itself.

In "The Parson's Tale," Geoffrey Chaucer wrote: "It is certain that envy is the worst sin that is; for all other sins [are] against one virtue, whereas envy is against all virtue and against all goodness." And a modern student of envy suggests that "Envy is to modern times what sex was to the Victorians, an obsession best forgotten, denied, or avoided."

*Ivan Illich once observed that in a consumer society
there are two kinds of slaves: the prisoners of addiction
and the prisoners of envy. "To be somebody" is the
overriding compulsion of the orphan generation.*

MADONNA KOLBENSCHLAG

GLUTTONY

Next on the list comes gluttony—in Latin, *gula* (such an expressive sound in that word!). Again we find insatiability—the denial of "enough." The opposite of gluttony is not abstinence but balance. More worthy of attention in today's world may be the realization that gluttony can apply to quality as well as quantity. The demand for "the best" can also signal imbalance. Gluttony is the overindulgence and overconsumption of anything to the point of waste. Peter Brown, in his landmark study *The Body and Society: Men, Women, and Sexual Renunciation in Early Christianity*, records that:

> *It was widely believed, in Egypt as elsewhere, that the first sin of Adam and Eve had been not a sexual act, but rather one of ravenous greed. It was their lust for physical food that led them to disobey God's command not to eat the fruit of the Tree of Knowledge. By so doing, they had destroyed the perfect physical equilibrium with which they had been first created.... In this view of the Fall, greed and, in a famine-ridden world, greed's blatant social overtones—avarice and dominance—quite overshadowed sexuality.*

For some in our obese nation, food has become fetish. Whether as "energy drinks," "organic food," in "four-star" restaurants, or specialized grocery stores, food is consumed as much to say who we are as to sate hunger. Status involves, among many other things, the ability to be more concerned about the quality of one's food than with its available quantity—which is perhaps too much taken for granted.

An industrious turkey farmer was always experimenting with breeding to perfect a better turkey.

His family was fond of the leg portion for dinner and there were never enough legs for everyone. After many frustrating attempts, the farmer was relating the results of his efforts to his friends at the general store get-together. "Well, I finally did it! I bred a turkey that has six legs!"

They all asked the farmer how it tasted. "Don't know," said the farmer. "Never could catch the son of a gun!"

❦

IT IS possible to enjoy food without making a fetish of it. Again, here, we find virtue inhabiting a middle—not so much a mean as the wide middle ground between two fairly obvious extremes. Except for the very poorest of the world's poor, to center one's existence on eating is to become less than human.

A very overweight man decided that it was time to shed a few pounds. He went on a new diet and took it seriously. He even changed his usual driving route on the way to the office precisely to avoid passing his favorite bakery. One morning, however, he arrived at the office carrying a large, sugar-coated, calorie-loaded coffee cake.

For this he was roundly chided by his colleagues, but he

only smiled, shrugged his shoulders, and said, "What could I do? This is a very special cake. What happened is that, by force of habit, I accidentally drove by the bakery this morning, and there in the window were trays full of the most scrumptious goodies.

"Well, I felt this was no accident that I happened to pass by this way, so I prayed, 'Lord, if you really want me to have one of those delicious coffee cakes, let me find a parking space right in front of the bakery.' And sure enough, on the ninth time around the block, there it was!"

WRATH

Anger—*ira*—is a "capital" defect not in its existence but in its persistence. There is nothing evil or "wrong" about experiencing anger. And so at issue here is not simple anger but *wrath*, named in the Latin *iracundia*, the very sound of which conveys enduring rage.

The emotions cannot in themselves be evil, sinful. They present our mixed human nature with a choice: Will we surrender to the brutish aspect of our being, or will we transcend some difficulty by tapping our spiritual "better selves"? We cannot choose whether or not to experience the emotions. We can choose what we do with that experience.

Two natives of Hong Kong were arguing loudly in the street. An American, who observed the altercation but could not speak the language, asked an Asian friend what they were arguing about.

"They are having a discussion about the ownership of a boat," came the reply.

"They're getting so wrought up, won't they start fighting soon?" the tourist asked.

"No," his friend said. "These men will not start fighting because each one knows the man who strikes the first blow admits his ideas just gave out."

❦

WRATH: A WORD that with its dragged-out *aah* sound hints its deeper meaning—not the emotion of anger but the clinging to it, the harboring of resentment. Wrath: a fixation, an obsession that consumes us. Wrath is embraced and nourished, fed constant tidbits of remembered violation. And wrath is especially vicious because of the deceitful way that, of all the capital sins, it can present itself as its opposite, justice. How readily we speak of "justified anger," but how silly sound such conjunctions as "enthusiastic sloth" or "measured gluttony" or "generous greed."

My neighbor was bit by a stray rabid dog. I went to see how he was and found him writing frantically.

I told him rabies could be cured and he didn't have to worry about a will.

He said, "Will!? What will? I'm making a list of the people I wanna bite."

❦

ANGER . . . WRATH . . . resentment . . . and revenge. "Anger craves revenge," observed Aquinas, quoting Augustine. For

Wrath's perversion of justice is precisely its demand to "get even." Wrath festers like a pus-filled sore, demanding to be lanced. Only in this case it is not the self but the other who is gored. Wrath is related to Envy but it is not the same—the mean hatred of Wrath can be more destructive than the morose regret of Envy. Envy bites its nails. Wrath scratches and tears with them.

Of course, things are not always this bad: There is the anger that does not become wrath.

A grandmother took her little grandson to the beach. They were having a good time when suddenly a huge wave came in and swept the boy out to sea. She fell down on her knees and pleaded to the heavens, "Please return my grandson—that's all I ask! Please!"

A moment later, lo and behold, a wave swelled in from the ocean and deposited the wet yet unhurt child at her feet. She checked him over to make sure that he was okay. He was fine. But then she looked up at the heavens angrily and said, "When we came, he had a hat!"

SLOTH—*ACEDIA*

The classic trap, the "noonday devil," *acedia*—is a kind of boredom in which nothing engages our interest or appeals to us. We wander about tediously, unable to find anything of interest. We may wish for another's company, but we also don't want to be bothered. The day seems endless: We raise our watch to our ear, to be sure it is running; check our cell phone, hoping for a message. Ennui oppresses us, and we keep looking for an ending—even an interruption—that is never there. "Why bother? What's the use? Nobody cares. Nothing matters, anyway."

Many commentators find in *acedia*/sloth both boredom and sadness. The most accurate translation of *acedia* is "self-pity," far more precise than "laziness" or "sloth," for it conveys both the utter melancholy of this condition and the self-centeredness on which it is founded.

As Evelyn Waugh observed in the Ian Fleming–edited study *The Seven Deadly Sins*: "The malice of sloth lies not merely in the neglect of duty (though that can be a symptom of it) but in the refusal of joy. It is allied to despair." Mary Louise Bringle, in her exploration of portrayals of "despair" in literature, brilliantly summarizes *acedia's* phenomenology as revealed by Alice Walker's Celie and Mary Gordon's Isabel:

> *Despair feels flat, dim, chill, and lonely; it smells faintly stale; it has no more taste than the white of an egg. The person in despair aches— sometimes dully, sometimes acutely—for a love which is lost, for a meaning gone sour, for an assurance of worth beneath the steady erosion of self-esteem. The feeling-tone of despair differs markedly from the searing red heat of anger. Compared to the surface sting of disappointment, despair is a deep and unremitting stab, reaming out a hollow wound at the very core of being.*

Acedia, especially if thought of as "sloth" or "laziness," hardly seems to merit listing as a "capital" or "deadly" sin. One reason for its gravity, as Aquinas noted, is that *acedia* weakens the will. Few things are as piteous as the self-pitying self—"melancholic self-centeredness" runs another attempt at describing *acedia*. In the words of writer Dorothy L. Sayers:

In the world [sloth] calls itself Tolerance; but in hell it is called Despair. It is the accomplice of the other sins and their worst punishment. It is the sin which believes in nothing, cares for nothing, seeks to know nothing, interferes with nothing, enjoys nothing, loves nothing, hates nothing, finds purpose in nothing, lives for nothing, and only remains alive because there is nothing it would die for.

"Melancholic self-centeredness" need not mean that one curls into a thumb-sucking lump. One problem with sloth being too often—and too treacherously—equated with "laziness" is that this notion propagates a false image. As Solomon Schimmel points out in his excellent analysis of *The Seven Deadly Sins,* "A paradox of sloth is its ability to mask itself in fervid but misdirected activity. In the absence of higher spiritual or moral aims, many people try to alleviate their underlying despair by the avid pursuit of pleasure. They hope thereby to fill their spiritual vacuum. Medieval writers emphasized that spiritual sloth did not preclude zeal and energy in secular matters."

The "answer" to *acedia*? As Lewis Hyde noted in his insightful study of poet John Berryman, *Alcohol and Poetry:* "The way out of self-pity and its related moods is to attend to something other than the self. This can be either the inner or the outer world, either dreams and visions which do not come from the self, or other people and nature. The point is that the self begins to heal automatically when it attends to the non-self."

Bahlul the Wise Fool, one of God's own, happened one day to meet the caliph Harun al-Rashid. "Where are you coming from like this, Bahlul?" the ruler asked him.

"From Hell," was the prompt reply.

Harun, astonished, put another question: "What were you doing there?"

Bahlul explained: "Fire was needed, Sire, so I thought of going to Hell to ask if they could spare a little. But the fellow in charge there said: 'We have no fire here.' Of course I asked him: 'How come? Isn't Hell the place of fire?' His answer was: 'I tell you, there really is no fire down here. Everybody brings his own fire with him when he comes.'"

In sheer amazement, Harun al-Rashid asked another question: "Tell me, Bahlul, what should I do so that I shan't take any fire down there?"

Bahlul the Wise Fool made off at top speed, crying: "Justice . . . Justice . . . Justice . . ."

⊗⊷⊙

"SIN": ALL spiritual traditions agree that the core problem is insatiable desire. Whatever is present is not enough. Buddhism locates the root of suffering in desire, while the Western tradition's *logismoi* identify the everyday forms desire takes. The "deadly sins," then, are not evil acts we commit; they are the roots of evil deeds, the life patterns that flow from viewing things in ways that make us the sort of people who will then do such things. Bad vision leads to bad choices.

The ultimate "evil" of the "capital sins" is that they make us excessively vulnerable to exploitation by those who would marshal our own desires against our own greater good. What can we do about it? For most of us, doing without desire is impractical if not impossible. But perhaps knowing our weaknesses—the aspects or parts of our life where experience suggests our desires sometimes get out of hand—we can guard against their exploitation. Virtue, recall, stands in the middle. So we can value ourselves without devaluing others or denying that we make mistakes, we can enjoy good things without centering our lives on their acquisition, we can admire the goods of others without thinking they should be ours, we can relish beauty without demanding to possess it. Above all, we can remember that spirituality can be found only in our actual experience.

A master gardener, famous for his skill in climbing and pruning the highest trees, examined his disciple by letting him climb a very high tree. Many people had come to watch.

The master gardener stood quietly, carefully following every move but not interfering with one word. Having pruned the top, the disciple climbed down and was only about ten feet from the ground when the master suddenly yelled: "Take care, take care!"

When the disciple was safely down an old man asked the master gardener: "You did not let out one word when he was aloft in the most dangerous place. Why did you caution him when he was nearly down? Even if he had slipped then, he could not have greatly hurt himself."

"But isn't it obvious?" replied the master gardener. "Right up at the top he is conscious of the danger, and of himself takes care. But near the end when one begins to feel safe, this is when accidents occur."

≈

One of the disconcerting—and delightful—teachings of the Master was: "God is closer to sinners than to saints."

This is how he explained it: "God in heaven holds each person by a string. When you sin, you cut the string. Then God ties it up again, making a knot—and thereby bringing you a little closer to Him. Again and again your sins cut the string—and with each further knot God keeps drawing you closer and closer."

PRAYER

Something happens to prayer in a culture dominated by
consumerism, scientism, and a technocratic mentality.
The mystery goes out of it. It becomes one more problem to solve.
Prayer loses its radical connection with the mystery of our deepest
self; it gets trapped in the nets of our individual egos with all their
strivings for power, security, possession, and success.

. . . Prayer is no-thing. It is not some thing we have. . . . Prayer has
nothing to do with having. It has everything to do with being.

RICHARD BYRNE

For many of us, at least sometimes, prayer is a pause, a respite from routine. But prayer can be—and perhaps should be—also a routine. We too easily forget who we are, why we are here. Prayer brings us back to such basic truths. The question for us, here, is how do we experience prayer?

Life may be brimming over with experience, but somewhere,
deep inside, all of us carry a vast and fruitful loneliness wherever

*we go. And sometimes the most important thing in a whole
day is the rest we take between two deep breaths, or the
turning inwards in prayer for five short minutes.*

ETTY HILLESUM

Father Thomas Hopko tells this story:

I once met someone who had gone to Mount Athos and met a
monk there who was in a very bad state, very dark, very bitter,
very angry. When asked what was the matter, he said, "Look at
me; I've been here for thirty-eight years, and I have not yet at-
tained pure prayer."

And this fellow was saying how sad he thought this was. Another man present said, "It's a sad story all right, but the sadness
consists in the fact that after thirty-eight years in a monastery
he's still interested in pure prayer."

⊗

YOU CAN make pure prayer an idol, too. Those are the worst forms
of idolatry.

*Prayer or any other benediction without love
and awe is like a bird without wings.*

RABBI SCHNEUR ZALMAN

As suggested in another segment, "... when you come right down
to it, there are only four basic prayers. Gimme! Thanks! Oops! and
Wow!... Wow! are prayers of praise and wonder at the creation.
Oops! is asking for forgiveness. Gimme! is a request or a petition.
Thanks! is expressing gratitude."

But what of those who do not believe in a personal God, who question or deny the existence of a supernatural being? Can they pray?

First, perhaps, it seems that both "Wow!" and "Thanks!" are always in some sense prayers, a recognition of some force or reality greater than the abilities of self, no matter uttered by whom to what. More realistically here, then, the question is: "Do they pray?" Each non-believer in the usual "God" must, of course, answer that question for herself or himself. But from reading, and conversations, listening carefully to those who are not theistic believers expounding on what they do believe, and the murmurings of our own hearts, we have formed some thoughts on this topic. Much of what we hear coheres well with the description of Buddhist prayer that appears on a website of that name:

> *Buddhist prayer is a practice to awaken our inherent inner capacities of strength, compassion and wisdom rather than to petition external forces based on fear, idolizing, and worldly and/or heavenly gain. Buddhist prayer is a form of meditation; it is a practice of inner reconditioning. Buddhist prayer replaces the negative with the virtuous and points us to the blessings of Life.*
>
> *For Buddhists, prayer expresses an aspiration to pull something into one's life, like some new energy or purifying influence and share it with all beings. Likewise, prayer inspires our hearts towards wisdom and compassion for others and ourselves. It allows us to turn our hearts and minds to the beneficial, rousing our thoughts and actions towards Awakening. If we believe in something enough, it will take hold of us. In other words, believing in it, we will become what we believe.*

This both contrasts with and complements a strong theistic understanding, which we draw from the Jewish Abraham Heschel and the Christian Evelyn Underhill:

> *To pray is to take notice of the wonder, to regain a sense of the mystery that animates all beings, the divine margin in all attainments. Prayer is our humble answer to the inconceivable surprise of living.*
>
> *. . . As a tree torn from the soil, as a river separated from its source, the human soul wanes when detached from what is greater than itself. Without the holy, the good turns chaotic; without the good, beauty becomes accidental.*
>
> ABRAHAM HESCHEL

> *[Too many modern religious believers] perpetually suggest that all we have to do is to grow, develop, unpack our own spiritual suit-cases; that nothing need be given us or done to us from beyond.*
>
> *Were the fullest possible development of his natural resources the real end of the being of man, this might be true enough. But all the giants of the spiritual life are permeated, penetrated through and through by the conviction that this is not the goal of human existence: that something must be given, or done to them, from the eternal world over-against us, without which man can never be complete. They feel, however variously they express it, that for us in our strange borderland situation there must be two orders, two levels of reality, two mingled lives, to both of which we are required to respond—the natural and the supernatural, nature and grace. . . .*
>
> EVELYN UNDERHILL

Others, pondering prayer, have offered helpfully memorable thoughts:

> *Prayer is a counterbalance to the nakedness of autonomy.*
> LAWRENCE S. CUNNINGHAM

> *Prayer is a habit of interior attentiveness, an activity*
> *that creates a formerly unknown self.*
> MARGARET MILES

> *Prayer is a waiting game. . . . Prayer is waiting on God. . . . I like to*
> *divide prayer into two basic categories: the first is formal, or what*
> *I call "Waste of Time Prayer." The second category is "Overflow*
> *Prayer": the sort of prayer that bubbles up spontaneously from*
> *somewhere deep inside during the course of the day.*
> SHEILA CASSIDY

Recall the four prayers: "Wow," "Oops!" "Thanks," and "Gimme." Our concern here is with the last—prayers of petition. Why pray prayers of petition? Believers even more than unbelievers find ridiculous the idea that finite human beings can somehow change an infinite God. Yet great religious teachers over the ages have recommended, even commanded, such prayer. How are we to understand this?

Two responses have been given. According to the first, widely embraced by believers, God's infinite knowledge knows from all eternity that certain events will take place because of prayers; therefore prayers do not change God but rather bring to fulfillment His eternal knowledge and will.

In the second understanding (which need not exclude the first), the purpose of prayer is to change not God but the pray-er. Just as between human beings it sometimes happens that a petition can change the attitude of the petitioner, so one's relationship with a Higher Power may undergo a change brought about by the exercise of the virtues inherent in the practice of praying—the humility of an admission of powerlessness in some circumstance, for example.

The prayer of petition may thus contain at least part of its own answer. Recognizing and acknowledging our separation from that which is greater than ourselves—the holy, the mysterious—we physically or mentally fall to our knees. Believing that "something will take hold of us," we let go (at least momentarily) of our demand for control and open ourselves to the possibility of awe and wonder. The first "answer" prayer offers is the acceptance that we do not have all the answers.

Rabbi Levi Yitzchok of Berditchev observed a man who was reciting his prayers very rapidly, mumbling the words in an unintelligible manner.

The rabbi approached the man and mumbled some nonsense syllables. "I'm sorry, Rabbi," the man said, "but I cannot understand what you are saying."

"Then why do you mumble your prayers unintelligibly?" the rabbi asked. "You should say your prayers distinctly so that each word can be understood."

The man responded, "When you hear an infant crying or saying nonsensical syllables, you may not understand what he wants, but his parents are sensitive to his sounds, and understand what each sound means. G-d is my Father. He understands my mumbling."

Rabbi Levi Yitzchok was thrilled. He had acquired a new plea to defend people's behavior.

❧

FOR GENUINE prayer involves listening. Although we are accustomed to hearing of "prayer and meditation" as virtually conjoined twins, and of prayer as "speaking" and meditation as "listening," such a disjunction is simplistic. Prayer is more conversation than monologue. When we ask another in person, even as we ask, we attend to the body language of that other. Essential to petition is an attentive *openness*. And the first openness is to change. The essence of prayer, in this view, is that it opens the pray-er to change, to some beneficent alteration.

An old man would sit motionless for hours on end in church. One day a priest asked him what God talked to him about.

"God doesn't talk. He just listens," was his reply.

"Well, then, what do you talk to him about?"

"I don't talk either. I just listen."

❧

OPENNESS—THE OPENNESS of the listening that is part of any appeal for "Help!" To what is the pray-er listening? God? The unconscious? A reservoir of experience? One's "better self"? Each must answer for herself or himself, even if not sure of that answer. For despite their differences, most moderns find it possible to pray together. Those prayers virtually always recognize and appeal to some Reality beyond the realm of self, and usually beyond the realm of everyday nature.

On the other hand—or is it "for example"?—when one of the authors was conversing with a non-believing acquaintance about writing this segment and asked whether prayer had any meaning to him, his response surprised and fulfilled: "It's nice to have moments when I'm not thinking about me."

A lion was taken into captivity and thrown into a concentration camp where, to his amazement, he found other lions who had been there for years, some of them all their lives, for they had been born there. He soon became acquainted with the social activities of the camp lions.

They had banded themselves into groups. One group consisted of the socializers; another was into show business; yet another was cultural, its purpose to carefully preserve the customs, tradition, and history of the times when lions were free; other groups were religious—they gathered mostly to sing songs about a future jungle where there would be no fences; some groups attracted those who were artistic by nature; others still were revolutionary, meeting to plot against their captors or against other revolutionary groups. Every so often a revolution would break out, one particular group would be wiped out, or the guards would be killed and replaced by another set of guards.

As he looked around, the newcomer observed one lion who always seemed deep in thought, a loner who belonged to no group and mostly kept away from everyone. There was something strange about him that commanded everyone's admiration but also everyone's hostility, for his presence aroused self-doubt. He said to the newcomer, "Join no group. These poor fools are busy with everything except what is essential."

"And what is that?" asked the newcomer.

"Studying the nature of the fence."

⸏⸎

PERSPECTIVE: The online journal *The Fix*, aimed at people interested in recovery from addiction, queried readers of its forum: "Why do many become more spiritual or religious when they recover from addiction?" The first two responses recovered on September 24, 2011, offered:

I think it is because the root cause of addiction is that we are longing for some inner joy. It's a spiritual longing that just going to church or believing in a set of rules will not fill. I really believe that our next step in our evolution will come with meditation. When more start to see that there can be a real connection to the universe. Not because the churches tell us but because we experience it for ourselves. (Lilyofthewoods)

. . . The answer to the original question is very simple. Most "real" alcoholics have lost the power of choice whether to drink or not. We discover that our way does not work. We become willing to consider something else. [Turning to] God solves our drink problem. Of course, he will allow us to continue with our other destructive behaviors, lying, pride, selfishness, etc. Until we have had enough of that and then become willing to ask God for help with that, too. In the beginning you don't have to believe in God. Just believe that there is a God, and you are not him. That is enough to start. The rest will become clear when you allow him to work in your life. No God, no Peace. Know God, know Peace. (SumIdiot)

What else can we say about the experience of prayer? Perhaps not much directly, but there are some stories. There is, for example, the story told by Tim Madigan, the biographer of television's Mister Rogers, about the day Fred Rogers met a boy with cerebral palsy. Mister Rogers asks the boy to pray for him.

> The boy had always been prayed for. The boy had always been the object of prayer, and now he was being asked to pray for Mister Rogers, and although at first he didn't know if he could do it, he said he would, he said he'd try, and ever since then he keeps Mister Rogers in his prayers and doesn't talk about wanting to die anymore, because he figures Mister Rogers is close to God, and if Mister Rogers likes him, that must mean God likes him, too.
>
> As for Mister Rogers himself... well, he doesn't look at the story in the same way that the boy did or that I did. In fact, when Mister Rogers first told me the story, I complimented him on being so smart—for knowing that asking the boy for his prayers would make the boy feel better about himself—and Mister Rogers responded by looking at me at first with puzzlement and then with surprise. "Oh, heavens no, Tim! I didn't ask him for his prayers for him; I asked for me. I asked him because I think that anyone who has gone through challenges like that must be very close to God. I asked him because I wanted his intercession."

⁂

MOST PEOPLE who pray, it seems safe to say, have some faith and hope that their prayers will make some sort of difference. And yet:

As the drought continued for what seemed an eternity, a small community of Midwest farmers was in a quandary as to what to do next. The rain was important not only to keep their crops healthy, but to sustain the townspeople's very way of living. As the problem became more urgent, the local church felt it was time to get involved and called a prayer meeting to ask for rain.

In what seemed a vague remembrance of a Native American ritual, the people began to arrive. The pastor on his arrival watched as the congregation continued to file in. He slowly made his way to the front to officially begin the meeting.

Everyone was taking the opportunity to visit across the aisles to socialize with close friends. The pastor's thoughts when he reached the front were on quieting those present and starting the meeting.

As he began to ask for quiet, his eyes scanned the crowd and he took note of an eleven-year-old girl sitting in the front row.

Her face was beaming with excitement as she quietly sat in her place. Next to her, poised and ready for use, was a red umbrella. The beauty and innocence of the girl made the pastor smile as he realized the faith she possessed. No one else in the congregation had brought an umbrella.

❦

WHEN MANY of the early alcoholics left the care of Sister Ignatia at St. Thomas Hospital in Akron, Ohio, in AA's earliest days, the late 1930s and early 1940s, they asked the nun to pray for them. Ignatia's consistent response was, "Pray for yourself: God loves to hear new voices!"

But many pray-ers cling to the more classic faith of such as Fred Rogers: Far better than praying for oneself is the prayer of someone else offered for you. The "Helping Others" motif that we explore in the segment on Recovery comes into full play here. Those conscious of recovering *need* to help, to be of service to others, and prayer certainly stands high among ways of helping—so long as the helping does not stop there. It is almost blasphemous to petition God to do something that one can also do oneself. Yes, intercession can help, but it often seems that God's answer is, "Okay, I'll help . . . through you. I will give you the strength and bless your efforts, but you have to do it." This awareness underlies the frequently heard caution, "Be careful what you pray for! You might get it!"

Also underlying that caution, of course, is the reminder that we do not always know what is best for us, that a prayer of petition may be answered, but not with the outcome for which we hoped.

One day the prophet Musa passed a beggar on the road, who clutched his robe and said: "Oh, Musa, prophet of Allah, please beg the Lord for me, that He may give me sustenance!" Musa continued on his journey and climbed the mountain, where he prayed to the Lord.

Finally, the Lord said: "Do you have anything to ask?"

Musa said: "Oh, Thou who knowest all and forgettest naught! This morning I saw a beggar who requested me to intercede on his behalf. He never receives a penny from anyone."

God said: "I do not wish him to receive anything." Musa went back to his house and spent the night praying.

The next morning, on his way to the mountain, Musa again saw the same beggar, who held him by his garment and asked him if he had any reply.

Musa answered: "Allah sends you His salaam, but He does not

wish to give you anything." The beggar insisted: "Oh, Nabii Musa, Holy Messenger, please ask Allah, exalted be His name, that He have mercy for once!"

Musa continued on his journey and climbed the mountain, where God spoke to him. Finally, God asked him if he had any questions. Musa repeated the beggar's prayer and God answered: "All right, for you I will change my decision once. That will be enough to show you."

Later that day it occurred to a passerby on the road to give a silver coin to the beggar. The beggar took the coin, went to the market, and bought a panga, a large, sharp knife. Then the beggar went and killed a man. The beggar was arrested, brought before the cadi, condemned to death, and executed.

And the Lord spoke to Musa: "Today you know why I did not wish that beggar to receive money. You begged it for him, and it was his undoing."

❧

THERE MAY be a more precise metaphor for prayer hidden in this story:

A young wife journeys up a mountain to visit a healer who lives as a hermit. There she asks him for a potion to help her minister to her husband, who has returned from a great war. The woman complains that her husband hardly speaks, angrily tosses food aside when she tries to serve meals, and sits looking out at the sea.

The hermit instructs her to pluck a whisker from the face of a tiger—a necessary ingredient in the potion she requests. Although dismayed at first, she finally comes up with a plan. She takes food to the cave of the tiger, remaining at a safe distance while the tiger comes out to eat.

For six months the woman takes food to the cave, each day coming a little closer to the tiger, until she is able to pat the tiger's head. On the next visit, while the tiger cuddles his head in her lap, the woman tenderly snips a whisker and returns triumphantly to the hermit with her prize.

Instead of using the whisker to mix a magical cure, the hermit tosses it into the fire. The woman cries out in alarm, questioning what seems a cruel and absurd gesture. The hermit replies: "This whisker is no longer needed . . . what could be more vicious than a tiger?"

Sometimes it seems that more important than any prayer itself is the faith and hope that undergirds the prayer. One purpose of faith—and of hope and charity—is to lift and carry us out of and *beyond* the narrow scope of ourselves . . . our-selfs. The ways of doing this are multitudinous, especially if we are not thinking of them.

An ignorant villager, having heard it is a good religious deed to eat and drink on the day before Yom Kippur, drank himself into a stupor. He awoke late at night, too late for Kol Nidrei services. Not knowing the prayers by heart, he repeated the letters of the alphabet over and over, asking the Almighty to arrange them into the words of the prayers.

The following day he attended the synagogue, and the rabbi inquired the cause of his absence at Kol Nidrei.

The villager confessed his transgression and asked whether his manner of reciting the prayers could be pardoned.

The rabbi responded: "Your prayer was more acceptable than mine because you uttered it with the entire devotion of your heart."

❧

SOMETIMES THE faith that underlies prayer may be very implicit in a somewhat different way.

A Sunday school teacher decided to have her young class memorize one of the most quoted passages in the Bible, Psalm 23. She gave the youngsters a month to learn the verse.

Little Rick was excited about the task—but he just couldn't remember the psalm. After much practice, he could barely get past the first line.

On the day that the kids were scheduled to recite in front of the congregation, Ricky was so nervous. When it came to his turn, he stepped up to the microphone and said proudly, "The Lord is my Shepherd, and that's all I need to know."

❧

PRAYER USUALLY has to do with faith—with belief. This next story is sort of on the unbeliever-believer cusp:

One Saturday afternoon, in a small Jewish village, two friends were taking a walk. One of them said to the other: "People are saying terrible things about you, things I can scarcely believe. They're claiming—may God preserve you from anything like this!—that you have lost your faith. Is this true?"

But the other friend refused to answer.

The questioner insisted to no avail, begging the other in the name of their venerable friendship of twenty years' standing. The friend who had been challenged persevered in his silence. At long last he allowed himself to be persuaded and made a promise: "Come to my place tomorrow. I will explain things to you."

The next morning, bright and early, the anxious friend presented himself and again asked if it was true his friend had lost his faith.

"What's that? Ah well, yes, it's true. I no longer believe in God."

"But that's shocking, horrible! Why didn't you want to tell me this yesterday?"

And the other responded: "Oh yes, yesterday, well, yesterday was the Sabbath. . . ."

❧

AND TO conclude, a happier story about *real* prayer . . . and more. This story is especially meaningful to us, who have passed most of our adult lives on or near university campuses. For we have known students like this . . . and churches like this. Deacons like this? That's a different story.

His name is Bill. He has wild hair, wears a T-shirt with holes in it, jeans, and no shoes. This was literally his wardrobe for his entire four years of college. He is brilliant. Kind of esoteric and very, very bright. He became a Christian while attending college.

Across the street from the campus is a well-dressed, very

conservative church. They want to develop a ministry to the students, but are not sure how to go about it. One day Bill decides to go there. He walks in with no shoes, jeans, his T-shirt, and wild hair. The service has already started and so Bill starts down the aisle, looking for a seat.

The church is completely packed and he can't find a seat. By now people are really looking a bit uncomfortable, but no one says anything. Bill gets closer and closer and closer to the pulpit and when he realizes there are no seats, he just squats down right on the carpet. (Although perfectly acceptable behavior at a college fellowship, trust me, this had never happened in this church before!) By now the people are really uptight, and the tension in the air is thick.

About this time, the minister realizes that from way at the back of the church, a deacon is slowly making his way toward Bill. Now, the deacon is in his eighties, has silver-gray hair, and a three-piece suit. A godly man, very elegant, very dignified, very courtly. He walks with a cane, and as he starts walking toward this boy, everyone is saying to themselves, "You can't blame him for what he's going to do. How can you expect a man of his age and of his background to understand some college kid on the floor?"

It takes a long time for the man to reach the boy. The church is utterly silent except for the clicking of the man's cane. All eyes are focused on him. You can't even hear anyone breathing. The people are thinking.

The minister can't even preach the sermon until the deacon does what he has to do, and now, they see this elderly man drop his cane on the floor. With great difficulty he lowers himself and sits down next to Bill and worships with him so he won't be alone. Everyone chokes up with emotion.

When the minister gains control he says,

"What I'm about to preach, you will never remember.

"What you have just seen, you will never forget."

CONFUSION

The doctor bent over the lifeless figure in bed. Then he straightened up and said, "I am sorry that your husband is no more, my dear."

A feeble sound of protest came from the lifeless figure in bed: "No, I'm still alive."

"Hold your tongue," said the woman. "The doctor knows better than you."

~

The librarian watched the old Japanese monk sitting in the corner of the library. The monk visited the library every day and would sit and meditate, his eyes closed, his countenance peaceful.

Months passed and the librarian could restrain himself no longer. "I see you here every day," he said to the monk, "but I never see you reading the sutras."

"I don't know how to read," the monk replied.

"Why, that's a disgrace!" the librarian exclaimed, shocked that the monk had never learned to read. "Shall I teach you how to read?"

"Yes. Please tell me," the monk said, pointing to himself, "what is the meaning of this character?"

⟨ೲ⟩

CONFUSION. SOMETHING within us occasionally suggests that we are made for other than we now are: We somehow fail to grasp the present. Some see this unease as a kind of deviation, a sign of maladjustment or illness. Others locate in it the essence of our humanity, which many seek to express in art. The one thing that is clear is that there seems to be some kind of confusion buried at the very core of our *be*-ing. This is not merely a difference in understandings; rather, it seems very difficult, even impossible, for many of us to simply be, simply to experience, simply to anything.

So let's try to look at this confusion, not with any plan or hope of somehow "solving" it or rendering it less confusing, but as a simple examination of how this core confusion might manifest or express itself in different ways in what is ultimately our spiritual life. Confusion comes in many forms. It often does not directly concern "the spiritual." In fact, most often our episodes of confusion seem as far away from "the spiritual" as anything can be— except, perhaps, in how we react to them.

One winter evening at the University of Buffalo, the world-famed violinist Jascha Heifetz was scheduled to perform a concert in Kleinhans Auditorium, a facility on the campus that seats 4,500 people. On the day of the concert, a blizzard hit Buffalo, as is common in January. When Heifetz got to the auditorium, exactly six of the seats were occupied. Heifetz walked out onto the stage, gazed at the six people, and said, "Look, this is silly. Let's go over to my room. I'll serve you all drinks and we'll talk for a while. We don't need to stay here."

Everyone was agreeable, except one person in the back of the auditorium, who immediately stood up and said, "Hey, I drove here all the way from Toronto to hear you sing, and by God, you're gonna sing!"

⸺⸱⸺

WHAT DO we do when we experience confusion? Usually, we get-further confused by and about the confusion itself! What should we do, then? Rejoice in the confusion! Confusion means that we don't understand something thoroughly: Welcome to the human condition! Zen and Christianity agree in honoring the concept of mystery, accepting the reality of mystery, not as something that "will eventually be solved," but as a hint of the nature of a reality greater than self. Confusion is often the sign of recognizing reality for what it is, a hint that we should accept our own finitude as it is. We are imperfect beings.

Sometimes, too, confusions may be more apparent than real.

Late one summer evening in Broken Bow, Nebraska, a weary truck driver pulled his rig into an all-night truck stop. The waitress had just served him when three tough-looking, leather-jacketed motorcyclists—of the Hell's Angels type—decided to give him a hard time. Not only did they verbally abuse him, one grabbed the hamburger off his plate, another took a handful of his French fries, and the third picked up his coffee and began to drink it. How would you respond?

Well, this trucker did not respond as one might expect.

Instead, he calmly rose, picked up his check, walked to the front of the room, put the check and his money on the cash register, and went out the door. The waitress followed him to put the money in the till and stood watching out the door as the big truck drove away into the night.

When she returned, one of the bikers said to her, "Well, he's not much of a man, is he?" She replied, "I don't know about that, but he sure ain't much of a truck driver. He just ran over three motorcycles on his way out of the parking lot."

⊶⊷

MANY CONFUSIONS, as this segment may illustrate, are humorous. Their denouement involves an unexpected, often disproportionate, twist. At its best, that quirk is innocent. Of course, "innocent" may depend on the eye of the beholder.

A woman answered the knock at her door and found a destitute man. He wanted to earn money by doing odd jobs, so she asked, "Can you paint?"

"Yes," he said, "I'm a pretty good painter."

"Well, here's a gallon of green paint and a brush. Go behind the house and you'll see a porch that needs repainting. Be very careful. When you're done, I'll look it over and pay you what it's worth."

It wasn't more than an hour before he knocked again. "All finished!" he reported with a smile.

"Did you do a good job?" she asked.

"Yes, but, lady, there's one thing I'd like to point out to you. That's not a Porsche back there. That's a Mercedes!"

THIS BOOK has so far not directly treated perhaps the greatest confusion surrounding the concept of spirituality—its relationship to *religion*. As noted in the segment Beyond "Spirituality," one of this age's slogans is "spiritual rather than religious." As not noted there, the way in which that shibboleth is tossed about can be painful to the many good people whose religion is deeply meaningful to them, who have not found in their faith the narrowness, moralism, and rigidity that has marred the religious experience of others.

At least as much as meanings of *spirituality* can vary, understandings of religion can be manifold. Those inclined to be critical sometimes point out that many practitioners of religion seem to hold a very demeaning opinion of God. Religious folk, they contend, often give lip service to God as creator of the universe and as loving parent. But, the critics continue, those who claim to be religious more often act as if God is some kind of reward/punishment factory: They are "good" in the hope of some reward, even to the point of attempting to bargain with their God. Or they are "good" because they fear God's punishment in this life or the next. Such bargaining seems, to many, to debase the idea of God.

But many religious people in reality identify more strongly with the following story:

It is not by chance that the first question in the Bible is that which God puts to Adam: "Where are you?"

"What?" cried a great Hasidic Master, Rabbi Shneur-Zalman

of Liadi. "God didn't know where Adam was? No, that's not the way to understand the question. God knew, Adam didn't."

⚬❧⚬

AS ONE contemporary religious thinker has insisted,

> *"Religious observance has nothing to do with receiving*
> *rewards or with God granting us anything.*
> *". . . The purpose of religion is to make us aware that we live*
> *in the presence of God, to help us become better people, to*
> *increase our sensitivity, and to amaze us through the miracles*
> *that surround us every moment. These are the real rewards.*
> *The goal is not that God change His behavior towards us, but*
> *that we change our behavior towards Him and our*
> *fellow human beings."*
>
> RABBI NATHAN LOPES CARDOZO

Too many, not only "spiritual" or "religious" but also "neither," in their demand for certainty seem inclined to fall into attitudes and practices that recall an Indian folktale:

A Hindu and a Muhammadan fakir were once disputing. The Hindu said that Rama was the greater while the Muhammadan insisted that Khuda was the greater. So they went to Raja Vikramaditya to decide the dispute. The raja ordered the Hindu to climb up a palm tree and jump down. As he jumped he called out to Rama and landed unhurt.

When the Muhammadan went up, seeing how the Hindu

had escaped, he began to think that he had better invoke both the deities. So with an invocation to both Rama and Khuda, he jumped and was dashed to pieces.

So the storyteller Kabir Das writes: "Do not sit on two boats when crossing a stream. You will fall between them and lose your life."

❦

WHOEVER CONFUSES *spiritual* and *religious* is trying to "sit on two boats." We name realities according to the actuality they have for us. Common courtesy suggests respecting the reality of thers, or at least that we try to understand that reality as they experience it. Such understanding neither requires nor implies embrace. But because we differ, understandings can be muddled.

. . . a little boy went into a grocery store and asked for extra-strength laundry detergent. As the clerk was finding it, he asked the boy what he wanted to use it for. The boy replied that he wanted to give his pet rat a bath.

The clerk advised, "Well, I think that this detergent is a bit strong for a rat. I am not sure I would use it."

The boy said he believed it would be all right. The grocer added: "Just be careful. This is awfully strong detergent."

About a week later, the boy came back. When asked by the grocer how his rat was, he said, "It died."

"I'm sorry to hear that," sympathized the clerk. "But I did tell you that the detergent was probably too strong."

"Oh, I really don't think it was the detergent," the boy replied. "I believe it was the spin cycle that did it."

⟊

THERE ARE many kinds of confusions—so many that confusions themselves can be confusing. Among that variety, the most heartening may be the most ingenuous.

One Sunday morning the minister noticed that little Craig was staring up at the large plaque in the foyer of the church.

The plaque was covered with names, and small American flags were mounted on either side of it. The ten-year-old boy had been staring at the plaque for some time, so the minister walked up, stood beside the boy, and said quietly, "Good morning, Craig."

"Good morning, Reverend," replied the young man, still focused on the plaque.

A long paused ensued. "Reverend Chesnut, what is this?" Craig asked.

"Well, son, it's a memorial to all the young men and women who died in the service."

Soberly they stood together, staring at the large plaque.

Little Craig's voice was barely audible when he asked, "Which service, the nine o'clock or the ten-thirty?"

⟊

SOME CONFUSIONS spring from a different kind of naïveté.

A young physician's story:

I was caring for a woman from Kentucky and asked, "So how's your breakfast this morning?"

"It's very good, except for the Kentucky jelly. I can't seem to get used to the taste," the patient replied.

I then asked to see the jelly and the woman produced a foil packet labeled "KY Jelly."

❧

CONFUSIONS: THE BEST of them can open to a wisdom that makes the very perplexity worthwhile. They less invite than compel more serious thought.

One day, a great sage was going up a mountain to pray. On the way he saw a worm crawling beneath. When he was praying he asked God, "Why did you create this worm?"

God said, "The worm just asked me that question about you."

❧

THE FARSI who told that story began by observing: "No creature's existence is in vain; our existence is not futile even if we think of ourselves as that." He continued, "All creatures are travelers on a journey . . . [but] are not aware of it. Each creature enters life for a unique purpose and a human being is most satisfied when he realizes his mission in life; the more distance between him and his mission, the more worry, anxiety and sadness that he has to deal with."

And perhaps the more confusion.

Supreme Court Justice Oliver Wendell Holmes had the reputation of being absent-minded. One day on a train out of Washington, Holmes was studying a pending case when the conductor asked for his ticket. The justice searched each pocket nervously, but to no avail.

"Don't be concerned, Mr. Justice Holmes," the conductor said. "We know who you are. When you return to Washington, you can send us the ticket at your convenience."

Holmes lowered his eyes and shook his head sadly. "Thank you, my good man, but you don't seem to understand the problem. It's not a question of whether I'll pay the fare. The problem is: Where am I going?"

⁂

ANOTHER SOURCE of frequent confusion arises from a well-known scriptural quotation: "An eye for an eye, a tooth for a tooth." Most of the time, we suspect, this quotation is interpreted as urging retaliation for some injury—that some injury be "paid back." But there is an alternative, and indeed more accurate, understanding: This principle is a *restriction, a limitation* on the "payback"—that it not be disproportionate to the original offense. The axiom, which appears in the code of Hammurabi as well as in the books of Exodus, Leviticus, and Deuteronomy, defines *and restricts* the extent of retribution permissible. It says, "No more than."

Sometimes confusion may even be deliberately engendered for a purpose, or perhaps be accidentally provoked by someone who has a different agenda.

Clarence Darrow was approached by a reporter who asked him for a prepared copy of a speech the legendary lawyer was scheduled to make that night.

Darrow, annoyed by the young man, handed him a blank piece of paper and turned to go.

"But, Mr. Darrow," the reporter said quickly, "this is the same speech you gave last week."

❧

When an Athenian crowd refused to hear him speak on an important matter, and hissed and booed, Demosthenes told them he wanted to tell a funny story and they listened.

"A certain youth," he began, "hired an ass to go from his home to Megara. At noon, when the sun was very hot, both he who had hired the ass and the owner of the animal were desirous of sitting in the shade of the ass, and fell to wishing each other away. The owner insisted that he had hired out only the ass and not the shadow. The other insisted that as he had hired the ass, all that belonged to the ass was his."

At this point in the story, Demosthenes turned to leave and the crowd clamored for him to finish the tale. "How is it you insist upon hearing the story of the shadow of an ass and will not give an ear to matters of great importance?" Demosthenes demanded, and the crowd finally permitted him to give the speech he had originally intended to make.

But he never resolved the fine point in the story he had begun telling.

❧

WE CANNOT help but think that had we been present, we would have insisted that Demosthenes finish the story of the ass's shadow. Did the ancient Greeks have contract law? According to Plutarch, Demosthenes—a lawyer as well as an orator and statesman—was "the most industrious of all pleaders." Had he ever argued such a case? We could find no direct evidence, but unwilling to leave our readers in the same predicament as Demosthenes's original audience, we pursued this investigation; precedent requires that we restrict our finding to the Notes.

∞

SOMETIMES, EVEN OFTEN, confusion arises when different people use different names for the same reality.

An Amish lady is trotting down the road in her horse and buggy when she is pulled over by a cop.

"Ma'am, I'm not going to ticket you, but I do have to issue you a warning. You have a broken reflector on your buggy."

"Oh, I'll let my husband, Jacob, know as soon as I get home."

"That's fine. Another thing, ma'am. I don't like the way that one rein loops across the horse's back and around one of his testicles. I consider that animal abuse. That's cruelty to animals. Have your husband take care of that right away!"

Later that day, the lady is home telling her husband about her encounter with the cop. "Well, dear, what exactly did he say?"

"He said the reflector is broken."

"I can fix that in two minutes. What else?"

"I'm not sure, Jacob...something about the emergency brake..."

∞

MOST OFTEN, people cause their own very unmysterious confusion because of tacit assumptions or unaware expectations, a variety of preconceived notions that may or may not adjust adequately to unexpected new circumstances. Two very different stories illustrate this truth.

A man boarded an airplane and took his seat. As he settled in, he glanced up and saw a very beautiful woman boarding the plane. He soon realized she was heading straight toward his seat. Lo and behold, she took the seat right beside his!

Eager to strike up a conversation, he blurted out, "Business trip or vacation?" She turned, smiled, and said, "Business. I'm going to the Annual Nymphomaniac Convention in Chicago." He swallowed hard. Here was the most gorgeous woman he had ever seen sitting next to him and she was going to a meeting for nymphomaniacs!

Struggling to maintain his composure, he calmly asked, "What's your business role at this convention?"

"Lecturer," she responded. "I use my experience to debunk some of the popular myths about sexuality."

"Really," he said, "what myths are those?"

"Well," she explained, "one popular myth is that African-American men are the most well endowed when, in fact, it's the Native American Indian who is most likely to possess that trait. Another popular myth is that French men are the best lovers, when actually it is the men of Jewish descent. We have, however, found that the best potential lover in all categories is the Southern redneck."

Suddenly, the woman became a little uncomfortable and blushed. "I'm sorry," she said, "I shouldn't really be discussing this with you. I don't even know your name."

"Tonto," the man said, "Tonto Goldstein. But my friends call me Bubba!"

A pastor realized that his church was getting into very serious financial troubles. While checking the church storeroom, he discovered several cartons of new Bibles that had never been opened and distributed. So at his Sunday sermon, he asked for three volunteers from the congregation who would be willing to sell the Bibles door-to-door for $10 each to raise the desperately needed money for the church.

Jack, Paul, and Louie all raised their hands to volunteer for the task. The minister knew that Jack and Paul earned their living as salesmen and were likely capable of selling some Bibles. But he had serious doubts about Louie, a local farmer who had always kept to himself because he was embarrassed by his speech impediment. Poor Louie stuttered badly. But, not wanting to discourage Louie, the minister decided to let him try anyway. He sent the three of them away with the backseat of their cars stacked with Bibles. He asked them to meet with him and report the results of their door-to-door selling efforts the following Sunday.

That day, anxious to find out how successful they were, the minister immediately asked Jack, "Well, Jack, how did you make out selling our Bibles last week?"

Proudly handing the reverend an envelope, Jack replied, "Using my sales prowess, I was able to sell twenty Bibles, and here's the two hundred dollars I collected on behalf of the church."

"Fine job, Jack!" the minister said, vigorously shaking his hand. "You are indeed a fine salesman and the church is indebted to you."

Turning to Paul, "And, Paul, how many Bibles did you sell for the church last week?"

Paul, smiling and sticking out his chest, confidently replied, "I am a professional salesman. I sold twenty-eight Bibles on behalf of the church, and here's two hundred and eighty dollars I collected."

The minister responded, "That's absolutely splendid, Paul. You are truly a professional salesman and the church is indebted to you."

Apprehensively, the minister turned to Louie and said, "And, Louie, did you manage to sell any Bibles last week?" Louie silently offered the minister a large envelope.

The minister opened it and counted the contents. "What is this? Louie, there's three thousand two hundred dollars in here! Are you suggesting that you sold three hundred and twenty Bibles for the church, door-to-door, in just one week?" Louie just nodded.

"That's impossible!" both Jack and Paul said in unison. "We are professional salesmen, yet you claim to have sold ten times as many Bibles as we could."

"Yes, this does seem unlikely," the minister agreed. "I think you'd better explain how you managed to accomplish this, Louie."

Louie shrugged. "I-I-I re-re-really do-do-don't kn-kn-know f-f-f-for sh-sh-sh-sure," he stammered.

Impatiently, Paul interrupted. "For crying out loud, Louie, just tell us what you said to them when they answered the door!"

"A-a-a-all I-I-I s-s-said wa-wa-was," Louis replied, "w-w-w-w-would y-y-y-you l-l-l-l-like t-t-to b-b-b-buy th-th-th-this B-B-B-B-Bible f-f-for t-t-ten b-b-b-bucks— o-o-o-or wo-wo-would yo-you j-j-j-just l-like m-m-me t-t-to st-st-stand h-h-here and r-r-r-r-read it t-to y-y-you?"

❦

DESPITE ALL the possible difficulties inherent in confusion, sometimes a bit of intentional discombobulation can be used as an effective teaching tool:

The daughter of Caesar said to Rabbi Y'hoshu'a ben Hananya: "Why is glorious wisdom contained in an ugly vessel like you?"

He said to her: "Does your father keep his wine in earthen vessels?"

She said to him: "In what else should he keep it?"

He said to her: "You people of importance should keep it in gold and silver!"

She immediately went and told her father. He put the wine into golden and silver vessels, and it soured. They went and told him. He said to his daughter: "Who told you this?"

She said to him: "Rabbi Y'hoshu'a ben Hananya."

He called him and said to him: "Why did you tell that to my daughter?"

Rabbi Y'hoshu'a ben Hananya replied, "What she told me, I told her."

Caesar said: "But there are also beautiful people who are scholars?"

"If they were ugly, they would be even greater scholars."

❦

MANY TIMES, as the examples illustrate, we ourselves are the cause of our own confusion, usually because of misguided expectations or incomplete or even erroneous knowledge. On some of these occasions, we may not even realize that we are confused.

Many classic wisdom tales attempt to warn their listeners against this type of confusion, for it can cause harm. It sometimes seems that we can be at our most dangerous precisely when we deem ourselves to be doing the most good.

The rainy season that year had been the strongest ever and the river had broken its banks. There were floods everywhere and the animals were all running up into the hills. The floods came so fast that many drowned except the lucky monkeys who used their proverbial agility to climb up into the treetops. They looked down on the surface of the water where the fish were swimming and gracefully jumping out of the water as if they were the only ones enjoying the devastating flood.

One of the monkeys saw the fish and shouted to his companion: "Look down, my friend, look at those poor creatures. They are going to drown. Do you see how they struggle in the water?"

"Yes," said the other monkey. "What a pity! Probably they were late in escaping to the hills because they seem to have no legs. How can we save them?"

"I think we must do something. Let's go close to the edge of the flood where the water is not deep enough to cover us, and we can help them to get out."

So the monkeys did just that. They started catching the fish, but not without difficulty. One by one, they brought them out of the water and put them carefully on the dry land. After a short time there was a pile of fish lying on the grass motionless. One of the monkeys said, "Do you see? They were tired, but now they are just sleeping and resting. Had it not been for us, my friend, all these poor people without legs would have drowned."

The other monkey said: "They were trying to escape from us because they could not understand our good intentions. But when they wake up they will be very grateful because we have brought them salvation."

⚬⚬⚬

IF ONE THEME is beginning to emerge from our exploration of confusions, it may be that of the treachery of expectations. Unrealistic—or even just plain carelessly inaccurate—expectations can also blight one's spiritual life. Too often they signal a lack of openness, an unreadiness for the gifts that may be otherwise awaiting us. To paraphrase William James, happiness can be quantified as the ratio between reality and our expectations: the higher our expectations, the smaller our satisfaction. There are, of course, different kinds of expectation.

There once was a powerful Japanese emperor who needed a new chief samurai. So he sent out a declaration throughout the entire known world that he was searching for a chief.

A year passed, and only three people applied for the very demanding position: a Japanese samurai, a Chinese samurai, and a Jewish samurai.

The emperor asked the Japanese samurai to come in and demonstrate why he should be the chief samurai. The Japanese samurai opened a matchbox, and out popped a bumblebee. *Whoosh* went his sword. The bumblebee dropped dead, chopped in half.

The emperor exclaimed, "That is very impressive!"

The emperor then issued the same challenge to the Chinese samurai, to come in and demonstrate why he should be chosen.

The Chinese samurai also opened a matchbox and out buzzed a fly. *Whoosh, whoosh, whoosh.* The fly dropped dead, chopped into four small pieces.

The emperor exclaimed, "That is very impressive!"

Now the emperor turned to the Jewish samurai and asked him to demonstrate why he should be the chief samurai. The Jewish samurai opened a matchbox and out flew a gnat. His flashing sword went *Whoosh.* But the gnat was still alive and flying around.

The emperor, obviously disappointed, said, "Very ambitious, but why is that gnat not dead?"

The Jewish samurai just smiled and said, "Circumcision is not meant to kill."

❧

EXPECTATIONS, OF COURSE, come in various guises. And at times they can be shattered in unexpected ways.

A new teacher was trying to make use of her psychology courses. She started her class by saying, "Everyone who thinks they're stupid, stand up!"

After a few seconds, Little Davie stood up. The teacher said, "Do you think you're stupid, Little Davie?"

"No, ma'am, but I hate to see you standing there all by yourself!"

❧

IT IS good to have a compassionate student in class. Some might think it preferable to be that compassionate student.

A certain man decided that he would seek the Perfect Master.

He read many books, visited sage after sage, listened, discussed, and practiced, but he always found himself doubting or unsure.

After twenty years he met a man whose every word and action corresponded with his idea of the totally realized man.

The traveler lost no time. "You," he said, "seem to me to be the Perfect Master. If you are, my journey is at an end."

"I am, indeed, described by that name," said the Master.

"Then, I beg of you, accept me as a disciple."

"That," said the Master, "I cannot do, for while you may desire the Perfect Master, he, in turn, requires only the Perfect Pupil."

୧୬

BACK TO "CONFUSION." Since we are dealing with spirituality, some may find it difficult to understand how there can be confusion even in a person of faith. Others may insist that there is an element of confusion even in faith itself. The philosopher Miguel de Unamuno offers helpful, even searing, light.

Those who believe that they believe in God, but without passion in their hearts, without anguish of mind, without uncertainty, without doubt, without an element of despair even in their consolation, believe only in the God idea, not in God himself.

Confusion. Sometimes it has to do with perspective. Maybe even in this book. Finally, then, a child's; then a neophyte disciple's.

A three-year-old boy went with his dad to see a litter of kittens. On returning home, he breathlessly informed his mother, "There were two boy kittens and two girl kittens."

"How did you know?" his mother asked.

"Daddy picked them up and looked underneath," he replied. "I think it's printed on the bottom."

❧

The Master taught that Truth is right before our eyes, and the reason we do not see it is our lack of perspective.

Once he took a disciple on a mountain climb. When they were halfway up the mountain the man glared at the under-brush and complained, "Where's the beautiful scenery you are always talking about?"

The Master smiled. "You're standing on top of it, as you will see when we get to the top."

RECOVERY

When the ill person begins to show an interest in
what is happening to others, those who are caring sigh
with relief. Recovery has commenced.
ALIDA GERSIE AND NANCY KING

The hallmark of recovery—and of spirituality—is *gratitude*.
Gratitude may, in fact, be a synonym for recovery.

This gratitude is not the mere saying of "thank you" to someone
who has gifted or otherwise benefited us, important as that is. For
characteristic of the most genuine gratitude is that it runs forward—
passing on to others the benefits of the gift one has received. Goodness spreads.

Gratitude begins in the vision of how much one has received, of
how gifted one has been. It begins to mature in the realization
that the only appropriate response to that reality is to pass it on—to,
in turn, gift others. Gratitude reaches full maturity in the living
out of that insight—and that full maturity is recovery.

Rabbi Hayyim had married his son to the daughter of Rabbi
Eliezer of Dzikov, who was a son of Rabbi Naftale of

Roptchitz. The day after the wedding, Rabbi Hayyim visited the father of the bride and said: "Now that we are related, I feel close to you and can tell you what is eating at my heart. Look! My hair and beard have turned white, and I have not yet atoned!"

"O, my friend," replied Rabbi Eliezer, "you are thinking only of yourself. How about forgetting yourself and thinking of the world!"

❧

THOSE WHO survive trauma, especially in matters related to health, are often referred to as "recovered" or "recovering." Some crisis has been lived through, survived; a significant turning point has been successfully traversed. Although its use has expanded in recent years, the term came to wider usage from its adoption by those experienced in addiction to describe their freedom from that affliction. "Recovery" in that context means "rejoining the human race," a rediscovery of one's basic humanity. In recovery we discover the place where we belong—sometimes by recognizing where we do not belong.

A man in a small Wisconsin city had been on the AA program for about three years and had enjoyed contented sobriety throughout that period. Then bad luck began to hit him in bunches. . . . At this point he cracked, and decided to go on an all-out binge. He didn't want to stage this in the small city, where everyone knew his sobriety record. So he went to Chicago, checked in at a North Side hotel, and set forth on his project. It was Friday night, and the bars were filled with a swinging crowd. But he was in no mood for swinging—he just wanted to get quietly, miserably drunk.

Finally, he found a basement bar on a quiet side street, practically deserted. He sat down on a bar stool and ordered a double bourbon on the rocks. The bartender said, "Yes, sir," and reached for a bottle.

Then the bartender stopped in his tracks, took a long, hard look at the customer, leaned over the bar, and said in a low tone, "I was in Milwaukee about four months ago, and one night I attended an open meeting. You were on the speaking platform, and you gave one of the finest AA talks I ever heard." The bartender turned and walked to the end of the bar.

For a few minutes, the customer sat there—probably in a state of shock. Then he picked his money off the bar with trembling hands and walked out, all desire for a drink drained out of him.

It is estimated that there are about eight thousand saloons in Chicago, employing some twenty-five thousand bartenders. This man had entered the one saloon in eight thousand where he encountered the one man in twenty-five thousand who knew that he didn't belong there.

❦

LIKE SPIRITUALITY itself, *recovery* cannot be defined, but it can be described. Like spirituality also, then, recovery is an *experience*—the kind of reality that is most like a skill, a practice, something that can be recognized but that eludes efforts to analyze it. For if it is broken down into "parts," no matter how those parts are arranged, the whole cannot be reconstituted. A skill, skillfully exercised, has both *flair* and *flow*—the kind of wholeness that does not admit of disjunction.

When Russian soldiers entered the town of Radin, the Jewish residents prepared special kosher meals for the Jewish soldiers in the czar's army. But then they saw their kindness and charity thrown back in their faces, as it were, as the soldiers devoured their food—and then lined up for the standard, non-kosher Russian rations.

When several people complained about this to the Chofetz Chaim, the saintly Rabbi Israel Meir Kagan, and suggested that they might as well stop preparing kosher food, he reflected with an insight that will stay with us for generations.

"Every Mitzvah* that a Jew does, every good deed, is not a fleeting act. It is an eternity. No matter what precedes or ensues, we must cherish each Mitzvah done by each and every person."

∾

THE BENEFITING of the caring person is not simply a Jewish or Judeo-Christian insight. Plato informs us of Socrates's practice and examples of *therapeia*. Each resulted "in the good or the improve-

---

* Mitzvah (MITS-vuh): Lit. commandment. Any of the 613 commandments that Jews are obligated to observe. It can also refer to any Jewish religious obligation, or more generally to any good deed (http://www.jewfaq.org/defs/mitzvot.htm).

ment of the care-giver rather than the recipient of the care. The good of the recipient or object of *therapeia* is incidental to the good of the care-giver."

Although perhaps not as pervasive as spirituality, recovery does occur in many settings. Recovery can be from an illness, or from grief, from some loss, or from something as mundane as losing one's balance. In each case, the process involves a return to some more desirable condition. What is also common to all experiences of recovery is a turning of attention from self to some reality outside the self—"catching one's balance" may be the most vivid as well as the most common example, attention shifting from momentary dizziness to the floor on which one's feet are now firmly planted or the banister on which one now gratefully leans. Recovery implies a "coming back," a *return* from some less than ideal state or condition to a situation of solidity.

But as the word is most commonly used today, so many think "recovery" has something to do with *spirituality* that a direct treatment of this connection seems advisable. Recovery is to Spirituality as a knife edge is to a knife blade—you can't have one without the other, for any experience of Recovery necessarily awakens gratitude. Recovery is like spirituality in that it is an ineffable experience. As soon describe in words the experience of making love, or of hitting a fast ball with the sweet spot on the bat, or what it feels like to stand on the side of the pool and watch your child execute a perfect somersault dive, or even what it feels like to "catch your balance." Words—language—limp.

Yet recovery, like spirituality, is real. Insofar as both can be described, each involves a right relationship with self, with others, and with larger reality. But those words, too, are too shallow. For recovery, like spirituality, if its reality is to be grasped, must be *experienced*—known, and felt, and more, in one's very *be*-ing. And part of this experiential reality is the discovery that recovery, like spirituality, works best when it is not talked about, even not thought about.

∽

Some Hasidim of the Maggid of Mezeritch came to him. "Rebbe, we are puzzled. It says in the Talmud that we must thank God as much for the bad days, as for the good. How can that be? What would our gratitude mean, if we gave it equally for the good and the bad?"

The Maggid replied, "Go to Anapol. Reb Zusya will have an answer for you."

The Hasidim undertook the journey. Arriving in Anapol, they inquired for Reb Zusya. At last, they came to the poorest street of the city. There, crowded between two small houses, they found a tiny shack, sagging with age.

When they entered, they saw Reb Zusya sitting at a bare table, reading a volume by the light of the only small window. "Welcome, strangers!" he said. "Please pardon me for not getting up, I have hurt my leg. Would you like food? I have some bread. And there is water!"

"No. We have come only to ask you a question. The Maggid of Mezeritch told us you might help us understand: Why do our sages tell us to thank God as much for the bad days as for the good?"

Reb Zusya laughed. "Me? I have no idea why the Maggid sent

you to me." He shook his head in puzzlement. "You see, I have never had a bad day. Every day God has given to me has been filled with miracles."

❦

I once asked Martin Marty [the Church historian]
for the shortest definition he could give me
of worship. And he said, "Gratitude." I
always thought that was terrific.

NORMAN LEAR

Recovery and Spirituality and Gratitude are related because they begin in the same place and have the same essence: an orientation toward *others*, a pointing outside the self. Our unspiritual selves are self-centered—turned in on self, attentive first if not exclusively to self and its supposed needs and real desires. Self is the only center of the sick, unspiritual universe.

An orientation toward others can take many forms.

One day Nasrudin Khoja and a group of his neighbors were going somewhere together. They all rode upon their donkeys. When they came to a hill, Khoja noticed that his donkey was sweating. He got down from its back and whispered into its ear, "I am sorry that you are working so hard that you are sweating."

His neighbors noticed Khoja get down from his donkey's back and whisper into its ear, and they were curious about this. "Khoja, what did you whisper to your donkey?" one of them asked.

"I told my donkey that I was sorry that he had to work so hard that he sweated," answered Khoja.

All his neighbors laughed, and one of them said, "Why did you do that? Donkeys do not understand human speech. They are not at all human."

"What I do is what concerns me. I did what is expected of a human being, and I do not care whether or not he understood what I said."

⚮

THE SUFI tell a story:

Past the seeker on the prayer rug came the crippled and the beggar and the beaten. And seeing them, the holy one went down into deep prayer and cried,

"Great God, how is it that a loving creator can see such things and yet do nothing about them?"

And out of the long silence, God said:

"I did do something about them. I made you."

⚮

AND IT works both ways: A genuine orientation toward others both flows from and begets the spiritual ideal of purity of heart, singleness of purpose. For theists, from God's point of view in this vision, "purity of heart" in the sense of singleness of purpose means the readiness to please Him, especially by acts of mercy and kindness toward others.

Said the Kotzker, "Take care of your own soul and of another man's body, not of your own body and of another man's soul."

❦

"PURITY OF HEART" means having a heart free from anger and ready to forgive, a *be*-ing centered outside one's self. The antithesis of purity of heart is resentment, the internally festering fascination with some wrong, real or imagined, that has been done to us. Rightly, from experience, the "Big Book" of Alcoholics Anonymous recognizes resentment to be "the number one offender," causing the destruction of those who cherish it. To be wrapped up in self, especially in how one's self has been "wronged," is an ultimate perversion.

Purity of heart suggests *straight* movement, and so coheres well with the understanding and portrayal of sin as *hamartia*, a swerving aside, a turning from the proper direction. Purity of heart aims to fulfill the Creator's aim in creating creatures—that they be beneficial to one another. *"I did do something about them. I made you."*

When Pachomius, the chief founder of community living among the Desert Fathers, urged his disciple, Theodore, to guard against evil thoughts, he pointed to those concerned with enmity and unkindness toward his brothers: "And if an evil thought comes into your mind, whether it be of hatred, unkindness, jealousy, distrust toward your brother, or of human vanity, remember immediately and say to yourself, 'If I consent to any one of these things, I shall not see the Lord.'"

Similarly, for that great summary compendium of Desert spirituality, Pseudo-Macarius's *Apophthegmata*, the sign of purity of heart is the absence of judgment, seeing no sin in others. "Seeing no sin"?

When the Master was a boy at school, a classmate treated him with persistent cruelty.

Now, older and contrite, the former classmate came to the monastery and was received with open arms.

One day he brought up the subject of his former cruelty, but the Master seemed not to recall it.

Said the visitor, "Don't you remember?"

Said the Master, "I distinctly remember forgetting it!" and they both melted in innocent laughter.

~∞~

TOO OFTEN, when we think of our relationship with a Higher Power, the tendency is to think only in terms of what we have received or hope to receive. Gratitude and petition are genuine prayers, gratitude especially fitting our condition. But petition harbors hidden possibilities for heroic sanctity. One might, for example, request the grace, the opportunity, to serve others.

A man was walking through the forest when he saw a fox that had lost its legs. The man wondered how the fox was able to stay alive. Then he saw a tiger come along with game in its mouth. The tiger ate its fill and left the rest of the meat for the fox.

The next day God fed the fox by means of the same tiger. The man wondered at God's greatness and said to himself, "I too shall just take my rest with full trust that the Lord will provide me with all I need."

He did this for many days but nothing happened, and he was almost at death's door when he heard a voice say, "O, you who are in the path of error, open your eyes to the truth! Follow the example of the life-giving tiger and stop imitating the disabled fox."

A PHILOSOPHICAL axiom suggests that "good is diffusive of itself"—the good *wants to* spread. This is, then, the surest test of genuine goodness—it gives of itself. Admittedly, the love of and responsibility for one's fellows can sometimes lead in strange directions.

It's late fall and the Indians on a remote reservation in South Dakota asked their new chief if the coming winter was going to be cold or mild.

Since he was a chief in a modern society, he had never been taught the old secrets.

When he looked at the sky, he couldn't tell what the winter was going to be like.

Nevertheless, to be on the safe side, he told his tribe that the winter was indeed going to be cold and that the members of the village should collect firewood to be prepared.

But, being a practical leader, after several days, he got an idea. He went to the phone booth, called the National Weather Service, and asked, "Is the coming winter going to be cold?"

"It looks like this winter is going to be quite cold," the meteorologist at the weather service responded.

So the chief went back to his people and told them to collect even more firewood in order to be prepared.

A week later, he called the National Weather Service again. "Does it still look like it is going to be a very cold winter?"

"Yes," the man at National Weather Service again replied, "it's going to be a very cold winter."

The chief again went back to his people and ordered them to collect every scrap of firewood they could find.

Two weeks later, the chief called the National Weather Service again. "Are you absolutely sure that the winter is going to be very cold?"

"Absolutely," the man replied. "It's looking more and more like it is going to be one of the coldest winters we've ever seen."

"How can you be so sure?" the chief asked.

The weatherman replied, "The Indians are collecting firewood like crazy."

❦

AN ORIENTATION toward others need not be painful; in fact it rarely is painful, but because there are heroes, there can be exceptional cases.

One day a penurious old man went to see Fazl-Rabi to discuss some matter or other.

Because of weakness and nervousness, the ancient stuck the iron point of his walking stick into Fazl-Rabi's foot.

Listening courteously to what the old man had to say, Fazl-Rabi said no word, although he went pale and then flushed, from the pain of the wound and the iron, as it stayed lodged in his foot.

Then, when the other had finished his business, he took a paper from him and put his signature to it.

When the old man had gone, delighted that he had been successful in his application, Fazl-Rabi allowed himself to collapse.

One of the attendant nobles said:

"My lord, you sat there with blood pouring from your foot,

with that old man in his dotage piercing your foot with his iron-tipped staff, and you said nothing, nothing at all."

Fazl-Rabi answered: "I made no sign of pain because I feared that the old man's distress might cause him to withdraw in confusion, and that he might abandon his application for my help. Poor as he was, how could I add to his troubles in that manner?"

❧

THE WISE and the caring show consideration in many ways. Sometimes a person wonders, "What is most important in recovery?"

A believer approached Rabbi Moche of Kobryn and asked: "How should I best use my days so that God will be contented with my actions?"

"There is only one possible option: to live with love," replied the rabbi.

Minutes later, another follower approached him and asked the same question.

"There is only one possible option: try to live with joy."

The first follower was taken aback.

"But the advice you gave me was different!"

"Not at all," said the rabbi. "It was exactly the same."

❧

RECOVERY IS a process, something that takes place over time. There is no "once and for all" in our relationships with a Higher Power OR with our fellow human beings. Again, recovery is perhaps best understood as a *skill* that needs to be practiced and can always be further developed.

In the book *First Things First*, Roger Merrill tells of a businessman named Fred who was moving into a new house. Fred decided to hire a friend to landscape his grounds. This friend had a doctorate in horticulture. She was extremely knowledgeable, extremely bright.

Well, Fred had a great vision for his grounds, but he was very, very busy. He traveled a lot, and so he kept emphasizing to his friend the need to create a garden in such a way that it would require very little maintenance on his part. He said that automatic sprinklers were an absolute necessity, and he was always on the lookout for labor-saving devices and other ways of cutting time.

Finally, his friend said to him, "Fred, I can see what you're saying, but there is one thing you need to deal with before we go any further. If there is no gardener, Fred, there is no garden."

❧

RECOVERY ... and gratitude ... and giving forward—how often do we link them in our minds, in our practice? At their deepest level, they are one. But we rarely live that deep awareness. Most often, in our habitual daily distraction, we see things separately. Even in our best moments we harbor firmly set ideas—we *know* what is good for us. We may even be quite sure of what is God's will for us.

In the remote mountains of northern Greece, there once lived a monk who had desired all of his life to make a pilgrimage to the Holy Sepulchre—to walk three times around it, to kneel, and to return home a new person. Gradually through the years he had saved what money he could, begging in the villages nearby, and finally, near the end of his life, had enough set aside to begin his trip. He opened the gates of the monastery and, staff in hand, set out with great anticipation on his way to Jerusalem.

But no sooner had he left the cloister than he encountered a man in rags, sad and bent to the ground, picking herbs. "Where are you going, Father?" the man asked. "To the Holy Sepulchre, brother. By God's grace, I shall walk three times around it, kneel, and return home a different man from what I am."

"How much money to do that do you have, Father?" inquired the man.

"Thirty pounds," the monk answered.

"Give me the thirty pounds," said the beggar. "I have a wife and hungry children. Give me the money, walk three times around me, then kneel and go back into your monastery."

The monk thought for a moment, scratching the ground with his staff, then took the thirty pounds from his sack, gave the whole of it to the poor man, walked three times around him, knelt, and went back through the gates of his monastery.

He returned home a new person, of course, having recognized that the beggar was Christ himself—not in some magical place far away, but right outside his monastery door, mysteriously close. In abandoning his quest for the remote, the special, the somehow "magical," the monk discovered a meaning far more profound in the ordinary experience close to home. All that he had given up came suddenly rushing back to him with a joy unforeseen.

To be surprised by grace is a gift still to be prized.

∞

THE UNION of Recovery and the Gratitude of Giving as a founda-
tion of experiential spirituality is not peculiar to the Christian or
Western tradition. A "Tricycle Daily Dharma" on "The Power of
Generosity" reminds:

> *Dana ("Giving") is the most fundamental of all Buddhist practices. It is*
> *the first topic in the Buddha's graduated talks, the first step on the*
> *bodhisattva's path to perfection, and the first of the ten paramitas*
> *(perfections) in the Mahayana tradition. It therefore sets the tone for*
> *all that follows in the spiritual journey.*
>
> *The act of giving purifies intention, the quality of mind with*
> *which any action is undertaken. For a brief moment, the giver's*
> *self-absorption is lifted, attachment to the gift is relinquished, and*
> *kindness towards the recipient is developed. All actions—of thought,*
> *word, and deed—undertaken for the sake of others rather than for one's*
> *own selfish purposes become transformed by the power of generosity.*

But there is another side to giving. Or, perhaps better, there is also
the gift of receiving. And again a Buddhist meditation on *Dana* well
frames this important aspect of the experiential spirituality of Recovery, the *full* experience of giving.

> *For the recipient, there is a kind of vulnerability in accepting a gift from*
> *a loved one. If you are disappointed—or even insulted—by the gift, or if*
> *you sense that the giver is not really in tune with who you are, how do*
> *you respond in a way that is not hurtful? Some people are close enough*
> *to each other to see the humor in this vulnerability, so that even failed*
> *gifts become occasions for deepening the bonds of affection. However,*

often people expect their gift to be a success, and if it is not, they take offense. Receiving a gift in that atmosphere puts pressure on the recipient. Not being appropriately enthusiastic could imply a rejection of that person and your relationship.

. . . Receiving is a powerful—and intimate—practice, for we are actually inviting another person into ourselves. Rather than focusing on our own practice, or on our own virtue, we can focus on providing an opportunity for someone else to develop generosity. In spite of its complexities and entanglements, the moment of exchange is one of simple connection and opening. That moment itself is unsullied. For that reason it is said that generosity is the discipline that produces peace.

And so Recovery . . . and Gratitude . . . and Giving . . . and Receiving. All are—or can be—spiritual. Each is an invitation to and can be a practice of looking outside of, beyond, our self.

A story from Brazil:

Shortly before he died, my father-in-law summoned his family.

"I know that death is only a passageway into the next world. When I have gone through it, I will send you a sign that it really is worthwhile helping others in this life." He wanted to be cremated and for his ashes to be scattered over Arpoador Beach while a tape recorder played his favorite music.

He died two days later. A friend arranged the cremation in São Paolo and—once back in Rio—we went straight to the beach armed with a tape recorder, tapes, and the package containing the cremation urn.

When we reached the sea, we got a surprise. The lid of the urn was firmly screwed down. We couldn't open it.

The only person around was a beggar, and he came over to us and asked: "What's the problem?"

My brother-in-law said: "We need a screwdriver so that we can get at my father's ashes inside this urn."

"Well, he must have been a very good man, because I've just found this," said the beggar.

And he held out a screwdriver.

WISDOM

Wisdom begins in wonder.
EDITH HAMILTON

The Master argued with no one, for he knew that what the arguer sought was confirmation of his beliefs, not the truth.

He once showed them the value of an argument:

"Does a slice of bread fall with the buttered side up or down?"

"With the buttered side down, of course."

"No, with the buttered side up."

"Let's put it to the test."

So a slice of bread was buttered and thrown up in the air. It fell buttered side up.

"I win!"

"Only because I made a mistake."

"What mistake?"

"I obviously buttered the wrong side."

Very often, argument is of little use. This is especially true when there is no clearly defined standard of evidence.

A Chicago matron was once seated next to Mrs. Cabot at a Boston dinner. During the crisp exchange of conversation, Mrs. Cabot advanced the information that "in Boston, we place all our emphasis on breeding."

To which the Chicago matron responded: "In Chicago, we think it's a lot of fun, but we do manage to foster a great many outside interests."

❧

An artist who wanted a home among the hills of Vermont was talking the matter over with a farmer who allowed that he had a house for sale. "I must have a good view," said the artist. "Is there a good view?"

"Well," drawled the farmer, "from the front porch yuh kin see Ed Snow's barn, but beyond that there ain't nuthin' but a bunch of mountains."

❧

ONE RATHER simple schema helps when we are confronted with confusing, because insufficiently explained, language or thought. Our schema is ancient and enduring. It is the distinction between *Knowledge* or *Intelligence* and *Wisdom* or *Understanding*. Each, let it be noted, can be an *entity* or a *process*—this is why we need two terms to delineate the product and practice of each.

Most people are more familiar and therefore comfortable with *knowledge*. It is, after all, our usual way of understanding reality. So let's begin with a few introductory notes on *wisdom*. Wisdom was defined/explained by the concentration camp–surviving psychiatrist Viktor Frankl as "knowledge plus: knowledge—and the knowledge of its own limits." Wisdom, it has also been suggested, is what sages and saints have always sought both to gain and to teach—the way of thinking distilled from the lives of saints and sages.

And so to our ten-point schema:

※

1. *Knowledge* seeks to collect facts, data—to amass a "body of knowledge." It is concerned with technique and focuses on *push* forces, efficient causality. Knowledge's "Why?" really asks, "How?"

Wisdom is concerned with *meaning*, and thus with "value." It searches for *pull* forces, final causality. Wisdom's "Why?" asks, "Wherefore? To what end?" seeking *reasons* rather than "causes."

> *... the humanness of human behavior cannot be revealed*
> *unless we recognize that the real "cause" of a given individual's*
> *behavior is not a cause but, rather, a reason. ... What, then,*
> *is the difference between causes and reasons? If you*
> *cut onions—you weep. Your tears have a cause.*
> *But you have no reason to weep. ...*
>
> VICTOR FRANKL

> *The person who knows "how" will always have a job.*
> *The person who knows "why" will always be his boss.*
>
> DIANE RAVITCH

Emphasizing action as to get away *from* something rather than to go *toward* something, to compensate for a lack rather than to seek to realize an aim, Helen Merrell Lynd has pointed out, "leaves no room for curiosity, thought, sympathy, tenderness, love, as well as humor."

As Mohandas Gandhi stepped aboard a train one day, one of his shoes slipped off and landed on the track. He was unable to retrieve it as the train started rolling. To the amazement of his companions, Gandhi calmly took off his other shoe and threw it back along the track to land close to the first shoe. Asked by a fellow passenger why he did that, Gandhi replied, "The poor man who finds the shoe lying on the track will now have a pair he can use."

⤫

2. *Knowledge* is primarily a method; it seeks and attains truth by experiment and aims at exactness, focusing on *quantity*, asking "How much?" Knowledge produces experts.

Wisdom is a vision. It seeks truth by understanding, is concerned with *adequacy*, and focuses on *qualities*. Wisdom questions "What kind of?" and produces artists.

> *Statistics are like bikinis: what they show is*
> *suggestive, but what they conceal is vital.*
> AARON LEVENSTEIN

> *When one has no character, one has to apply method.*
> ALBERT CAMUS

Sam Levinson tells the story of the birth of his first child.

The first night home the baby would not stop crying. His

wife frantically flipped through the pages of Dr. Spock to find out why babies cry and what to do about it. Since Spock's book is rather long, the baby cried for a long time.

Grandma was in the house, but since she had not read books on child rearing, she was not consulted. The baby continued to cry until Grandma could stand it no longer and she shouted downstairs, "For heaven's sake, Sarah, put down the book and pick up the baby!"

This zeal for uncriticizable statements and precisely verifiable
measurements should certainly be encouraged, but not
without warning that in pursuing Certainty, the Absolute, one is
likely to leave Man, the thinking reed, forsaken in the rear....
"You can't make a leaf grow by stretching it."

HELEN MERRELL LYND

Once there was a poor, blind, old man, and he and his wife had no children. He had a hard life, but the man never complained. One day Elijah came to him as he was sitting by the river, and he said, "Even though your life has been hard, you never complained, so God will grant you one wish." The poor man smiled. "What a wish! I'm blind, I'm poor, and I am childless. How will one wish satisfy all my problems? But give me twenty-four hours and I'll come back with a wish."

So he went home and told his wife what had happened. She smiled at him and said, "Eat well and sleep soundly, for I know what you should wish." (Now think: What would he wish for? Remember the problem: He's blind, he's poor, he's childless....)

Here's his wish. He came back the next day and he said to Elijah, "I wish to see my children eat off golden plates."

The wish was granted, and the man and his wife lived happily for the rest of their days.

❧

3. *Knowledge* can be and must be added to, even replaced; it advances. We find knowledge in textbooks or articles that we read once, perhaps use, and then may "refer to."

Wisdom is less added to than deepened. We find it in "classics," works that we reread and ponder because we change more than they do. With each new reading and pondering, we have a sense of profiting because we *have* "seen them before."

An old country doctor was celebrated for his wisdom. "Dr. Sage," a young man asked, "how did you get so wise?"

"Weren't hard," said the doc, "I've got good judgment."

"Well, Doc, how does one get good judgment?"

"That's easy," said Doc Sage. "Good judgment comes from experience. And experience—well, that comes from having bad judgment."

Nobody ever reads the same book twice.
ROBERTSON DAVIES

Nathaniel Hawthorne's son, Julian, also an author, was mistaken for his father by an adoring fan. "Oh, Mr. Hawthorne," she cried, "I've read *The Scarlet Letter*, and I think it's a real masterpiece."

"Oh, that," Hawthorne replied, dismissing the book with a

wave of his hand, "that was written when I was only four years old."

> *A classic is a book that has never*
> *finished saying what it has to say.*
>
> ITALO CALVINO

⸜⸜

4. *Knowledge* gives answers: one "possesses" knowledge, and therefore can sell/merchandise it.

Wisdom suggests new perspectives on ultimate questions: one does not "possess" it but rather is possessed by it. Those who claim to sell wisdom are regarded as charlatans.

> *When we ask the ultimate questions, whether about*
> *the direction of our own lives or about the meaning of*
> *existence, the outcome of thinking is not an answer but*
> *a transformed way of thinking, not propositions to assent*
> *to but heightened power of apprehension.*
>
> HELEN MERRELL LYND

> *One never "possesses" his story, any more than one "possesses" an*
> *identity or a faith: in each case, one is rather possessed by it.*
>
> ERNEST BECKER

THE HISTORY OF MEDICINE . . .

2010 BC—HERE, EAT THIS ROOT.

1000 AD—THAT ROOT IS HEATHEN. HERE, SAY THIS PRAYER.

1850 AD—THAT PRAYER IS SUPERSTITION. HERE, DRINK THIS POTION.

1940 AD—THAT POTION IS SNAKE OIL. HERE, SWALLOW THIS PILL.

1980 AD—THAT PILL IS INEFFECTIVE. HERE, TAKE THIS ANTIBIOTIC.

2010 AD—THAT ANTIBIOTIC DOESN'T WORK ANYMORE. HERE, EAT THIS ROOT.

> *"What we call basic truths are simply the ones*
> *we discover after all the others."*
>
> ALBERT CAMUS

❧

5. The source of *Knowledge* is leisure, either the possession of it or the desire for it.

The source of *Wisdom* is suffering. As Aeschylus first (as far as we know) dramatized, "wisdom's price is suffering, and it is always paid unwillingly, although sent in truth as a gift from the gods."

> *Out of suffering have emerged the strongest souls;*
> *the most massive characters are seared with scars.*
>
> EDWIN HUBBELL CHAPIN

> *There is an ancient tribal proverb I once heard in*
> *India. It says that before we can see properly we*
> *must first shed our tears to clear the way.*
>
> LIBBA BRAY

> *But a mermaid has no tears, and therefore*
> *she suffers so much more.*
>
> HANS CHRISTIAN ANDERSEN,
>
> *The Little Mermaid*

Jimmy received a parrot for Christmas. The parrot was fully grown, with a very bad attitude and even worse vocabulary.

Jimmy tried to change the bird's attitude by constantly saying polite words, playing soft music, anything that he could think of.

Nothing worked. He yelled at the bird, and the bird got worse. He shook the bird, and the bird got even more rude. Finally, in a moment of desperation, Jimmy put the parrot in the freezer.

For a few moments he heard the bird squawking, kicking, and screaming. Then, suddenly, there was absolute quiet. Jimmy was frightened that he might have actually hurt the bird and quickly opened the freezer door.

The parrot calmly stepped out onto Jimmy's extended arm and said, "I'm sorry that I offended you with my language and my actions, and I ask your forgiveness. I will endeavor to correct my behavior."

Jimmy was astounded at the change in the bird's attitude and was about to ask what had changed him, when the parrot continued, "May I ask what the chicken did?"

❦

6. *Knowledge* attends to and focuses on realities as things, tending to analyze, to take apart.

Wisdom attends to and examines realities as personal, inclining to synthesize, to view and embrace *wholes*.

> *A hundred love-letters are probably not worth a dollar;*
> *But one love-letter may be worth more than a hundred dollars.*
>
> UNKNOWN

A lawyer was questioning a farmer about an accident. The lawyer said to the farmer, "Tell me what happened right after the accident, when you reportedly said, 'I feel fine!'" The farmer then began to speak, "Me and my cow Bessie were driving down the road."

At this the lawyer interrupted, saying, "Please answer my question. Didn't you say you felt fine immediately following the accident?" Turning to the judge, the lawyer asked that the witness be instructed to answer the question.

The judge looked at the farmer and said, "Please answer the question." The farmer began again, "Me and my cow Bessie were driving down the road."

The lawyer interrupted once again. "Your Honor, please instruct the witness to answer my question." The judge looked at the lawyer and then at the farmer and then back to the lawyer and said, "Let's just allow the witness to tell his story."

The farmer began once again. "Me and my cow Bessie were driving down the road. When we crossed the intersection, this big truck hit us broadside. I flew out of our truck in one direction and Bessie flew out in the other. I regained consciousness just as the highway patrol officer arrived. He went over, looked at poor Bessie lying there on the road, then he came over and told me she was injured and in pretty bad shape. Then he went back to Bessie, pulled out his gun, and shot her dead. He then came back to me and asked me how I felt. I said, 'I feel fine.'"

Rabbi Israel Salanter was very scrupulous in his observance of all the six hundred and thirteen precepts prescribed by the religious code. It was his custom whenever the Passover holidays came around, to personally supervise the making of matzos in his town. He wished to make sure that it was done according to the time-honored ritual regulations.

On one such occasion, when he was confined by illness, his disciples volunteered to supervise the baking of the matzos.

"Instruct us, Rabbi," they said. "Tell us the most important thing we have to watch out for."

"My sons, see that the women who bake the matzos are well paid," was Rabbi Israel's brief reply.

❧

7. *Knowledge* locates human identity and uniqueness in the capacity to think.

Wisdom locates human identity and uniqueness in the capacity to love.

> *while you and i have lips and voices which*
> *are for kissing and to sing with*
> *who cares if some oneeyed son of a bitch*
> *invents an instrument to measure Spring with!*
>
> E. E. CUMMINGS

Buddha was once threatened with death by a bandit called Angulimala.

"Then please fulfill my dying wish," said Buddha. "Cut off the branch of that tree."

One slash of the sword, and it was done! "What now?" asked the bandit.

"Put it back again," said Buddha.

The bandit laughed. "You must be crazy to think that anyone can do that."

"On the contrary, it is you who are crazy to think that you are mighty because you can wound and destroy. That is the task of children. The mighty know how to create and heal."

∞

8. *Knowledge* insists on the separation of "fact" and "value," carefully distinguishing between data and interpretations.

Wisdom insists that "What can I know?" and "How shall I live?" are not totally unrelated questions—one reason for its reliance on *stories*.

The comic strip *For Better or For Worse* is about family life, a mother and dad and two kids. In one early episode, the first three panels show the mother tossing and turning in her bed, worrying about her ten-year-old son, Michael. She says, "Are we too tough on Michael? Are we not tough enough? Do we give in too often? Too seldom? Do we listen? Do we understand? Maybe I nag too much. Am I a good parent? Where are the answers? How does one know what to do?"

In the last panel, we see Michael lying awake in his bed saying, "Trouble with grownups is they think they know everything."

> *Few people know how much you have to know*
> *in order to know how little you know.*
>
> WALTER ONG

On the first day of school, a teacher asked her class, "Who here is a Mets fan?"

Every student knew that she loved the Mets, so they all replied by raising their hands, except for one girl, Rosie.

The teacher asked, "Who do you like, little girl?"

Rosie replied, "I'm a Yankees fan and I hate the Mets."

The teacher asked why and Rosie told her that her parents were Yankees fans, so she was, too.

The teacher said to the class, "So if Rosie's parents were idiots, what would that make her?"

Rosie chimed in, "A Mets fan!"

⁂

9. *Knowledge* searches out and is fascinated with "the new."

Wisdom assumes the connectedness of reality, encouraging mindfulness of "the old"; it tends to prefer that which has endured the test of time.

A young man had just gotten his driving permit. He asked his father, who was a rabbi, if they could discuss his use of the family car. His father took him into his study and said: "I'll make a deal with you. You bring your grades up, study your Talmud a little, get your hair cut, and then we'll talk about it."

After about a month, the boy came back and again asked his father if they could discuss his use of the car. They again went into the father's study, where the father said: "Son, I've been very proud of you. You have brought your grades up, you've studied the Talmud diligently, but you didn't get your hair cut."

The young man waited a moment and then replied: "You know, Dad, I've been thinking about that. You know Samson had long hair, Moses had long hair, Noah had long hair, and even Jesus had long hair."

The rabbi said: "Yes, and they walked everywhere they went."

Upon entering a little country store, the stranger noticed a sign reading, Danger! Beware of dog! posted on the door.

Inside he noticed a harmless old hound dog asleep on the floor near the cash register. He asked the store's owner, "Is that the dog folks are supposed to beware of?"

"Yep," the proprietor answered. "That's him."

The stranger couldn't help being amused. "That certainly doesn't look like a dangerous dog to me." He chuckled. "Why in the world did you decide to post that sign?"

"Because," the owner replied, "before I posted that sign, people kept tripping over him."

∞

10. *Knowledge* accepts only what has been (or can be) in some sense proven.

Wisdom acknowledges the possibility of the existence of that which escapes strict proof, holding that faith in the existence of certain realities has to precede the ability to see their operation.

"Prove that you love me" = *"Prove you are sane"*:
the very effort to do so destroys that which cannot be objectified.

A couple of Alabama hunters are out in the woods when one of them falls to the ground. He doesn't seem to be breathing and his eyes are rolled back in his head.

The other guy whips out his cell phone and calls 911. He gasps to the operator, "My friend is dead! What can I do?"

The operator, in a calm, soothing voice, says, "Just take it easy. I can help. First, let's make sure he's dead."

There is a long silence, then a shot is heard. . . .

The hunter says, "Okay, now what?"

❧

"WILL THIS be on the test?" "Will there *be* a test?" That depends . . . but in the meantime . . . some final questions for further thought about knowledge and wisdom:

Knowledge or Wisdom: Which is more easily faked?

Despite all our technical and technological adeptness, the reality that almost any one individual can readily command vastly more knowledge and incredibly greater force than any ancient royal court or army, are we really better prepared to face death than peoples of earlier times?

What about facing life?

Knowledge and wisdom seem to be but one of several "both/and" realities at the core of human being, of *be*-ing human. Yet the human story hints a consistent pattern of demands or assumptions (which are more dangerous?) that these realities are or be either-or. Why? And so what?

In general, it seems, our interest and expertise focus on the *knowledge* of our own culture, on the *wisdom* of foreign and strange cultures. We tend to know and attend most to their art, literature, religion. That generalization, if valid, is an item of knowledge. What wisdom might it suggest?

❧

HOH ELDER Leila Fisher speaks:

"Did you ever wonder how wisdom comes? There was a man, a postman here on the reservation, who heard some of the Elders talking about receiving objects that bring great power. He didn't know much about such things, but he thought to himself that it would be a wonderful thing if he could receive such an object which can only be bestowed by the Creator. In particular, he heard from the Elders that the highest such object a person can receive is an eagle feather. He decided that was the one for him. If he could just receive an eagle feather, he would have all the power and wisdom and prestige he desired.

"But he knew he couldn't buy one and he couldn't ask anyone to give him one. It just had to come to him somehow by the Creator's will.

"Day after day he went around looking for an eagle feather. He figured one would come his way if he just kept his eyes open. It got so he thought of nothing else. That eagle feather occupied his thoughts from sunup to sundown. Weeks passed, then months, then years. Every day the postman did his rounds, always looking for that eagle feather, looking as hard as he could. He paid no attention to his family or friends. He just kept his mind fixed on that eagle feather. But it never seemed to come. He started to grow old, but still no feather. Finally, he came to realize that no matter how hard he looked, he was no closer to getting the feather than he had been the day he started.

"One day he took a break by the side of the road. He got out of his little jeep mail-carrier and had a talk with the Creator. He said: 'I'm so tired of looking for that eagle feather. Maybe I'm not supposed to get one. I've spent all my life thinking about that feather. I've hardly given a thought to my family and friends. All I cared about was the feather, and now life has just about passed me by. I've missed out on a lot of good things. Well, I'm giving up the search. I'm going to stop looking for that feather and start living. Maybe I have time enough left to make it up to my family and friends. Forgive me for the way I have conducted my life.'

"Then and only then a great peace came into him. He suddenly felt better inside than he had in all these years. Just as he finished his talk with the Creator and started getting back in his jeep, he was surprised by a shadow passing over him. Holding his hands over his eyes, he looked up into the sky and saw, high above, a great bird flying over. Almost instantly it disappeared. Then he saw something floating down ever so lightly on the breeze—a beautiful tail feather. It was his eagle feather! He realized that the feather had come not a single moment before he had stopped searching and made his peace with the Creator.

"He finally learned that wisdom comes only when you stop looking for it and start truly living the life the Creator intended for you.

"That postman is still alive and he's a changed person. People come to him for wisdom now and he shares everything he knows. Even though now he has the power and the prestige he searched for, he no longer cares about such things. He's concerned about others, not himself.

"So now you know how wisdom comes."

Notes

In this richly diverse age, when reading takes place in various electronic modes as well as from print media, research and reference offer new possibilities. Even with a book in hand, most readers have more ready access to online resources than to physical libraries. Online resources offer a bountiful variety of possibilities and connections. Accordingly, while we do cite many print resources in the Notes to this book, when online resources are available, and especially when we have used them in our own research, we point to them and, when possible, link to them.

For the benefit, then, especially of those who use this book in print format, we include reference URLs both raw and translated to a shortened format, using http://v.gd which, as of February 2014, has excellent protection against malware intrusions. v.gd uses six characters, is case-sensitive, and begins by telling you where it will take you, allowing you to verify that the site is as intended and therefore most likely safe.

Further comments that do not fit into the text also on occasion appear in the Notes.

NOTES ON INTRODUCTION

page 2: "The governor resigned": Anthony de Mello, *One Minute Nonsense* (Chicago: Loyola, 1992), [original English edition by Gujarat Sahitya Prakash, Anand, India, 1992], 53. Courtesy of Gujarat Sahitya Prakash (booksgsp@gmail.com).

page 3: "A word about *be*-ing": This is a virtually ageless conundrum, going back at least to Parmenides; for a brief treatment of the beginning of "the problem of 'is,'" cf. Robert N. Bellah, *Religion in Human Evolution: From the Paleolithic to the Axial Age* (Cambridge, MA: Belknap-Harvard, 2011), 377.

page 3: "There was once a Sufi": Idries Shah, *The Magic Monastery* (London: Jonathan Cape, 1972), 32.

page 5: The plagiarism quote appears in many places, but we came across it first in an article by Hugh Thomson Kerr Jr., professor of theology at Princeton Theological Seminary and senior editor of the ecumenical religious quarterly *Theology Today* from 1950 until his death in 1992: "Preacher, Professor, Editor," *Theology Today* 45:1 (April 1988), 2.

page 6: The Martin Buber quotation is from his preface to *Tales of the Hasidim* (combined edition), (New York: Schocken, 1991 [1947]).

page 6: Anne Lamott on "grace," from, *Traveling Mercies: Some Thoughts on Faith* (New York: Anchor, 2001 [1999]), 143.

page 8: Anthony de Mello on the sources of stories, from *The Prayer of the Frog*, vol. 1 and vol. 2 (Anand, India: Gujarat Sahitya Prakash, 1989), xxiii.

NOTES ON BEYOND "SPIRITUALITY"

page 9: Pulitzer Prize–winning novelist Marilynne Robinson spoke at Harvard University in 2008: "Credo," *Harvard Divinity Bulletin* 36:2 (Spring 2008).

page 9: The stories of "Reb Yerachmiel ben Yisrael" may be found at "The Virtual Rebbe," http://www.hasidicstories.com/Articles/Learning_From_Stories/virtual.html—table_contents, http://v.gd/SMKmSb; they are the work of Rabbi Rami M. Shapiro, author of *Open Secrets: The Letters of Reb Yerachmiel ben Yisrael* (Monkfish Book Publishing) and appear here with his kind permission.

page 10: Alan Watts and "effing the ineffable": cf. Louis Nordstrom and Richard Pilgrim, "The wayward mysticism of Alan Watts," *Philosophy East and West*, 33:3 (July 1980), 381; an interesting treatment may be found at http://christinaondrus.com/writing.html, http://v.gd/JSS6EK (accessed August 13, 2013).

page 11: D. H. Lawrence, *Women in Love* (Mineola, NY: Dover, 2002 [1920]), 353.

page 12: On the origins of religion and spirituality, we rely primarily on the Native American stories that we know; but cf. also George E. Vaillant, *Spiritual Evolution* (New York: Broadway, 2008) and Robert N. Bellah, *Religion in Human Evolution* (Cambridge, MA: Belknap-Harvard, 2011).

page 13: Two brothers: Wilkie Au, *By Way of the Heart* (New York: Paulist, 1989), 46, citing Belden C. Lane, "Rabbinical Stories: A Primer on Theological Method," *Christian Century* 98:41 (December 16, 1981), 1307–1308.

page 15: Joan Robinson's *Economic Philosophy* (1962) is quoted in Fred Hirsch, *Social Limits to Growth* (Cambridge, MA: Harvard, 1976), 87.

page 16: The cobbler: Anthony de Mello, *The Prayer of the Frog*, vol. 1, 9.

page 16: "Spiritual rather than religious": on this distinction, the literature is vast; see, e.g., Peter C. Hill, et al., "Conceptualizing Religion and Spirituality: Points of Commonality, Points of Departure," *Journal for the Theory of Social Behaviour* 30:1 (2000), 51–77; Penny Long Marler and C. Kirk Hadaway, "'Being Religious' or 'Being Spiritual' in America: A Zero-Sum Proposition?," *Journal for the Scientific Study of Religion* 41:2 (Jun. 2002), 289–300; Sandra M. Schneiders, I.H.M.,

"Religion and Spirituality: Strangers, Rivals, or Partners?," http://www.liturgy.
co.nz/spirituality/reflections_assets/schneiders.pdf, http://v.gd/UX23gH, (accessed August 7, 2013), and "Religion vs. Spirituality: A Contemporary Conundrum," *Spiritus: A Journal of Christian Spirituality* 3:2 (Fall 2003), 163–185; also
Philip Sheldrake, "Spirituality and the Integrity of Theology," *Spiritus* 7 (2007),
93–98; Amy Hollywood, "Spiritual But Not Religious: The vital interplay between submission and freedom," *Harvard Divinity Bulletin* 38:1&2 (Winter/
Spring 2010). Of special interest may be "Spiritual But Not Religious? Please Stop
Boring Me," a Huffington Post blog column http://www.huffingtonpost.com/
lillian-daniel/spiritual-but-not-religio_b_959216.html,http://v.gd/CIsUAc,that
drew much attention when published. A commentary on that column, http://
v.gd/rGE3QO (this one is absolutely too long to offer unshortened), although
written from a denominational perspective, merits thoughtful reading for its
treatment of community.

page 17: The use of *beyond* as a verb was pioneered by literary scholar and philosopher Kenneth Burke, who first applied it to Aristotle's use of catharsis in his
Rhetoric; cf. Kenneth Burke, "I, Eye, Ay: Emerson's Early Essay on 'Nature':
Thoughts on the Machinery of Transcendence," *The Sewanee Review* 74.4 (1966):
875–895; Richard M. Coe, "Defining rhetoric—and us," *Journal of Advanced Com-
position* 10.1 (1990): 39–52. "Beyond" is treated at greater depth in the segment on
Wonder.

page 17: The Master Shaku Soen story is from Irmgard Schloegl, *The Wisdom of the Zen
Masters* (New York: New Directions, 1975), 21.

page 17: Stephen Bamber's "The Spiritual Self" may be found at http://www.william-
whitepapers.com/pr/Dr. Stephen Bamber on The Spiritual Self.pdf, http://v.gd/
tGMEfF (accessed October 10, 2013).

page 18: Jeffrey M. Georgi, "Spirituality, AA and Religion," *The Counselor* (1999) 26.

page 19: The Ava caravan story may be found in Maung Htin Aung, *Burmese Monk's
Tales* (New York: Columbia University Press, 1966), 107–108.

page 20: The Reb Yerachmiel stories that follow and the text and quotation that follow them appear at "The Virtual Rebbe," http://www.hasidicstories.com/Arti-
cles/Learning_From_Stories/virtual.html—table_contents,   http://v.gd/
SMKmSb; as noted above, they are the work of Rabbi Rami M. Shapiro, author of
Open Secrets: The Letters of Reb Yerachmiel ben Yisrael (Monkfish Book Publishing)
and appear here with his kind permission; the Asher Yotzor is actually recited as
one leaves the bathroom. Gratitude to Rabbi Shais Taub, author of *God of Our
Understanding: Jewish Spirituality and Recovery from Addiction* (Jersey City, NJ:
KTAV, 2011), for this information and clarification.

page 24: Edward Kinerk, "Toward a Method for the Study of Spirituality," *Review for
Religious* 40:1 (1991), 3–4, italics added.

page 24: Edward C. Sellner, *Soul-Making: The Telling of a Spiritual Journey* (Mystic, CT:
Twenty-Third Publications, 1991).

page 24: Jerome Dollard, quoted by Thomas Prugh, "Alcohol, Spirituality and Recovery," *Alcohol Health and Research World* 10:2 (Winter 1985/86), 28-31, 53.

page 24: D. H. Lawrence is quoted without specific citation in *Parabola* (Fall 2011).

page 24: Sandra Marie Schneiders, "Religion vs. Spirituality: A Contemporary Conundrum," 165.

page 25: Einstein and counting: according to Quote Investigator, this quotation often credited to Einstein is more accurately attributed to William Bruce Cameron: http://v.gd/4bEXRY,http://quoteinvestigator.com/2010/05/26/everything-counts-einstein/ (accessed August 7, 2013).

page 25: On "way of life, way of being," cf. Pierre Hadot, *Philosophy as a Way of Life* (Oxford, UK: Blackwell, 1995), subtitled "Spiritual Exercises from Socrates to Foucault"; also, pursuing the same point more directly, Robert C. Solomon, *Spirituality for the Skeptic* (New York: Oxford, 2002).

NOTES ON EXPERIENCE

page 27: The Montaigne quotation is from his essay "Of Experience," which may be found at http://oregonstate.edu/instruct/phl302/texts/montaigne/montaigne-essays-8.html—XXI, http://v.gd/Z3x3bu (accessed August 8, 2013).

page 27: Sandra Marie Schneiders' words appear in "Religion vs. Spirituality: A Contemporary Conundrum," *Spiritus: A Journal of Christian Spirituality* 3:2 (Fall 2003), 165.

page 28: The cowboy and the Indian: Anthony de Mello, *The Prayer of the Frog*, vol. 1, 46.

page 28: "Unawareness is the root of all evil": cf. Simon Tugwell, *Ways of Imperfection* (Springfield, IL: Templegate, 1985), 16.

page 29: On "participation prior to . . . belief," cf. Margaret Miles, *Practicing Christianity* (New York: Crossroad, 1988), p. 89: "In the twentieth century, a secular privileging of intellectual and psychological understanding has led to a widespread assumption that change in behavior follows, rather than precedes, insight. . . . In contrast to twentieth-century consensus, most historical people thought it obvious that insight follows change; changed behavior—changed activities—produce insight. . . . We do not take seriously enough the constant monitory reminders in historical devotional manuals that practices are a sine qua non of understanding." The admonitions of William James, John Dewey, and others to "Act yourself into a new way of thinking" recapture the classic understanding.

page 29: Carol P. Christ, *Diving Deep & Surfacing: Women Writers on Spiritual Quest* (Boston, MA: Beacon, 1980), 5.

page 29: The William James quotation is from *The Principles of Psychology*, vol. 1 (New York: Cosimo, 2007 [1890]), 402.

page 29: A stronger version of the Viennese surgeon story is told of Sophia by David W. Jones, *For the Love of Sophia: Wisdom Stories from Around the World and Across the Ages* (Nashville, TN: Valjean, 2010), 3.

page 30: "aroma and taste": The lack of attention to aroma has been lamented, for example, by Herbert Weiner in his study *9½ Mystics: The Kabbala Today* (New York: Holt, Reinhart & Winston, 1969), 232–233: ". . . smell seems to be one of the senses which has been eliminated from modern worship. Only the Catholic and Orthodox censers offer a reminder of the central role which incense and odor once played in religion. . . . This elimination from worship of a sense which mystical literature has always recognized as the most spiritual of men's sensory faculties is probably part of the general disembodiment of religion. To recognize the mood-evocative power of perfume in the relations of man and woman, while ignoring its possibilities in the romance of man and God, is surely a mistake."

page 30: "The scholar approached the Master": lightly adapted from Anthony de Mello, *Taking Flight* (New York: Doubleday-Image, 1990), 70.

page 31: A version of the two rabbinic sons story may be found at http://rabbionan-arrowbridge.blogspot.com/2009_10_01_archive.html, http://v.gd/FEi3wn.

page 32: See the Randy Pausch entry in Wikipedia or, better, Wikiquote; for those who have not yet seen *The Last Lecture*, http://www.youtube.com/watch?v=ji5_MqicxSo, http://v.gd/dBxIH2 .

page 32: Gadamer is quoted by Martin Jay, *Songs of Experience* (Berkeley, CA: University of California, 2005), 402.

page 32: Dying rabbi: William J. Bausch, *In the Beginning, There Were Stories* (Mystic, CT: Twenty-Third Publications, 2004), 93–94.

page 33: St. Bernard in Jean Leclercq, *The Love of Learning and the Desire for God* (New York: Fordham University, 1982 [1961]), 5.

page 33: Wendy Doniger O'Flaherty, *Other Peoples' Myths* (New York: Macmillan, 1988), 23.

page 34: The story of Naaman is related in *2nd Kings*, chapter 5.

page 35: The samurai and monk story is told by Ram Dass and Paul Gorman in *How Can I Help?* (New York: Knopf, 1985), 99–100.

page 36: A version of "Fishing in a bed of roses" may be found in *The Trout Bait Recipe Book*, http://www.troutbaitrecipes.com/0000004576au/th345thurslc98790/trout 1315ebookfinal2009.pdf, http://v.gd/hOvgTO (accessed November 27, 2013), 23.

page 37: Huxley is quoted without citation by Laurence J. Peter, *Peter's Quotations* (New York: William Morrow & Co., 1977), 185; it is attributed by Wikiquote to *Texts and Pretexts* (1932), 5.

page 38: The James quotation is from op. cit., 244.

page 39: To speak of the "heart" carries dangers. Too much soft sentimentality has been wrapped around the image of this bodily organ. As philosopher Martha

Nussbaum details in *Upheavals of Thought: The Intelligence of Emotions* (Cambridge, UK: Cambridge University, 2001), "the heart" does not signify merely feelings: classically, in the true imagery of the imagination, the "head" generates ideas while the "heart" produces understanding; for an earlier discussion of the point, see Thomas Taaffe, "Education of the Heart," *Cross Currents* 49:3 (Fall 1999).

page 39: Mary Midgley, "Against Humanism," The New Humanist.org.uk, 125:6 (Nov./ Dec. 2010): http://rationalist.org.uk/articles/2419/against-humanism, http://v.gd/ 7OyUCL (accessed October 13, 2013).

page 40: The Aish quotation is from the daily newsletter of October 23, 2011.

page 40: For the Egyptian use and understanding of "heart," cf. Bellah, *Religion in Human Evolution*, 239; for ancient China, Bellah, op. cit., 445, 464f., 468–471; the quotation on early biblical literature is from Michael Downey, *A Blessed Weakness: The Spirit of Jean Vanier and l'Arche* (San Francisco, CA: Harper & Row, 1986), 58.

page 41: The Rabbi Baer story is drawn from Kenneth Paul Kramer, Martin Buber's *Spirituality: Hasidic Wisdom for Everyday Life* (Lanham, MD: Rowman & Littlefield, 2012), 22, and the *puppik* story from Zalman Schachter and Edward Hoffman, *Sparks of Light: Counseling in the Hasidic Tradition* (Boulder, CO: Shambhala, 1983), 107.

page 41: The interpretation of Jonathan Edwards is by Richard Lovelace, "Edwards' Theology: Puritanism Meets a New Age," *Christian History* magazine 8 (1985), 18–19.

page 42: The quotation following is from Page Smith, *Killing the Spirit* (New York: Penguin, 1990), 200.

page 42 "the wisdom of the heart's experience": For a sensitive, in-depth exploration of the imagery of the heart in ancient and early Christian times, see Peter Brown, *The Body & Society* (New York: Columbia University, 1988). For a useful albeit brief discussion of the significance of "heart" image and language on the cusp between the medieval and modern worlds, cf. the treatment of Blaise Pascal by Robert Bellah, *Religion in Human Evolution*, 108ff.

page 43: James's Cambridge words are reported by Jackson Lears, "The Thought Experimenter," *Nation*, February 8, 2007.

page 44: The "Uncertainty" quotation is also from Lears, again quoting James, the italics Lears's.

NOTES ON WONDER

page 45: The full Tolstoy quotation, from his *Essays, Letters and Miscellanies*, runs: "If, then, I were asked for the most important advice I could give, that which I considered to be the most useful to the men of our century, I should simply say: in the name of God, stop a moment, cease your work, look around you."

page 45: The Moltmann quotation is from his article "The Unity of the Triune God," *St. Vladimir's Theological Quarterly* 28:3 (1984), quoting St. Gregory of Nyssa.

page 45: Rachel Carson's "The Sense of Wonder" first appeared in the *Woman's Home Companion* in July 1956, 25-27, 46-48, under the title "Help Your Child to Wonder"; available at library.fws.gov/Carson/WHC-july56.pdf, http://v.gd/HaIhAv (accessed October 19, 2013).

page 46: Specifically on "reverence," cf. Paul Woodruff, *Reverence: Renewing a Forgotten Virtue* (New York: Oxford, 2001), a work that nicely complements the Robert C. Solomon book *Spirituality for the Skeptic*, noted above.

page 46: Elpenor's "A Drunkard's Progress" comes from *Harper's* magazine, October 1986.

page 46: Marilynne Robinson's "Credo," op. cit.

page 47: Rabbi Marc Gellman's "The Right Way to Pray?" was reported by Zev Chafets in the *New York Times*, September 16, 2009.

page 48: "Questions like that": The writer John Updike did think on such questions. He wrote: "Ancient religion and modern science agree: we are here to give praise. Or, to slightly tip the expression, to pay attention. Without us, the physicists who have espoused the anthropic principle tell us, the universe would be unwitnessed, and in a real sense not there at all. It exists, incredibly, for us. This formulation (knowing what we know of the universe's ghastly extent) is more incredible, to our sense of things, than the Old Testament hypothesis of a God willing to suffer, coddle, instruct, and even (in the Book of Job) to debate with men, in order to realize the meager benefit of worship, of praise for His Creation. What we beyond doubt do have is our instinctive intellectual curiosity about the universe from the quasars down to the quarks, our wonder at existence itself, and an occasional surge of sheer blind gratitude for being here." http://www.brainpickings.org/index.php/2012/09/17/the-meaning-of-life/, http://v.gd/QcrWnt (accessed August 13, 2013).

page 48: William H. Herr's "To the Unknown God" appeared in *The Critic* (Summer 1994).

page 49: Thoughts on "victims" as an aftermath of the Enlightenment can be found in Christopher Lasch, *The True and Only Heaven: Progress and Its Critics* (New York: W. W. Norton, 1991); Charles J. Sykes, *A Nation of Victims: The Decay of the American Character* (New York: St. Martin's Press, 1992); and Joseph Amato, *Victims and Values: A History and a Theory of Suffering* (Westport, CT: Greenwood, 1990).

page 49: Morris Mandel's thought appears in the *Jewish World Review*, April 13, 2011, http://www.jewishworldreview.com/0411/index041311.php3, http://v.gd/aoru3z (accessed October 19, 2013).

page 49: On the distinction between *logos* and *muthos* as it was developed by the ancient Greeks, cf. Bellah, *Religion in Human Evolution*, 389–390. This distinction is more fully developed in the segment on Wisdom.

page 50: The "Oops!" story was told by Rabbi Hirsch Chinn at a 1994 "Spiritual Day" put on in New York City by JACS (Jewish Alcoholics, Chemically Dependent Persons, and Significant Others).

page 51: The insight about mythic stories is usually attributed to the fourth-century Roman historian and mystic Sallustius.

page 51: "Beyond": There is a special spiritual richness in this word; as Robert N. Bellah notes in *Religion in Human Evolution*, 9: "Without the capacity for self-transcendence, for seeing the realm of daily life in terms of a realm beyond it, without the capacity for 'beyonding,' as Burke put it, one would be trapped in a world of what has been called dreadful immanence. For the world of daily life seen solely as a world of rational response to anxiety and need is a world of mechanical necessity, not radical autonomy. It is through pointing to other realities, through beyonding, that religion and poetry . . . break the dreadful fatalities of this world of appearances." The reference to Kenneth Burke is to his *Language as Symbolic Action*: "to beyond . . . to see something in terms of something beyond it"; 199–200, 298–299; cf. also Benjamin I. Schwartz, "The Age of Transcendence," *Daedalus* 104:2 (Spring 1975), 1–7, writing of "a strain towards transcendence . . . a kind of standing back and looking beyond. . . ."

page 52: The Brahman and the milkmaid story has been adapted from several sources, including the telling by Heinrich Zimmer, "Walking on Water: A Parable of Liberation," *Parabola*, August 1990.

page 53: On Awesome, cf. Neal Whitman, "The Greatest Love of 'Awe,'" http://www.visualthesaurus.com/cm/dictionary/the-greatest-love-of-awe/ http://v.gd/i6GeWE (accessed August 18, 2013).

page 53: Paul Brockelman's, *The Inside Story: A Narrative Approach to Religious Understanding and Truth* (Albany, NY: SUNY Press, 1992) remains a worthy read.

page 54: The Philip K. Dick reality quotation is from "How To Build a Universe That Doesn't Fall Apart Two Days Later," available at http://deoxy.org/pkd_how2build.htm, http://v.gd/0cMEml (accessed November 27, 2013).

page 54: The puzzle-mystery point is interestingly made at http://v.gd/ZpKcj4, http://www.farnamstreetblog.com/2012/02/whats-the-difference-between-a-puzzle-and-a-mystery/, accessed November 28, 2013.

page 54: Ken Kesey was interviewed by Robert Faggen in *The Paris Review*, Spring 1994, "The Art of Fiction."

page 55: C. S. Lewis's *The Abolition of Man* was originally published in 1944; it is available in a 2001 reprint from HarperCollins.

page 55: The Einstein quotation is drawn from his 1930 essay "The World as I See It."

page 56: Maurice Friedman, *A Dialogue with Hasidic Tales: Hallowing the Everyday* (New York: Human Sciences Press, 1988).

page 56: Aldous Huxley's little-known 1925 *Those Barren Leaves* is available as a free pdf download at http://cewebinocy.webs.com/apps/blog/show/prev?from_id=23685296 (accessed October 19, 2013), http://v.gd/DfSheN.

page 59: The shohet story is told by Zalman Schachter-Shalomi in *Spiritual Intimacy* (Northvale, NJ: Jason Aronson, 1991).

page 60: Excerpts from Lao Tzu, *Tao Te Ching: A New English Version*, by Ursula K. Le Guin. This translation may be found at http://www.bopsecrets.org/gateway/ passages/tao-te-ching.htm, http://v.gd/wPgh7T, about halfway down the long page (accessed August 5, 2013).

NOTES ON COMMUNITY

page 61: Mark Nepo, "Unfinished Painting," *Parabola* (Winter 2011).

page 61: The Mennonite farmer story is from "The Testament of Friends," *The Christian Century*, February 28, 1990, 212, reported by Paul H. Jones, "Tarry at the Cross: A Christian Response to the Holocaust," *Perspectives* 7:3 (March 1992), 15.

page 62: Peter Kropotkin, *Mutual Aid: A Factor of Evolution* (London: William Heinemann, 1907), 61ff.; more recently, Frans de Waal, *The Age of Empathy* (New York: Three Rivers/ Random House, 2009); Edward O. Wilson, *The Social Conquest of Earth* (New York: Liveright/Norton, 2012).

page 63: The well-known Rabbi Hillel quotation is from *Ethics of the Fathers* 1:14.

page 64: "pay attention to yourself": was imprinted irrevocably on the Western tradition by Evagrius Ponticus, who is treated at depth in *The Spirituality of Imperfection*, pp. 74 ff.; for its expression in another tradition, see http://www .brahmakumaris.org/interactive/cottmessages/detail.html?itemid=0edc2890-6519-47b4-b625-a4729cb4ac8f, http://v.gd/1uVx9A (accessed October 10, 2013).

page 64: "Participation in community": A helpful treatment of the role of stories in communities may be found in Julian Rappaport, "Narrative Studies, Personal Stories, and Identity Transformation in the Mutual Help Context," *Journal of Applied Behavioral Science* 29:2 (June 1993), 239–256; also Julian Rappaport and Ronald Simkins, "Healing and Empowering Through Community Narrative," *Prevention in Human Services* 10:1 (1991), 29–50.

page 64: "The company of the saints": For two different traditions, see http://www. beingfrank.co.nz/in-the-company-of-saints-we-become-saints, http://v.gd/ 1vxJSX and http://www.satnaam.info/index.php?option=com_content&task= view&id=169&Itemid=22, http://v.gd/r9wpzn (both accessed August 10, 2013).

page 64: The Breytenbach quotation is from "Why Are Writers Always the Last to Know?," *New York Times Book Review*, March 28, 1993.

page 64: Heaven and Hell and spoons comes from Terry Webb, *Tree of Renewed Life* (New York: Crossroad, 1992), 33.

page 65: "94-year-old man": "Metropolitan Diary," *New York Times*, November 6, 1996.

page 66: "shared story": "People listen to stories not merely to learn something new (communication), but to relive, together, the stories that they already know, stories about themselves (communion)." Wendy Doniger O'Flaherty, *Other Peoples' Myths*, 148.

page 68: G[ilbert] K[eith] Chesterton, *What's Wrong With the World* (New York: Dodd, Mead & Co., 1918 [1910]) (available on Project Gutenberg http://www.gutenberg .org/files/1717/1717-h/1717-h.htm, http://v.gd/mqpxFi).

page 68: On the lack of "a sense of community": cf. Mary Ann Glendon, *Rights Talk: The Impoverishment of Political Discourse* (New York: Free Press, 1991).

page 69: On depression, shame, and community, cf. Thomas J. Scheff, "Shame and Community: Social Components in Depression," *Psychiatry* 64:3 (Fall 2001), 212–224; also Scheff, "Shame and the Social Bond: A Sociological Theory," *Sociological Theory* 18:1 (March 2000), 84–99.

page 69: Gilbert C. Meilaender, *The Theory and Practice of Virtue* (Notre Dame, IN: University of Notre Dame Press, 1984), 165–176 & passim; also Glendon, *Rights Talk*.

page 70: Rabbi Hillel Goldberg, "What is Greatness?" *Jewish World Review*, November 16, 2001; the whole piece is reproduced at http://www.jewishworldreview.com/ hillel/greatness.asp, http://v.gd/6YQGLb (accessed August 10, 2013).

page 71: Lawrence Kushner, *The Book of Words* (Woodstock, VT: Jewish Lights Publishing, 1993), 43.

page 72: William James, *The Varieties of Religious Experience: A Study in Human Nature* (New York: Longmans, Green: 1903 [1902]), 31–32.

page 73: St. Basil: Andrew Louth, "The Eastern Fathers: The Cappadocians," in Cheslyn Jones, Geoffrey Wainwright, and Edward Yarnold (eds.), *The Study of Spirituality* (New York: Oxford University Press, 1986), 165; see also Clifford Hugh Lawrence, *Medieval Monasticism* (London: Longman, 1984), 10.

page 73: Dag Hammarskjöld, *Markings* (New York: Ballantine, 1964), 85.

pages 73: Our study of Buber has been much informed by Steven Kepnes, *The Text as Thou: Martin Buber's Dialogical Hermeneutics and Narrative Theology* (Bloomington, IN: Indiana University, 1992), 111ff., especially the note on 187.

page 74: "Why Moses?": David N. Bell, *Wholly Animals: A Book of Beastly Tales* (Kalamazoo, MI: Cistercian Publications, 1992), 101.

page 74: "I begin to realize": Martin Buber, "The Man of Today and the Jewish Bible," *Israel and the World: Essays in a Time of Crisis* (New York: Schocken, 1948), 99; see also Donald J. Moore, "Buber's Challenge to Christian Theology," *Thought* 62:247 (December 1987), 395: "After years of study and interpretation of Hasidic texts and stories, Buber became convinced that at the heart of Hasidism was the simple message that we cannot approach the divine in any other way than by becoming human. To become human is what each individual person is created for."

page 75: Elie Wiesel, *From the Kingdom of Memory* (New York: Summit, 1990), 76.

page 76: The "nameless survivor" story is found in Yaffa Eliach, *Hasidic Tales of the Holocaust* (New York: Oxford, 1982), 107, quoting what a survivor had told Arnost Lustig.

NOTES ON DARK

page 78: The Kafka quotation is from a letter to Oskar Pollak, November 8, 1903; cited from Max Brod (ed.), *Briefe*, 1902-1924 (New York: Schocken, 1958), 27; translation from Frederick R. Karl, Franz Kafka, *Representative Man* (New York: Ticknor & Fields, 1991), 98.

page 78: The de Unamuno quotation is from Miguel de Unamuno, *The Tragic Sense of Life in Men and in Peoples*, trans. J. E. Crawford Flitch (London: Macmillan, 1921 [1913]), 135.

page 79: The Lida story is via Liesl Schillinger, "Disturbing the Comfortable," *New York Times*, November 22, 2009, review of Ludmilla Petrushevskaya, "Incident at Soloniki," in *There Once Lived a Woman Who Tried to Kill Her Neighbor's Baby* (London: Penguin, 2009), 12–14.

page 80: The Grushenka story is also retold by Schillinger, loc. cit.

page 81: The Murdering Mule story may be found on the Aish "All Jokes" page: http://www.aish.com/j/j/a/, http://v.gd/DQV8eb (accessed November 27, 2013).

page 81: Eugene O'Neill, "Even as a Child," http://v.gd/QPhUQS (accessed October 19, 2013), http://www.poemhunter.com/poem/even-as-a-child/.

page 82: "only one arm and one leg": see http://www.snopes.com/military/amputee.asp, http://v.gd/YY44Hx (accessed November 27, 2013).

page 84: There are many versions of The Little Snow Girl story, all based on a Russian folktale: we have adapted one from the World Folktales website: http://www.eslstation.net/theREALWF/Synopsis_Snow_girl.htm, http://v.gd/dN8jQx (accessed August 18, 2013).

page 86: "it faced a blank wall": William J. Bausch, *A World of Stories for Preachers and Teachers*, 243.

page 89: The Etzioni piece appeared as "Good Grief" in the *New York Times*, October 7, 2006.

page 90: The second long quotation is from Alida Gersie, op. cit., 149.

page 91: The John Bowker quotation is from *The Meanings of Death* (Cambridge, UK: Cambridge University Press, 1991), 42.

page 91: This de Unamuno quote is from op. cit., 17.

page 94: The final text quotation comes from Colman McCarthy, "Sister Maureen's Women Worth Fighting For," *National Catholic Reporter* 26:3 (November 3, 1989).

NOTES ON LISTENING

page 95: David Michael Levin, *The Listening Self* (London: Routledge, 1989), 17.

Notes

page 95: Søren Kierkegaard, *Either/Or*, vol. 1, trans. David F. Swenson and Lilian Marvin Swenson (Princeton, NJ: Princeton University Press, 1959 [1944]), 66.

page 95: Charles Horton Cooley proposed and built upon the looking-glass image; links to most of Cooley's works may be found at http://www.sociosite.net/topics/sociologists.php—COOLEY, http://v.gd/0Bdcnb (accessed October 19, 2013). Although using different imagery, Jonathan Haidt makes substantially the same argument in *The Righteous Mind* (New York: Vintage, 2012), see especially chapter 4.

page 96: "The Silk Drum" has been adapted from various sources, including P. L. Travers, *Parabola* 5:2 (1980).

page 98: Donald P. McNeill, Douglas A. Morrison, and Henri Nouwen, *Compassion* (New York: Doubleday, 1982), 13–14.

page 98: Earle M., *Physician, Heal Thyself* (Minneapolis: CompCare, 1989), 203.

page 100: Herbert Weiner, *9½ Mystics: The Kabbala Today*, 14–15; see also Levin, op. cit., 35: "The future of the world which the humanism of the Enlightenment inaugurated seems to call, now, for the restitution of the Hebraic tradition, a tradition that has always emphasized the communicativeness of listening more than the possessiveness of vision."

page 100: On Benedict, http://www.osb.org/rb/ and http://www.intratext.com/IXT/LAT0011/_P1.HTM, http://v.gd/1p2R1A (accessed August 10, 2013); "Obsculta" is sometimes rendered "Ausculta"; for Bernard, http://blog.gaiam.com/quotes/authors/saint-bernard-clairvaux , http://v.gd/tMPh36, and scroll down a bit.

page 101: math homework: http://www.ebaumsworld.com/jokes/read/382544/, http://v.gd/s1Chf1 (accessed October 30, 2013).

page 102: "which only you can hear": http://hasidicstories.com/Articles/Learning_From_Stories/virtual.html [another Reb Yerachmiel story—see initial note at Beyond "Spirituality," above.]

page 103: Much of what appears here on Carol Gilligan was inspired by or in reader's dialogue with Mihaly Csikszentmihalyi, "More Ways Than One to Be Good," review of Carol Gilligan et al. (eds.), *Mapping the Moral Domain, New York Times Book Review*, May 28, 1989.

page 104: "Two stars shining": Anthony de Mello, *The Prayer of the Frog*, vol. 2, 110.

page 104: "Being claimed by what is being said": the works of Hans-Georg Gadamer express this as fully and thoroughly, although not always as clearly as those of other thinkers. Two quotations germane to this segment: "We cannot understand without wanting to understand, that is, without wanting to let something be said." Also: "When you look at something, you can also look away from it by looking in another direction. But you cannot 'hear away.'" Hans-Georg Gadamer, *Truth and Method* (New York: Continuum, 2004 [1975]), 458.

page 105: "knowing that I'm still with her": Bausch, *A World of Stories for Preachers and Teachers*, 285.

page 105: "Listen yourself into a new way of seeing": "Vision is a spectator," John Dewey wrote. "Hearing is a participator."

page 108: Joshua Bell: http://www.washingtonpost.com/wp-dyn/content/article/ 2007/04/04/AR2007040401721.html, http://v.gd/Js5tV2 (accessed August 10, 2013); the story appeared in the *Washington Post*, April 8, 2007; be sure to scroll down and turn up your speakers: This article includes four thirty-second clips of Bell's performance.

page 110: the brick: http://www.simplyjune.org/2011/11/brick.html, http://v.gd/OJ-DiMt (accessed October 17, 2013).

page 111: J. R. R. Tolkien, "On Fairy Stories," *Tree and Leaf* (Boston, MA: Houghton Mifflin, 1965).

page 111: the cricket and the coins: Bausch, *A World of Stories for Preachers and Teachers*, 339.

NOTES ON FORGIVENESS

page 113: William Arthur Ward is one of America's most quoted writers of inspirational maxims; see his Wikipedia entry: http://en.wikipedia.org/wiki/ William_Arthur_Ward, http://v.gd/gKX5Fz (accessed October 30, 2013).

page 113: John Patton, *Is Human Forgiveness Possible?* (Nashville, TN: Abingdon, 1985), 16.

page 113: The "Paco" story is labeled "Bits & Pieces, October 15, 1992, p. 13" and may be found at http://www.sermonillustrations.com/a-z/f/forgiveness.htm, http:// v.gd/X0jy0q (accessed October 31, 2013).

page 113: Hannah Arendt, *The Human Condition* (Chicago, IL: University of Chicago, 1958), 241.

page 114: Dag Hammarskjöld, *Markings*, 105.

page 114: Paul Tillich, *The New Being* (New York: Charles Scribner's Sons, 1955), 13.

page 114: William R. Miller, "As We Forgive," Sermon at St. Andrew Presbyterian Church, Albuquerque, NM, November 4, 2007, available at http://www.william rmiller.net/download/As We Forgive.pdf, http://v.gd/J7ePnN. (accessed August 10, 2013); an excellent published treatment is H. J. N. Horsbrugh, "Forgiveness," *Canadian Journal of Philosophy* 4:2 (Dec. 1974), 269–282.

page 114: Abbot Anastasius: cf. Thomas Merton, *The Wisdom of the Desert*, Google eBook, XVII; for another perspective on "forgiving is not forgetting," see D. M. Dooling, "This Word Forgiveness," *Parabola* 12:3 (August 1987), 6–9: "If forgiving were equivalent to forgetting, it would make it possible to believe that forgiving is indeed an act that human beings are capable of initiating, since forgetting comes quite easily to humankind; but in fact we are incapable of that large act of acceptance and exchange unless we are acted upon by something greater than ourselves."

page 118: The Sufi story: for a deeper treatment of condoning, see R. S. Downie, "Forgiveness," *The Philosophical Quarterly* 15:59 (Apr. 1965), 130–131.

page 118: Marilynne Robinson, "Credo," op.cit.

page 119: A slightly different version of the snake tale may be found in Roger D. Abrahams, *African Folktales* (New York: Pantheon, 1983), 140–141.

page 120: Denis Donoghue, "Whose Trope Is It Anyway?" reviewing Richard Poirier, *The Renewal of Literature: Emersonian Reflections, The New York Review of Books* 34:11 (June 25, 1987), 6.

page 120: For a telling context of Niebuhr on forgiveness, see http://www.mbird.com/2010/10/cruelty-of-righteous-people/, http://v.gd/cxwQSZ, especially the final paragraph (accessed August 11, 2013).

page 121: Steen Halling, et al., "Exploring Self-Forgiveness," unpublished paper, Seattle University; a useful development of this research may be found at http://upetd.up.ac.za/thesis/available/etd-06172004-123504/unrestricted/02chapter2.pdf, http://v.gd/cmelya (accessed August 11, 2013).

page 122: Gordon E. Marino, "The Epidemic of Forgiveness," *Commonweal* 122:6 (March 24, 1995), 10, quoting Bishop Butler.

page 122: Lewis Hyde, *The Gift* (Edinburgh: Canongate, 2006), 60.

page 122: Anne Lamott, *Traveling Mercies: Some Thoughts on Faith* (New York: Anchor, 2001 [1999]), 213, who also said, ibid. 134: "Not forgiving is like drinking rat poison and then waiting for the rat to die."

page 122: The Padshah tale is from *Sa'di, Tales from the Gulistan* (London: Philip Allan, 1928), 3.

page 123: Marino, op. cit., 10; Marino points out that as Jeffrie G. Murphy and Jean Hampton argue in *Forgiveness and Mercy* (Cambridge, UK: Cambridge University Press, 1988), 17 et passim, "the concept of forgiveness is traditionally bound up with the idea of a restored relationship . . . and it takes two to restore a relationship."

page 124: On self-forgiveness see also Julie C. Hall & Frank D. Fincham, "Self-Forgiveness: The Stepchild of Forgiveness Research," *Journal of Social and Clinical Psychology* 24:5 (2005), 621–637.

page 124: The swimming image is from George Aichele Jr., "Poverty and the Hermeneutics of Repentance," *CrossCurrents* 38:4 (Winter 1988–1989), 461.

page 125: Steen Halling, "Shame and Forgiveness," *The Humanistic Psychologist* 22:1 (Spring 1994), 79.

page 125: The Readers' Guide point is made by Doris Donnelly, *Learning to Forgive* (Nashville, TN: Abingdon, 1979), unpaged "Introduction."

page 126: "Resentment is the number one offender": *Alcoholics Anonymous*, 64.

page 127: On the connection between forgiveness and gratitude, see Loren Toussaint & Philip Friedman, "Forgiveness, Gratitude, and Well-Being: The Mediating Role of Affect and Beliefs," *Journal of Happiness Studies* 10 (2009), 635–654; a more popular treatment appears at http://www.byregion.net/articles-healers/ HeartHealing.html, http://v.gd/FGGMYQ (accessed August 11, 2013).

page 127: Rabbi Abiah: Louis I. Newman, *Maggidim and Hasidim* (New York: Bloch, 1962), 95.

page 128: For Islam and the divine names and the primacy of compassion, see Charles Le Gai Eaton, *Islam and the Destiny of Man* (Albany, NY: SUNY Press, 1985).

page 128: Rabbi Benjamin Blech, "Forgive the Terrorists?", http://www.jewish-worldreview.com/0911/love_terrorists.php3, http://v.gd/jIKFsW (accessed October 12, 2013).

page 129: Rabbi Levi Yitzhak: Susan Handelman, "Emunah: The Craft of Faith," *CrossCurrents* 42:3 (Fall 1992), 308.

NOTES ON HUMOR

page 130: The opening story is from Nathan Ausubel, *A Treasury of Jewish Folklore* (New York: Crown, 1948), 264.

page 131: Niebuhr is quoted by Doris Donnelly, "Divine Folly: Being Religious and the Exercise of Humor," *Theology Today* 48:4 (January 1992), 387; Anne Lamott, *Plan B: Further Thoughts on Faith* (New York: Riverhead Books, 2005), 66.

page 131: E. B. White, "Some Remarks on Humor," *A Subtreasury of American Humor* (New York: Modern Library, 1948 [1941]).

page 132: "Holy Fools" and puncturing and pomposity: in addition to Doris Donnelly, "Divine Folly," see M. Conrad Hyers, *Zen and the Comic Spirit* (London: Rider & Co., 1974), 40; also William J. Bausch, *Storytelling: Imagination and Faith* (Mystic, CT: Twenty-Third Publications, 1984), 138; for the Russian *yurodivuie* as "fools for Christ's sake," cf. Sergius Bolshakoff, *Russian Mystics* (Kalamazoo, MI: Cistercian Publications, 1980), 49.

page 132: Tan-hsia: Belden C. Lane, "Merton as Zen Clown," *Theology Today* 46:3 (October 1989), 260–61; see also Hyers, op. cit., 104–05, with plate illustrating "Tan-hsia burning the Buddha-image."

page 133: James Thurber was quoted in the *New York Post* of February 29, 1960.

page 134: "The collapse of categories": George Santayana argued that at the heart of comedy lies a confusion of categories ordinarily kept distinct, like applying the formulae of theology to cookery or of cookery to theology: *The Sense of Beauty* (New York: Charles Scribner's Sons, 1896), 188.

page 134: "the union of opposites": cf. Peggy V. Beck, "In the Company of Laughter," *Parabola* 11:3 (Fall 1986), 18–25.

page 134: Jan Knappert, *Myths and Legends of the Swahili* (Nairobi: Heinemann Educational Books, 1970), 6.

page 134: The Bono story and the story behind it come in many forms, as can be verified at http://www.snopes.com/music/artists/bono.asp, http://v.gd/eKlpIJ (accessed August 11, 2013).

Notes

page 135: The Barbara Walters story is apparently another urban legend: http://urban legends.about.com/library/bl_land_mines.htm, http://v.gd/Ry5Hgn (accessed August 11, 2013).

page 139: "four-letter words": David Minkoff, *Oy! The Ultimate Book of Jewish Jokes* (New York: St. Martin's, 2005), 395.

page 139: Mississippi grandma: various at http://www.snopes.com/legal/grandma-court.asp, http://v.gd/5nPDfq (accessed October 26, 2013).

page 141: The Arthur Miller–Marilyn Monroe Passover story was told by Joseph Epstein, "Two Passover Jokes," *Commentary* (April 6, 2011).

page 142: Mrs. Moskowitz: Stan Pollack, *The Golden Age of Tongue Kissing: Brooklyn 23, NY* (New York: Xlibris, 2002), 54.

page 144: The long quotation on anecdote is from Hyers, op. cit., 150.

NOTES ON GRAY

page 147: Robert N. Bellah, et al., *The Good Society* (New York: Knopf, 1991), 51.

page 147: Michael Roemer, *Telling Stories* (Lanham, MD: Rowman & Littlefield, 1995), 85.

page 147: Frank C. Senn, "Lutheran Spirituality," in Frank C. Senn (ed.), *Protestant Spiritual Traditions* (New York: Paulist, 1986), 19.

page 148: "Upon your hearts": Jacob Needleman told this Hasidic story to Parker Palmer, who included it in his monograph "The Broken-Open Heart: Living with Faith and Hope in the Tragic Gap," *Weavings* 24:2 (2008).

page 148: Matisse and Renoir: Paulo Coelho, *Stories for Parents, Children and Grandchildren*, vol. 1 (n.p.: Lulu, 2008), 34.

page 149: David J. Wolpe, *In Speech and In Silence* (New York: Henry Holt, 1990), 26–27.

page 150: for Sappho: http://www.poemhunter.com/poem/mother-i-cannot-mind -my-wheel-2/ , http://v.gd/adJwul (accessed November 29, 2013).

page 150: Henry Alonzo Myers, *Tragedy: A View of Life* (Ithaca, NY: Cornell, 1965), 151.

page 150: Rabbi Moshe Leib: in Nochem Gringas, "Judaism, Addiction and Faith: The Spiritual Odyssey of Recovery," in S. J. Levy and S. B. Blume (eds.), *Addictions in the Jewish Community* (New York: Federation of Jewish Philanthropies, 1986), 265–296.

page 151: Bonnie Brandel, presentation at Guest House, Lake Orion, MI, October 1988.

page 152: The quotation is usually attributed to Anton Chekhov, but: http://marissa bidilla.blogspot.com/2009/06/any-idiot-can-misattribute-quote.html, http:// v.gd/Q32aYq (accessed August 11, 2013).

page 152: The Bryan story appears in Edmund Fuller, *Thesaurus of Anecdotes* (New York: Crown, 1942), 139.

page 154: Michael Roemer, op. cit., 247.

page 154: The Bedouin story: Inea Bushnaq, *Arab Folktales* (Cairo: American University in Cairo: 1986), 44.

page 156: For the Godparent story, http://www.storyfest.com/sacred-story-blog/father-cosmas-tells-how-god.html, http://v.gd/aJYorR, and scroll down quite a way (accessed August 11, 2013).

page 158: G[ilbert] K[eith] Chesterton, *What's Wrong with the World* (New York: Dodd, Mead & Co., 1918 [1910]), 35 (available on Project Gutenberg http://www.gutenberg.org/files/1717/1717-h/1717-h.htm, http://v.gd/mqpxFi).

page 158: Abraham Maslow is quoted by Rollo May, *The Cry for Myth* (New York: W. W. Norton, 1991), 294; the italics are May's.

page 158: Elie Wiesel, interview in *U.S. News & World Report*, October 27, 1986.

page 158: The Vaillant story is told by Joshua Wolf Shenk, "What Makes Us Happy?" *The Atlantic*, June 2009, 47–48; a fuller version appears in Vaillant's book *Spiritual Evolution*, 91–92.

page 159: The basket story is adapted from Alida Gersie, *Storymaking in Bereavement* (London: Jessica Kingsley, 1991), 254.

page 161: The next Roemer quotation is from op. cit., 247 (yes, the same page!).

page 161: The prayer book: Martin Buber, *Tales of the Hasidim*, (Random House e-Book, 2013), n.p.

page 161: The white hen: this Yoruba, Nigeria, story is told by Denis O'Sullivan, S.M.A. http://www.afriprov.org/index.php/african-stories-by-season/14-animal-stories/69-the-sacrifice-of-the-white-hen.html, http://v.gd/VKpUTz (accessed August 11, 2013).

page 162: The Siddur story is from Project Genesis, June 16, 2011, http://v.gd/rOcTU1 http://www.projectgenesis.org/554/open-your-heart-and-then-your-eyes/ (accessed October 12, 2013).

NOTES ON MEMORY

page 164: Kushner, *The Book of Words*, 87.

page 165: The Barrie quotation is from his rectorial address, May 3, 1922, St. Andrew's University, Scotland.

page 165: Benjamin Blech, http://www.aish.com/ci/s/What-Was-Saved-from-the-Hurricane.html, http://v.gd/1Vr4jQ (accessed October 12, 2013).

page 165: For a useful summary of the importance of memory, cf. Jacklyn Jeffrey & Glenace Edwall, *Memory and History* (Lanham, MD: University Press of America, 1994), especially Elizabeth Loftus, "Tricked by Memory."

page 165: Miguel de Unamuno, *Tragic Sense of Life*, 8.

page 166: Several versions of the young sage story can be found online; see also John Navone, "Heroes, Saints and Leaders: Models for Human Development," *Studies in Formative Spirituality* 11:1 (February 1990), 23–34: "Human growth and development is a question of having the right heroes, saints and leaders, the right models

of human development. From our earliest years we are shaped by our relationships to our parents and to the significant others whose life stories impinge upon
our own. Our earliest conduct is imitative rather than deliberately learned and
chosen.... We seldom, if ever, act according to principles and rules stated in
words and logically arranged. Rather we act according to models and stories."
page 166: Brockelman, *The Inside Story*, 58.

page 167: The "because He loves stories" story is usually attributed to Elie Wiesel, *The
Gates of the Forest* (New York: Schocken, 1995 [1966]), although it has also been
attributed to Knesset Yisrael (Reuven Zak, 1900) by Ellen Frankel, *The Classic
Tales: 4,000 Years of Jewish Lore* (Northvale, NJ: Jason Aronson, 1989), 551, attrib-
uting the English version to Martin Buber, *The Later Masters*. In his retelling of
the story in *Souls on Fire: Portraits and Legends of Hasidic Masters* (New York:
Summit, 1972), 167–168, Wiesel ends it differently, as detailed in the footnote.

page 168: "Of what story": Alasdair MacIntyre, *After Virtue* (Notre Dame, IN: University of Notre Dame, 1981), 201.

page 168: The Kierkegaard quote is one translation of his Journals IV A 164 (1843); see
Kierkegaard: *Papers and Journals: A Selection* (London: Penguin, 1996) trans.
Alastair Hannay, 63, 161.

page 168: George S. Howard, "Culture Tales," *American Psychologist* 46:3 (March 1991),
192.

page 168: Brian Swimme, "The Resurgence of Cosmic Storytellers," *The Way* 29:1
(January 1989), 27.

page 169: Barry Lopez, *Crow and Weasel* (n.p.: North Point Press, 1990), 60.

page 169: Edward S. Casey, *Spirit and Soul* (Dallas, TX: Spring Publications, 1991), 179.

page 169: Walter Benjamin, "The Storyteller," in *Illuminations* (New York: Schocken,
1969), available at http://slought.org/files/downloads/events/SF_1331-Benjamin.
pdf, http://v.gd/NkvUHH, 4–5 (accessed August 11, 2013).

page 171: Quotation adapted from Terry Eagleton, *Literary Theory: An Introduction*
(Minneapolis: University of Minnesota, 1983).

page 171: Marilynne Robinson, *Housekeeping* (New York: Farrar, Straus & Giroux,
1980), 194; see also Wendell Berry's novel *Remembering* (Berkeley, CA: Counter-
point, 2008 [1988]) and the study by Edward S. Casey, *Remembering: A Phenomenological Study*, 2nd ed. (Bloomington, IN: Indiana University Press, 2000).

page 172: "Re-membered": from Robert McAfee Brown, "Three Sides of Memory,"
Christianity and Crisis (February 20, 1989), 31; this insight is explored at greater
depth by Barbara Myerhoff, "Life History Among the Elderly: Performance, Vis-
ibility, and Re-Membering," in Jay Ruby (ed.), *A Crack in the Mirror: Reflexive Perspectives in Anthropology* (Philadelphia: University of Pennsylvania, 1982),
99–117.

page 172: Rupert Brooke: "Thought For The Day," 19 Aug 2001, from bobmich@
attglobal.net.

page 173: On memory and "mourning": cf. Casey, *Remembering*, 273 and note on 353.

page 173: David Eagleman, "Metamorphosis," in *Sum: Forty Tales from the Afterlives* (New York: Vintage, 2010), 23.

page 173: Adorno is quoted by Martin E. Marty in a review of Forrest G. Wood's *The Arrogance of Faith: Christianity and Race in America from the Colonial Era to the Twentieth Century, Commonweal* 118:2 (January 25, 1991).

page 173: "'Memory' as key word": Wiesel, *From the Kingdom of Memory*, 194, 201.

page 174: Abba Moses the Black: Austin Hughes, "The Spirituality of the Desert Fathers," in Maurice Couve de Murville (ed.), *The Unsealed Fountain: Essays on the Christian Spiritual Tradition* (Dublin: Veritas, 1987), 44.

page 175: Piaget and Inhelder are quoted by David Thelen, "Memory and American History," *Journal of the American Historical Association* 75:4 (March 1989).

page 176: Rabbi's wife's servant: Martin Buber, *Tales of the Hasidim,* (Random House e-Book, 2013), n.p.

page 176: Morris Berman, *The Reenchantment of the World* (Ithaca, NY: Cornell University Press, 1981), 19.

page 177: Robert N. Bellah, et al., *Habits of the Heart: Individualism and Commitment in American Life* (Berkeley, CA: University of California, 1985), 81.

page 177: Paul Tournier, *The Meaning of Persons* (Cutchogue, NY: Buccaneer, 1957), 109.

page 177: James Hillman, *Healing Fiction* (Barrytown, NY: Stanton Hill, 1983), 42.

page 177: Ronald David Laing, *Self and Others,* 2nd ed. (Baltimore, MD: Pelican, 1969[1961]), 93.

page 179: Stories find us: Anne A. Simpkinson, "Sacred Stories," *Common Boundary* (November–December 1993), 11(6), 25–31.

page 179: The computer: proximately from Jamie Kalven, "Found in Translation," *University of Chicago Magazine* (June 1992), 36.

page 179: "No 'now'": in literature, cf. Jean-Paul Sartre, *Portrait of the Anti-Semite*; in Søren Kierkegaard, see "A" on "the aesthete" in *Either/Or.*

page 179: "Lovemaking" etc.: Christopher Lasch, *The Minimal Self* (New York: Norton, 1984), 247.

page 180: The snail: quoted by Adriano Francis Vatta, "Incidence, clinical appraisal and treatment of haemonchosis in small ruminants of resource-poor areas in South Africa" (submitted in partial fulfillment of the requirements for the degree Magister Scientiae), Department of Veterinary Tropical Diseases, Faculty of Veterinary Science, University of Pretoria, Onderstepoort, Gauteng, South Africa, August 2001, ii.

NOTES ON VIRTUE

page 182: Jonathan Glover, "God Loveth Adverbs," *London Review of Books* 12:22 (November 22, 1990), 12.

page 182: Aristotle and courage: a useful treatment of Aristotle's virtue ethics may be found at http://www.drury.edu/ess/reason/Aristotle.html, http://v.gd/sqGZVV (accessed October 10, 2013).

page 183: A variant version of the Feldkirch story was found at the town's website—http://www.bodensee-vorarlberg.com/multimedia/Broschueren/FeldkirchCityGuide2011_E.dist.pdf, http://v.gd/3QzkPC, p. 20, in February 2013); it has since been removed (October 18, 2013); a version also appeared on several websites after "9-11": http://v.gd/00FYxt, http://v.gd/6KdqYY, http://v.gd/ME69uU, credited to Steve Goodier.

page 184: On the four cardinal virtues, see the writings of Josef Pieper, perhaps especially *The Four Cardinal Virtues* (Notre Dame, IN: Notre Dame, 1966).

page 184: Several versions of "The Old Man and His Dog" story appear online: cf. e.g. http://llerrah.com/oldmanandhisdog.htm, http://v.gd/3fNOFw or http://www.christinyou.com/pages/mananddog.html, http://v.gd/Urrqyv (accessed October 18, 2013).

page 187: Gratitude-an-denken: cf. William Barrett, *Irrational Man: A Study in Existentialist Philosophy* (New York: Doubleday/Anchor, 1962 [1958]), 235.

page 187: There are several versions of the blind man begging story; we draw on Gabriel Daly, "Widening Horizons," *The Tablet* 244:7811 (March 31, 1990), 419–20.

page 188: Dag Hammarskjöld, *Markings*, 151.

page 188: Carl and Hans: Bausch, *A World of Stories for Preachers and Teachers*, 246.

page 190: humility: Simon Tugwell, *Ways of Imperfection* (Springfield, IL: Templegate, 1985), 84.

page 192: altruism: A helpful treatment of the topic, from which we borrow here, may be found in Robert Wuthnow, *Acts of Compassion* (Princeton, NJ: Princeton University Press, 1991), 45.

page 192: The Lincoln story is recounted by Rabbi Yonason Goldson, "Is Altruism a Programmed Response?" Jewish World Review.com, June 22, 2011, http://v.gd/v5SQjj, http://www.jewishworldreview.com/0611/goldson_altruistic_robots.php3 (accessed October 19, 2013): the whole article merits reading.

page 193: Genuine and false humility: Elie Wiesel, *Sages and Dreamers* (New York: Summit, 1991), 428–429.

page 194: "golden tripod": Alexander Eliot, "The Story of the Seven Sages," in "Astonishing Delphi," *Harvard Magazine* 92:4 (March–April 1990), 18–20.

page 195: "When night ends and day begins": Paulo Coelho, *Stories for Parents, Children and Grandchildren*, vol. 1 (n.p.: Lulu, 2008), 64.

page 196: There are many descriptions online of Mrs. Kendal and the Elephant Man.

page 198: The Vaclav Havel quotation is from *The New York Review of Books*, January 24, 2012.

page 198: The review of Susan Neiman and the following quotation are by Tim Black, *Spiked*, July 26, 2009, reviewing Susan Neiman, *Moral Clarity: A Guide for Grown-Up Idealists* (New York: Harcourt, 2008).

page 198: The St. Francis of Assisi story is from Hester Goodenough Gelber, "A Theater of Virtue: The Exemplary World of St. Francis of Assisi," in John Stratton Hawley (ed.), *Saints and Virtues* (Berkeley, CA: University of California, 1987), 33.

NOTES ON SIN

page 201: "sexual anorexia": Anthony de Mello, *More One Minute Nonsense* (Chicago, IL: Loyola, 1993), [original English edition by Gujarat Sahitya Prakash, Anand, India, 1992], 10. Courtesy of Gujarat Sahitya Prakash (booksgsp@gmail.com).

page 204: Churchill & Cripps: from DmacsMac@aol.com, July 23, 1999.

page 205: On postmodern pride, browse the definitions available at http://www.onelook.com/?w=PRIDE&ls=a, http://v.gd/Kcpl5q (accessed August 11, 2013).

page 206: Rabbi Elimelekh: Coelho, *Stories for Parents, Children and Grandchildren*, vol. 1 (n.p.: Lulu, 2008), 56.

page 207: On avarice, cf. John Ortberg, *When the Game Is Over, It All Goes Back in the Box* (Grand Rapids, MI: Zondervan, 2007), 189.

page 208: Window and mirror: Frankel, *The Classic Tales*, 552–553.

page 208: Fox and bird: Bausch, *A World of Stories for Preachers and Teachers*, 308.

page 209: Monkey and pot: Coelho, *Stories for Parents, Children and Grandchildren*, vol. 1 (n.p.: Lulu, 2008), 23.

page 213: On envy, cf. Henry Fairlie, *The Seven Deadly Sins Today* (Notre Dame, IN: University of Notre Dame, 1979), 64; Thomas Aquinas, *Summa Theologica*, II-II, q. 36, a. 2; and especially Joseph H. Berke, *The Tyranny of Malice* (New York: Summit, 1988), 13; but also Peter Walcot, *Envy and the Greeks: A Study of Human Behaviour* (Warminster: Aris & Phillips, 1978), 7, quoting Helmut Schoeck.

page 215: "what sex was to the Victorians": Joseph H. Berke, *Why I Hate You and You Hate Me: The Interplay of Envy, Greed, Jealousy and Narcissism in Everyday Life* (Google eBook, 2012).

page 216: The quotation is from Madonna Kolbenschlag, *Lost in the Land of Oz: The Search for Identity and Community in American Life* (San Francisco, CA: Harper & Row, 1988), 42ff.

page 216: On Adam's and Eve's first sin, cf. Peter Brown, *The Body and Society: Men, Women, and Sexual Renunciation in Early Christianity* (New York: Columbia University, 1988), 220.

page 218: Ninth time around the block: Bausch, *A World of Stories for Preachers and Teachers*, 390.

page 218: The tale of the Hong Kong arguers is told by Zig Ziglar, *Secrets of Closing the Sale* (New York: Penguin/Berkley, 1984), 271.

page 219: Aquinas quotes Augustine at *Summa Theologica* I-II, q. 46, a. 2.

page 220: The envy-wrath comparison is by Henry Fairlie, op. cit. 104.

page 220: An excellent twenty-first-century description of acedia may be found at http://www.nytimes.com/2011/12/25/books/review/their-noonday-demons-and-ours.html?pagewanted=all&_r=1& , http://v.gd/MIJl9j (accessed August 11, 2013).

page 221: On the self-pity aspect, cf. especially Solomon Schimmel, *The Seven Deadly Sins: Jewish, Christian and Classical Reflections on Human Nature* (New York: Free Press, 1992), 193; and William McDonough, "Sin and Addiction: Alcoholics Anonymous and the Soul of Christian Sin-Talk," *Journal of the Society of Christian Ethics* 32:1 (2012), 45; see also http://logismoitouaaron.blogspot.com/2010/03/demon-of-noondayst-cassian-evagrius-on.html, http://v.gd/gqbR1F (accessed August 11, 2013); a highly readable study is Kathleen Norris, *Acedia & me* (New York: Riverhead Books, 2008); especially stimulating is the final section, "Acedia: A Commonplace Book."

page 221: Mary Louise Bringle, *Despair: Sickness or Sin?* (Nashville, TN: Abingdon, 1990), 33.

page 221: On acedia and the will, cf. Thomas Aquinas, op. cit., II-II, q. 35, a. 3, a. 4; also McDonough, op. cit., 47.

page 221: The Dorothy L. Sayers excerpt is from "The Other Six Deadly Sins," an address given to the Public Morality Council at Caxton Hall, Westminster, October 23, 1941: available at http://www.lectionarycentral.com/trinity07/Sayers.html, http://v.gd/VsDx4v (accessed August 11, 2013); see also Janice Brown, *The Seven Deadly Sins in the Work of Dorothy L. Sayers* (Kent, OH: Kent State University, 1998), capturing Sayers's portrait of "the empty heart, the empty brain, the empty soul," 39.

page 222: "Melancholic self-centeredness" cf. Lewis Hyde, *Alcohol and Poetry: John Berryman and the Booze Talking* (Dallas, TX: Dallas Institute Publications, 1986), 14. This brief booklet, which we recommend to anyone interested in alcoholism, can be downloaded via https://www.google.com/—bav=on.2,or.r_cp.r_qf.&fp=161ec0fe335c48c5&q=berryman+hyde, http://v.gd/qJvzEq, and click on "[PDF] Alcohol and Poetry—Lewis Hyde". [Note that this leads to a document file, not a website.]

page 222: On "the paradox of sloth," cf. Schimmel, op. cit., 201.

page 222: The Bahlul story is from Sheikh Muzaffer Ozak Al-Jerrahi, Irshad: *Wisdom of a Sufi Master* (Amity, NY: Amity House, 1988), 61.

NOTES ON PRAYER

page 226: The opening is adapted from Richard Byrne, "Approaching Prayer as Mystery," *Spiritual Life* 34:1 (Spring 1988), 12–13, 14.

page 226: Etty Hillesum, *An Interrupted Life: The Diaries, 1941–1943* and *Letters from Westerbork* (New York: Henry Holt, 1996 [1981–Dutch]), 93; for those unacquainted with Etty Hillesum, we highly recommend reading the brief biography at http://www.gratefulness.org/giftpeople/hillesum.htm, http://v.gd/oQVP94 (accessed October 11, 2013).

page 227: Thomas Hopko, "Living in Communion: An Interview with Father Thomas Hopko," *Parabola* 12:3 (August 1987), 57.

page 227: The Schneur Zalman quotation is via Schachter and Hoffman, *Sparks of Light*, 110.

page 227: Rabbi Marc Gellman, in Zev Chafets, "The Right Way to Pray?" *New York Times*, September 16, 2009.

page 228: http://buddhistfaith.tripod.com/buddhistprayer/id5.html, http://v.gd/srUpK3 (accessed August 12, 2013).

page 229: Abraham Heschel, *Man's Quest for God*, as quoted by John Garvey (ed.), *Modern Spirituality* (Springfield, IL: *Templegate*, 1985), 9–10.

page 229: Evelyn Underhill, Mixed Pasture, as quoted by Garvey, op. cit., 17–18.

page 230: Lawrence S. Cunningham, "Old Prayers Made New," *Theology Today* 44:1 (October 1987), 362.

page 230: Margaret Miles, *Practicing Christianity* (New York: Crossroad, 1988), 126.

page 230: Sheila Cassidy, "Stalking the Spirit," *The Tablet* 246: 7909 (March 7, 1992), 305–306.

page 230: The "God's infinite knowledge" understanding, cf. Thomas Aquinas, *Summa Theologica*, II-II, q. 83, a. 2.

page 231: The mumbling pray-er story is from Rabbi Abraham J. Twerski, *Living Each Day* (Brooklyn, NY: Mesorah Publications, 1988), 351.

page 235: Tim Madigan, *I'm Proud of You: My Friendship with Fred Rogers* (Los Angeles, CA: Ubuntu Press, 2012), 79.

page 236: The umbrella: http://llerrah.com/redumbrella.htm, http://v.gd/1iSwik (accessed August 12, 2013).

page 236: Mary C. Darrah, *Sister Ignatia: Angel of Alcoholics Anonymous* (Chicago, IL: Loyola University, 1991).

page 237: The Musa story is from Jan Knappert, *Myths and Legends of the Swahili* (Nairobi: Heinemann, 1970), 48.

page 238: The tiger's whisker story appears in several places online, but it is drawn here from a workshop offered by Tina Alston, "Storytelling: A Tool of Healing for Vietnam Veterans and Their Families," Agent Orange Class Assistance Program Symposium, Washington, D. C., 1994, 7 (handout).

page 240: The Sabbath story is from Arnold Mandel, quoted by Michel Sales, "The Fulfillment of the Sabbath," *Communio 21* (Spring 1994), 33.

page 241: The "Bill" story was originally found at "Clergy Corner," *The Valley Chronicle*, March 1, 2012: http://www.thevalleychronicle.com/local-news/community/item/1439-clergy-corner-his-name-was-bill (accessed February 10, 2013). It does not appear there on August 12, 2013), but versions can be found at: http://www.centrestreetumc.com/Messenger 2012/2012 10 Messenger.pdf, http://

v.gd/Kx6Fnj, 8; and http://groups.yahoo.com/group/FavoriteStories/message/12, http://v.gd/qeonPZ, story #6; and http://www.rankdirection.com/manteysamuel .wordpress.com, http://v.gd/ylkzE2 (all accessed August 12, 2013).

NOTES ON CONFUSION

page 245: The Heifetz story is adapted from Karl Weick, "Summary and Dialogue" in Paul Woodruff and Harry A. Wilmer (eds.), *Facing Evil: Light at the Core of Darkness* (LaSalle, IL: Open Court, 1988), 240.

page 249: Rabbi Nathan Lopes Cardozo, "The Almighty as an Idol: The Tragedy of the Religious," Jewish World Review.com , http://v.gd/dnTRfQ , http://www.jew-ishworldreview.com/0811/cardozo_tragedy_of_the_religious.php3 (accessed October 12, 2013).

page 249: Kabir Das: Kanwarjit Singh Kang and Diljit Kaur Kang (comps. & eds.), *151 Folk Tales of India* (Delhi: Ajunta Publications, 1988), 6.

page 250: On "differing" realities, a challenging discussion, concerning Christianity and Islam, may be found in the "Comments" at http://www.firstthings.com/on-thesquare/2013)/02/benedict-face-to-face-with-islam, http://v.gd/j6SIw0 (accessed August 12, 2013).

page 250: spin cycle: Steve Goodier, *Joy Along the Way* (Salt Lake City UT: Life Support System, 2002), 57.

page 252: The questioning worm: Hossein Dezhakam, *Crossing the Zone 60 Degrees Below Zero* (trans. Saeed Moeini), privately published, but may be accessed at http://www.facesandvoicesofrecovery.org/pdf/International/Iran_Crossing_the_Zone.pdf, http://v.gd/j5IE0X, 147 (accessed August 12, 2013); the continuing paragraph that follows is from private e-mail correspondence with Hossein Dezhakam, founder of Congress60, an Iranian program for substance abusers, the work's author.

page 253: In the Hammurabi Code and Hebrew Law, the "eye for eye" was to restrict compensation to the value of the loss. Thus, it might be better read "only one eye for one eye"; cf. Gunther Plaut, *The Torah—A Modern Commentary* (New York: Union of American Hebrew Congregations, 1981), 571ff.

page 253: Darrow: http://anecdotage.com/articles/11545/, http://v.gd/y5PRsl (accessed October 19, 2013).

page 254: Demosthenes: Fuller, *Thesaurus of Anecdotes*, 135–137.

page 254: On Demosthenes as pleader, cf. Plutarch: *Lives of the Noble Grecians and Romans*, trans. John Dryden, rev. Arthur Hugh Clough (New York: The Modern Library, n.d.), 1025.

page 254: Since we are ignorant of contract law in ancient Greece, we consulted with a Washington, D.C.-based twenty-first-century American attorney, Aleksandra Doran, who, while admitting that she had never worked on a case involving an ass (four-legged), suggested the following: "Depends on the language of the contract. If it says, 'May use the ass to transport a burden from here to Megara,' the ass's owner has a slightly better claim; but I think that claim is weak, period (while someone else is using the ass, the owner shouldn't retain any residual use in it unless there's a specific carve-out in the contract, because reserving other uses could interfere with the purpose for which it was hired). If the contract says that the renter may have the ass for so many hours and move it where he likes, well, that includes wherever it would cast a shadow over him, in which case I'd say he's the clear winner. If I were the renter, I would argue that I assumed that, like the standard ass-renting contract, this one included the shadow (as it travels with the ass), and that that was the good for which I had negotiated my price; if the owner wanted the shadow back, I get a ten-percent discount."

page 259: Rabbi Y'hoshu'a ben Hananya: Raphael Patai, *Gates to the Old City* (Detroit, MI: Wayne State University, 1981), 219.

page 260: The benevolent monkeys: this traditional Tanzanian folktale can be found at http://www.afriprov.org/index.php/african-stories-by-season/14-animal-stories/ 67-how-the-monkeys-saved-the-fish.html, http://v.gd/sEsoES (accessed August 12, 2013).

page 263: The perfect pupil: Idries Shah, *Wisdom of the Idiots* (New York: Dutton, 1971), 162.

page 263: "Belief in God": Miguel de Unamuno, *Tragic Sense of Life*, 193.

NOTES ON RECOVERY

page 265: Alida Gersie & Nancy King, *Storymaking in Education and Therapy* (London: Jessica Kingsley, 1990), 225.

page 265: "Goodness spreads": Thomas Aquinas, *Summa Theologica*, I, q. 5, a. 4.

page 266: Rabbi Eliezer: Thomas D. Zweifel and Aaron L. Raskin, *The Rabbi and the CEO: The Ten Commandments for 21st Century Leaders* (New York: SelectBooks, 2008), 169.

page 266: The alcoholic in Chicago: [Anonymous], *Came to Believe . . .* (New York: A.A. World Services, 1973), 74–75.

page 267: On "skill, a practice," cf. Alasdair MacIntyre, *After Virtue* (Notre Dame, IN: University of Notre Dame, 1981).

page 268: "therapeia": David M. Parry, "Holiness as service: *Therapeia* and *hyperetike* in Plato's Euthyphro," *The Journal of Value Inquiry* (1994) 28: 529–539; the "helper-therapy principle" was formulated and popularized by Frank Riesmann, "The 'helper' therapy principle," *Social Work* 10:2 (1965), 27–32.

page 271: Norman Lear, interview with Thomas M. Landy, "What's Missing from This Picture," *Commonweal* 119:17 (October 9, 1992), 20.

page 271: Nasrudin's donkey: Warren S. Walker and Ahmet E. Uysal, *Tales Alive in Turkey* (Cambridge, MA: Harvard, 1966), 235.

page 272: The seeker: Gregory Corrigan, *Disciple Story* (Notre Dame, IN: Ave Maria, 1989), 99.

page 273: "Purity of heart": Juana Raasch, "The Monastic Concept of Purity of Heart and Its Sources," *Studia Monastica* 11 (1969), 273: "In the Demonstrations of Aphraates, purity of heart is envisioned from God's point of view to mean readiness to please him, especially by acts of mercy and kindness towards men, with whom God identifies, and by having a heart free from anger and ready to forgive."

page 273: *Alcoholics Anonymous* (New York: A.A. World Services, 1939), 64.

page 273: Pachomius: Raasch, op. cit., 300.

page 273: The *Apophthegmata Patrum* consists of stories and sayings attributed to the Desert Fathers and Desert Mothers from approximately the fifth century CE. They describe the spiritual practices and experiences of early Christian hermits living in the desert of Egypt, typically in the form of a conversation between a younger monk and his spiritual father.

page 275: Weather: http://voices.washingtonpost.com/capitalweathergang/2008/11/winter_weather_joke.html, http://v.gd/b9A41C (accessed August 12, 2013).

page 276: Fazl-Rabi: Idries Shah, *The Way of the Sufi* (New York: Dutton, 1970), 63–64.

page 278: Fred the gardener: Stephen R. Covey, A. Roger Merrill, Rebecca R. Merrill, *First Things First* (New York: Fireside/Simon & Schuster, 1995 [1994]), 77.

page 278: The Greek monk: Belden C. Lane, *Landscapes of the Sacred* (New York: Paulist, 1988), 191–192.

page 280: Andrew Olendzki, "Dana: The Practice of Giving," *Parabola* (Summer 2003); see also the "Kindred Spiritualities" website, http://kindredspiritualities.blogspot.com/2011/05/dana-practice-of-giving.html, http://v.gd/RLwjE3 (accessed August 12, 2013). The quotation that follows is from the same site.

page 281: The screwdriver: Paulo Coelho, *Stories for Parents, Children and Grandchildren*, vol. 2 (n.p.: Lulu, 2008), 8.

NOTES ON WISDOM

page 283: The Edith Hamilton quote is from *The Greek Way* (New York: Norton, 1983 [1930]), 119, which attributes this quotation to Socrates, but that has been challenged, with explanation, at http://www.perishablepundit.com/index.php?date=02/11/09&pundit=5, http://v.gd/U79UfD (accessed August 12, 2013). On balance, reading that explanation and its sources, we think the proper attribution of the idea, even if not of its precise English verbalization, should be to Plato's Socrates.

page 285: Our ten-point schema of course reflects the ancient distinction between art and science, the Greek differentiation of *logos* and *muthos*, noted in Wonder.

page 285: Viktor Frankl, *The Unconscious God* (New York: Simon & Schuster, 1975 [1948]), 137.

page 285: Diane Ravitch, commencement address at Reed College, Portland, OR; *Time*, June 17, 1985.

page 286: Helen Merrell Lynd, *On Shame and the Search for Identity* (New York: Harcourt, Brace & World, 1958), 98.

page 286: The Aaron Levenstein quotation is attributed to Brand Autopsy, no date given.

page 286: Albert Camus, *The Fall* (New York: Vintage, 1956), 11.

page 287: Helen Merrell Lynd, op. cit., pp. 129-130, quoting Henry A. Murray.

page 287: Elijah and the poor man: Bausch, *A World of Stories for Preachers and Teachers*, 288.

page 288: "Dr. Sage": Brian Cavanaugh, T.O.R., *The Sower's Seeds* (rev. and ex. edition) (Mahwah, NJ: Paulist, 2004), 33.

page 288: Robertson Davies in excerpt from a talk included in "The Tanner Lectures on Human Values, volume 13, 1992," edited by Grethe B. Peterson (University of Utah).

page 288: Julian Hawthorne: Robert Hendrickson, *American Literary Anecdotes* (New York: Facts on File, 1990), 102.

page 289: Italo Calvino, "Why Read the Classics?" in *Why Read the Classics?* trans. Martin McLaughlin (New York: Vintage, n.d.)—Kindle edition, no pagination.

page 289: Lynd on "ultimate questions": op. cit., 251.

page 289: Ernest Becker, *The Denial of Death* (New York: Macmillan/Free Press, 1973).

page 290: Camus, *The Fall*, 84.

page 290: Aeschylus: Edith Hamilton, *The Greek Way*, 59; see also Andre-Jean Festugière, *Personal Religion Among the Greeks* (Berkeley: University of California, 1954), making the point that this understanding marked the rebellion of moral conscience against the idea of hereditary penalty: "Suffering, then, teaches. At the least, it teaches pity," 33.

page 290: "Out of suffering": although usually attributed to Kahlil Gibran, Wikiquote credits Edwin Hubbell Chapin for this quotation, as reported in Josiah Hotchkiss Gilbert, *Dictionary of Burning Words of Brilliant Writers* (1895).

page 290: Libba Bray, *The Sweet Far Thing* (New York: Ember/Random House, 2007), 785.

page 292: Rabbi Israel Salanter: David Greenberg and Eliezer Witztum, *Sanity and Sanctity: Mental Health Work Among the Ultra-Orthodox in Jerusalem* (New Haven, CT: Yale, 2002), 108, citing Nathan Ausabel, *A Treasury of Jewish Folklore* (New York: Crown, 1948).

page 293: e. e. cummings: quoted by George Vaillant, *Spiritual Evolution* (New York: Broadway Books, 2008), 183, citing an original manuscript in the Harvard Houghton Library.

page 294: Walter Ong, quoted by Robert B. Lawton, "The Scholar's Life," *America* 164:12 (March 30, 1991), 366.

Notes

page 296: Knowledge as proven: see Gordon C. S. Smith and Jill P. Pell, "Parachute Use to Prevent Death and Major Trauma Related to Gravitational Challenge: Systematic Review of Randomized Controlled Trials," *International Journal of Prosthodontics 2006*, 19: 126–128; originally appeared in the *British Medical Journal* 2003; 327: 1459–1461; this absolutely essential article may be obtained at http://www.ncbi.nlm.nih.gov/pmc/articles/PMC300808/, http://v.gd/B8z8E0 (accessed October 19, 2013).

page 296: Wisdom and faith: see, e.g., the discussion in Leszek Kolakowski, *Religion* (New York: Oxford, 1985), 53–54.

page 297: Spoken by Hoh Elder Leila Fisher in Steve Wall & Harvey Arden, *Wisdomkeepers* (Hillsboro, OR: Beyond Words, n.d.), 74ff.

Sources

These are some of the books in which we found versions of some of the stories told in this book. As noted in the Introduction, most of these stories we first heard were told by friends or acquaintances or sent by them in postal or e-mail correspondences. But for those interested in finding still more such stories, the following are a good place to start.

Ausubel, Nathan. *A Treasury of Jewish Folklore* (New York: Crown, 1948).

Bausch, William J. *Storytelling: Imagination and Faith* (Mystic, CT: Twenty-Third Publications, 1984).

——. *A World of Stories for Preachers and Teachers* (Mystic, CT: Twenty-Third Publications, 1998).

Buber, Martin. *Tales of the Hasidim: The Early Masters* (New York: Schocken, 1948).

——. *Tales of the Hasidim: Later Masters* (New York: Schocken, 1948).

Bushnaq, Inea. *Arab Folktales* (Cairo: American University in Cairo, 1986).

Coelho, Paulo. *Stories for Parents, Children and Grandchildren*, vol. 1 (n.p.: Lulu, 2008).

——. *Stories for Parents, Children and Grandchildren*, vol. 2 (n.p.: Lulu, 2008).

de Mello, Anthony, *One Minute Nonsense* (Chicago, IL: Loyola, 1992) [original English edition by Gujarat Sahitya Prakash, Anand, India, 1992].

——. *More One Minute Nonsense* (Chicago, IL: Loyola, 1993) [original English edition by Gujarat Sahitya Prakash, Anand, India, 1992].

——. *The Prayer of the Frog*, vol. 1 (Anand, India: Gujarat Sahitya Prakash, 1989).

——. *The Prayer of the Frog*, vol. 2 (Anand, India: Gujarat Sahitya Prakash, 1989).

Frankel, Ellen. *The Classic Tales: 4,000 Years of Jewish Lore* (Northvale, NJ: Jason Aronson, 1989).

Friedman, Maurice. *A Dialogue with Hasidic Tales: Hallowing the Everyday* (New York: Human Sciences Press, 1988).

Newman, Louis I. (trans. & comp.), *The Hasidic Anthology: Tales and Teachings of the Hasidim* (New York: Schocken, 1963 [1934]).

Shah, Idries. *The Way of the Sufi* (New York: Dutton, 1970).

Wiesel, Elie. *From the Kingdom of Memory* (New York: Summit, 1990).

——. *Sages and Dreamers* (New York: Summit, 1991).

Index

Index

Index

Index

Index

Ward, William Arthur, 113
Watts, Alan, 10–11
Waugh, Evelyn, 221
Weiner, Herbert, 100
White, E. B., 131
Wiesel, Elie, 75, 158, 167n, 173, 193
Wilde, Oscar, 32
Wilson, E. O., 63
wisdom
    concern with meaning and reasons, 285–86
    deepening through repeated exposure, 288–89
    embrace of realities as personal and whole, 291–93
    endurance despite ambiguity and confusion, 175–76
    faith in unprovable realities, 296–97
    human identity as capacity to love, 293–94
    impossibility of possessing, 289–90
    mindfulness of time-tested realities, 295–96
    origin in wonder, 283
    through prayer, 228
    as reality distinct from knowledge, 284–85, 297
    receipt of, 298–99
    suffering as source of, 290–91

synthesis of fact and value, 294–95
unteachability of, 2
value of argument, 283–84
as vision with focus on qualities, 286–88
Wolpe, David, 149
Women in Love (Lawrence), 11
wonder and awe
    everyday reality, 45–46, 56
    existence of *beyond*, 51–53
    experience of mystery, 53–56, 60, 229
    versus forfeiture of miracle, 56
    as foundation of religion, 12, 47–48, 55–56
    implied limitations, 48
    openness to, 12, 231
    at root of wisdom, 283
    versus scientific mastery over nature, 48–50
    through simplicity and innocence, 56–59
    two-sided nature of, 46–47
wrath, 218–20

Yerachmiel ben Yisrael, 9–10, 20–21, 102–3
Y'hoshu'a ben Hananya, 259
Yitzhak, Levi, 129

Zalman, Schneur, 227
Zen anecdotal materials, 143–44

If you enjoyed this book, visit

www.tarcherbooks.com

and sign up for Tarcher's e-newsletter to receive
special offers, giveaway promotions, and
information on hot upcoming releases.

TARCHER
PENGUIN

Great Lives Begin with Great Ideas

Connect with the Tarcher Community

• • •

Stay in touch with favorite authors!
Enter weekly contests!
Read exclusive excerpts!
Voice your opinions!

Follow us

 Tarcher Books

@TarcherBooks

If you would like to place a bulk order
of this book, call 1-800-847-5515.